T5-BBP-538

FREE TRADE

and the New
Right
Agenda

FREE TRADE

and the New Right Agenda

JOHN W. WARNOCK

New Star Books
Vancouver

BRESCIA COLLEGE
LIBRARY
56578

Copyright © 1988 by John W. Warnock
All Rights Reserved

First Printing June 1988
1 2 3 4 5 92 91 90 89 88

Canadian Cataloguing in Publication Data

Warnock, John W., 1933-
Free trade and the new right agenda

Bibliography: p.
ISBN 0-919573-80-0 (bound). — ISBN 0-919573-79-7 (pbk)

1. Canada - Commerce - United States.   2. United
States - Commerce - Canada.   3. Free trade and
protection - Free trade.   4. Canada - Economic
policy - 1971-   5. Right and left (Political
science).   6. Economic history - 1971-   I. Title.
HF1766.W37 1988   382.0971'073   C88-091313-4

This book is published with assistance from
the Canada Council and the Department of Communications

Printed and bound in Canada

New Star Books Ltd.
2504 York Avenue
Vancouver, B.C.
V6K 1E3

BRESCA COLLEGE
LIBRARY

To Delia, Robert and Duff, and their generation, who must now decide what kind of Canada they want for themselves and their children

ACKNOWLEDGEMENTS

This book has benefited enormously from the help of a large number of colleagues and friends over the past few years. I would particularly like to thank those who have taken the time to read drafts of all or part of the manuscript: Peter Bakvis, Harold Bronson, John Dillon, Cy Gonick, Jim Harding, Betty Warnock, Chris Willette and Kay Willson. While writing the book, there were others whom I consulted and who provided me with invaluable information and guidance: Duncan Cameron, Bruce Campbell, Bill Carroll, Tony Clark, Marjorie Cohen, Steve Dorey, Daniel Drache, Bill Hamilton, Dennis Howlett, John Lang, Bill Luttrell, Scott Sinclair and Larry Wagg. My views on the actual Reagan/Mulroney free trade deal were sharpened by discussions with my colleagues on the Pro-Canada Network research team. There are other close friends without whose personal support this effort would not have been possible; special thanks goes to Lorne Brown, Doug Daniels, Murray Dobbin, Ellen Gould and Joe Roberts. The staff at the University of Regina Library was most co-operative and helpful. The manuscript was greatly improved by my editor, Gail McConnell. Of course, I am completely responsible for the text as it now appears. A grant from the Boag Foundation helped defray my expenses during the writing of the book. Finally, I would like to thank the people at New Star Books, especially Lanny Beckman.

John W. Warnock
Regina, Saskatchewan
December 23, 1987

CONTENTS

LIST OF TABLES AND FIGURES

INTRODUCTION

The Mulroney Free Trade Deal

How many Canadians remember that in the 1983 campaign for the leadership of the Conservative Party, Brian Mulroney strongly opposed a bilateral free trade agreement with the United States? He actually said, "Don't talk to me about free trade. That issue was decided in 1911. Free trade is a danger to Canadian sovereignty. You'll hear no more of it from me." Sir John A. Macdonald called free trade with the United States "veiled treason." Brian Mulroney has now lifted the veil.

On October 5, 1987, the Mulroney government and the Reagan administration announced that they had reached a basic agreement on a comprehensive bilateral free trade agreement between Canada and the United States. President Reagan declared that the "the U.S./ Canada free trade agreement is a new economic constitution for North America." The Canadian prime minister proclaimed that the new agreement would result in a net increase of 350,000 jobs for Canadians and would permanently end regional disparities. The defence of the deal began immediately, using some very strong language aimed at would-be opponents. The chief Canadian negotiator, Simon Reisman, informed Canadians that they could all expect a 25% increase in their real income and that those who opposed the deal were engaging in the "big lie technique" used by Nazi Germany. The Minister of Finance, Michael Wilson, told a gathering of high-profile businessmen in New York that Canadians opposed to the agreement were "dominated by fear and weak of will."

There is no question that everyone, opponents and defenders, can agree that free trade with the United States would represent the most far-reaching change that Canada has faced since Confederation. The question is, what kind of deal was reached on October 5? The first thing to become apparent was that it was a hasty deal, reached under

9

serious, even unreasonable, time constraints. The free trade agreement between Canada and the United States was negotiated under the "fast track" system established by the U.S. Congress. Under the U.S. Constitution, the Congress has the responsibility for foreign and interstate commerce. The only authority that the executive branch of the goverment has in the area of foreign commerce is that delegated by the Congress. In the 1984 *Trade and Tariff Act*, the U.S. Congress granted the president the authority to sign bilateral free trade agreements with Israel and Canada. Agreements are different from treaties, which have a higher status under the Constitution and require approval by two-thirds of the Senate. However, under the provisions of this Act, the president had to inform the Congress by October 5, 1987, of his intentions to sign such agreements, and the agreements themselves had to be submitted to Congress for approval no later than January 5, 1988. After Congress began consideration of the agreements, they had ninety days to approve or reject them by a simple majority vote in both the House of Representatives and the Senate. Under the act, the Congress could not amend the agreements. In April 1985 the U.S. government signed a free trade agreement with Israel.

The actual negotiations between Canada and the United States did not begin until May 1986, which left only seventeen months to work out a deal. As the deadline approached, it did not appear possible for the two governments to reach an agreement within the designated time period. Many Canadians feared that the Mulroney government would pull another "Meech Lake Accord": in early June of 1987 the prime minister and the ten provincial premiers were locked up for nineteen uninterrupted hours during which, thanks largely to the process of exhaustion, they reached an agreement on the Canadian Constitution. The result was unsatisfactory to a great many Canadians, but the prime minister and the premiers did not permit any democratic ratification of the agreement. There were no elections and no referendums on the Accord. While there were a few scattered public hearings, the prime minister and the premiers rejected any possibility of amending the Accord. Party leaders throughout the country, both those in power and those in opposition, used party discipline to try to obtain unanimous approval of the Accord in the provincial legislatures and the House of Commons. The only serious oppositions came from the Canadian Senate. Would the free trade agreement follow the same pattern?

The business press in Canada closely followed the free trade negotiations. By the middle of September 1987 they reported that there were many outstanding issues still to be resolved. The key demands by the Mulroney government had not been accepted by the U.S. government. Our negotiators had requested exemption from the protectionist U.S. trade laws which harassed Canadian exporters. They had demanded that the long process of appearing before the U.S. International Trade Commission, the U.S. Department of Commerce and the U.S. courts be replaced by an impartial trade disputes panel which would have the power of binding arbitration. The Canadian negotiators wanted this new dispute panel actually to replace the existing U.S. procedures. Canada was requesting the special treatment appropriate to its proposed status as a close partner in a free trade agreement. U.S. negotiators and key Congressional leaders were taking the position that Canada could not be granted a special status without affecting their other trading partners, and that they could not ratify international agreements that would, in effect, deny U.S. firms access to existing trade legislation and the courts.

The Canadian government also wanted exemption from the very protectionist omnibus trade bill that had passed the U.S. House of Representatives and the Senate in 1987. Each branch of the Congress had passed a different version of the new trade bill. The two versions were stalled in a joint committee of the two houses, as their representatives tried to work out a compromise. From the beginning, the president opposed the legislation and vowed to veto any final bill. However, the bill's original overwhelming support in both houses suggested that its supporters in Congress might have the two-thirds majority needed to override a presidential veto. It was widely agreed that the omnibus trade bill would cause further problems for Canadian exports to the United States. Key Congressional leaders were unwilling to exempt Canada from this new legislation. Furthermore, they made it clear that they planned to give priority to the omnibus bill over any U.S./Canada free trade agreement.

Canada further insisted that both countries be allowed to introduce legislation and programs to assist those sectors of private industry and labour which would be hard hit by the free trade agreement. Industries protected by tariffs would have to adjust to the impact of increased competition. However, the U.S. negotiators were dead set against this demand as they had no intention of offering similar help to American firms and workers.

As well, Canada wanted national treatment for Canadian firms in the area of U.S. government procurement policy, by which they would be eligible to build on government contracts. Not only was the U.S. government resisting open access to federal contracts, they took the position that they could not bind state and municipal governments to provide such access.

At the same time, U.S. negotiators were pressing for American access to key areas of the Canadian economy. On investment policy, the U.S. was demanding that Canada give up the right to screen foreign takeovers of Canadian companies. After the Ontario provincial election of September 1987, U.S. officials insisted that several aspects of the Canada/U.S. Auto Pact had to be changed. The Reagan administration also put forth a set of rules which defined government subsidies acceptable to the American government, but which offered no changes to the existing U.S. laws which Canadian governments and businesses had found so objectionable.

Then on September 23, 1987, the Mulroney government dramatically cut off the free trade talks with the United States. Simon Reisman walked out of the negotiations in Washington declaring that U.S. officials were "not responding on elements fundamental to Canada's position," in particular, the establishment of a joint disputes tribunal with the power to make binding decisions. Most observers felt this move was a play to shift the negotiations to a higher, more political level, involving the prime minister and the president. Most of the provincial premiers, even Grant Devine of Saskatchewan, supported the breaking off of the talks.

In a letter to the U.S. Secretary of the Treasury, James Baker, who now assumed responsibility for the free trade talks, Michael Wilson set forth the bottom line of the Canadian position. The deal must include five elements: removal of all tariffs and most non-tariff barriers over ten years, while no new barriers were to be introduced; balanced and improved access for agriculture and food products; no changes in the Auto Pact unless they "improve prospects for Canadian and U.S. production, trade and employment"; clear and predictable rules of trade, objectively interpreted, subject to an impartial tribunal; and clear definitions of fair and unfair trade practices, including what was an acceptable government subsidy.

Negotiations were resumed on October 1 at a higher political level. Canada was represented by Michael Wilson, Pat Carney, Minister of International Trade, and Derek Burney, chief of staff to Brian Mulroney. They met with James Baker and the U.S. trade representative, Clayton Yeutter. However, it became widely known that the U.S. government was holding fast in certain areas. Echoing the position of U.S. business interests, they were insisting on strict limitations on the ability of Canadian governments to give financial support to culture, regional development and domestic industries in general. They particularly objected to Canadian subsidies to resource industries.

Shortly before the final negotiations began, Giles Gherson, Washington reporter for *The Financial Post*, outlined the key elements of the deal that remained to be settled. Canada was still insisting on a bilateral disputes tribunal. However, the U.S. compromise proposal offered only to make it a court of last resort. On the issue of government subsidies, agreement seemed impossible. The United States had continued to refuse to phase out their tariffs (which were, on average, only one-half those of Canada) over a five-year period.

For the United States, the major outstanding issues remained Canadian screening of foreign business takeovers, access to the Canadian financial services sector, protection for Canadian periodicals and for radio and television broadcasters, changes in the Auto Pact, and right of establishment and national status for U.S. firms wishing to operate in the service sector in Canada. Jennifer Lewington, Washington reporter for *The Globe and Mail*, quoted U.S. sources who argued that the Canadian government had to make concessions on a variety of issues related to market access, including provincial liquor board restrictions, investment regulations, copyright and patent law, telecommunications and the Auto Pact.

Finalizing the free trade deal did indeed turn out to be a repeat of the Meech Lake Accord process. On Friday, October 3, the top negotiators met for thirteen and one-half hours. On Saturday, October 4, they met for another fourteen hours. The basic principles of the deal were worked out by 11 p.m. that Saturday night, and at 11:54 p.m. President Reagan formally notified the U.S. Congress that a deal had been made, six minutes before the legal deadline.

The Free Trade Agreement

On October 5, the U.S. government released their text of the summary of the tentative free trade agreement, and the Canadian version appeared two days later. These contained only the basic principles of the agreement. The actual complete text was to be drafted over the next two months. Those who had been following the debate over the issue were astonished by how much the Canadian government had surrendered and how little they got in the deal. When the final text was released on December 11, 1987, very few changes had been made.

The Canadian negotiators did not get exemption from the omnibus trade bill before the Congress. On October 9, Pat Carney conceded that the free trade agreement would not protect Canada from the omnibus trade bill or any other changes that the Congress might make in U.S. trade law before the agreement came into effect on January 1, 1989. This was reiterated by Simon Reisman during his press conference on December 11. U.S. Congressional leaders announced that they intended to take up the omnibus bill before they considered the Canada/U.S. free trade agreement.

There was nothing in the agreement that provided for government assistance to businesses or workers in adjusting to the impact of the removal of tariffs. Such subsidies could be classified as "unfair trade practices" under existing U.S. legislation. Lacking any protection in the free trade agreement, it is doubtful, then, that such adjustment programs can be introduced. Brian Mulroney nevertheless announced that a Conservative government would introduce a "massive program" of employment adjustment. However, he was quickly contradicted by his Minister of Finance, Michael Wilson, who noted that only existing programs for the unemployed would be used.

It proved impossible to arrive at a definition of an acceptable government subsidy or of an "unfair trade practice." Since the Mulroney government could not accept the American position paper on this very important issue, it was put aside. Under the agreement the two countries would continue to enforce their existing trade legislation. A lower-level working group would be created to try to reach a new agreement in this area. If the two countries could not reach an agreement in seven years, then either party would be able to terminate the agreement after giving six months' notice. In the meantime, U.S. industries would be free to pursue their attacks on a wide variety of Canadian programs which they feel are "subsidies" to their Canadian competitors. Thus, while the provincial governments were being asked to give support to the free trade agreement, they did not know what the outcome would be in a very significant area of provincial concern, regional development programs.

Both countries agreed to reduce the impact of government procurement policies. The agreement broadens and deepens the obligations of both countries under the GATT code on government procurement policies. The new threshold level for open bidding, that is, the level below which contracts could be awarded with no bidding, or limited bidding, was set at US$25,000 in each country. However, there is no mention in the agreement of government purchasing at the state, provincial or municipal level. It does specifically exclude broadening Canadian access to U.S. military contracts.

The Canadian government claims that this section of the agreement will open up US$3 billion in opportunities in the United States and about US$0.5 billion in Canada. This seems to be only a small gain. Even so, the American negotiators point out that while about 40% of Canadian contracts were above the previous threshold, only "a minor percentage" of U.S. procurements were below the threshold. Proportionally, therefore, Canada is opening up a much higher percentage of their procurements to U.S. entities. Furthermore, under the new rules, the Canadian government will no longer be able to give preference to firms who invest in Canada.

Finally, there was the key Canadian demand, the trade disputes tribunal which was to have the power of binding arbitration. From the beginning, the Mulroney government and almost all of the provincial premiers insisted that this was an absolute minimum requirement for any Canadian acceptance of a free trade agreement with the United States. The agreement does provide for the creation of five-member binational disputes panels, to be chosen from a roster provided by both countries. Each country would nominate two members, with the deciding fifth member being either jointly approved, selected by the four other panel members, or chosen by lot. The new binational panel would replace judicial review in both countries. Under the agreement the panel would have to make a decision within 315 days, which could reduce the time of a trade dispute appeal, as court cases take years to complete. However, it is not at all certain that this aspect of the agreement will stand up to legal challenge, as U.S. interests insist that the government has no power to remove the right of an injured party to seek redress in the courts.

Moreover, the binational panel does not in fact replace the existing system of settling disputes currently established under U.S. trade laws. It is only tacked onto the end, in place of a judicial review. Canadian exporters challenged by U.S. competitors would still have to go through the long, expensive process of defending themselves through the present U.S. system. Furthermore, a binational panel could not overrule U.S. legislation. It could only determine whether or not American rules and procedures used in a given action against a Canadian exporter conformed to existing American law. Finally, the decisions of such a panel would not carry any binding authority; they would be merely "declaratory opinions." In the end, each national government would then decide whether or not to accept it. If one government refused, then the only alternative available to the other would be retaliatory action. It is not surprising that the "binary dispute panel," the key Canadian provision in the agreement, was quickly attacked by politicians, businessmen and farmers as inadequate and no improvement over the status quo.

In this instance, the status quo may actually be better than what was achieved in the free trade agreement for a number of reasons. The binational panels proposed would be more political than the current approach of appealing to a disputes panel under the General Agreement on Tariff and Trades (GATT). Representatives of the disputing parties are excluded from a GATT tribunal, and the GATT tribunals use international trade law rather than U.S. trade law. GATT tribunals also use international precedents rather than U.S. precedents. In addition, under the current system, Canadian industries which have been subject to the present U.S. trade action system can appeal to the U.S. Court of International Trade, which has been quite fair and impartial in its decisions, which are binding. However, this final route of appeal has been removed under the agreement. But worst of all, by formally participating in this process the Canadian government would legitimize existing U.S. trade law which in many areas is contrary to the general principles of the GATT. One very important area is regional development programs, which are sanctioned by the GATT and widely used everywhere. Why should the Mulroney government agree to sanction the U.S. unilateralist approach?

Canadian Concessions

While Canada's negotiators did not get very much from the Americans, they made major concessions in the areas of energy, investment, tariffs, the Auto Pact, agriculture, and the financial and service sectors. The most controversial are briefly summarized below.

Energy. Much to the surprise of everyone, the free trade agreement included a continental energy policy. The Mulroney government granted the United States "non-discriminatory access" to *all* Canadian energy supplies and agreed to prohibit restrictions on imports and exports. Canada is expressly forbidden to use "quantitative restrictions, taxes, minimum import or export price requirements, or any other equivalent measure." Even if the national reserve is inadequate to meet Canadian requirements, as is the case with conventional oil, Canada must provide the United States with "proportional access to the diminishing supply." The United States is guaranteed the right to consume Canada's non-renewable energy resources. In return, Canada gets the right to supply them! Under the terms of the agreement, provincial governments would no longer be able to give Canadian industries or even individual firms preferential energy prices over buyers in the United States. This prohibition covers provincial crown corporations that provide electricity. One immediately thinks of how Quebec, Ontario, Manitoba and British Columbia have used low-cost electric power to encourage the development of energy-intensive industries like pulp and paper and smelting. If the agreement is implemented, provincial industrial and commercial rates may not be lower than those offered to U.S. customers. Furthermore, the National Energy Board would no longer be able to apply the "least cost alternative test" to Canadian energy exports, under which energy exports cannot be sold at a lower price than what the U.S. customer would pay from an alternative source. The new rules will allow Canadian natural gas and electrical power to be exported to the United States at even lower prices.

Investment. American control of the Canadian economy is a serious issue in Canada, but few Americans think that Canadian business expansion into the United States is a threat. Given this fundamental imbalance, when the agreement grants "national treatment" to each country in the establishment of new business enterprises and the acquisition of existing businesses, it is hardly a *quid pro quo*, or a mutual concession. Both countries agree: not to adopt policies which require minimum levels of national ownership in domestic firms; not to require forced divestiture from ownership; not to require foreign firms taking over domestic firms to meet certain performance requirements (e.g., investment or jobs); to provide fair standards for expropriation and compensation; and to allow free transfer of profits and other remittances to the home country. The effect of this section of the agreement would be to prohibit all future Canadian governments from adopting policies designed to increase the level of Canadian ownership of the economy. The Mulroney government even agreed to change the already feeble rules on screening foreign business takeovers by limiting the review process to very large corporations. The agreement would also tie the hands of provincial governments, as they would be prohibited from giving preference to Canadian or local firms in government-supported development projects. The provisions on investment go far beyond a free trade agreement and create new rules which are normally associated with common market arrangements.

Tariffs. All tariffs would be removed within ten years, beginning

January 1, 1989. Different products have different schedules for phasing out tariffs, but they are the same for both countries. Canadian negotiators were unable to get the United States, which is by far the stronger economy, to agree to remove its tariffs more quickly than Canada. In fact, Canada would be removing tariffs at an average rate of about 10% per year, while the United States would be removing tariffs at an average rate of about 5%. Thus, in reality, Canada would be removing its tariffs twice as fast as the United States.

The Auto Pact. From the beginning, the Mulroney government insisted that the 1965 Canada/U.S. Auto Pact would not be on the negotiating table. However, there were very strong political interests in the United States that insisted on changes in the Auto Pact, without which they would oppose the entire free trade agreement. The Auto Pact safeguards which guarantee continued production of automobiles in Canada are discussed in Chapter 12. The Auto Pact is an example of managed trade, not free trade. For every North American car sold in Canada, one had to be produced in Canada, with 60% of its content being Canadian. A penalty duty of 9.2% is imposed on any manufacturer not complying with these guidelines. The free trade agreement would eliminate this penalty over a ten-year period. New content rules allow automobiles and trucks to enter Canada duty-free if they contain 50% North American content. But, as the Automotive Parts Manufacturers of Canada point out, under the free trade agreement imports could have 100% North American content but no Canadian content. Finally, Canada agreed to immediately surrender the power to remit or waive duties linked to export performance; Canadian duty remission schemes linked to local production would end by 1995. These were major concessions. They make it difficult for the premier of Ontario, David Peterson, to accept the free trade agreement. During the campaign leading up to the September 1987 election, he promised to oppose any agreement which made such changes in the Auto Pact.

Agriculture. Major changes were proposed for agriculture. All provincial government protections for the wine industry and grape growers would be phased out. All agricultural tariffs are to be eliminated over a ten-year period, including seasonal duties on fruits and vegetables. The Canadian horticultural industry can expect devastation if the agreement is implemented. The Canadian import quotas for poultry, poultry products and eggs would be increased as of January 1, 1989. The Canadian Wheat Board could be undermined by the elimination of its power to grant import licences for wheat, barley, oats and corn. Wheat farmers would lose the two-price system, under which they receive higher prices for domestic sales. The general thrust of the agreement "against protectionism and for trade liberalization," plus the specific commitment "to improve access to each other's [agricultural] markets through the elimination or reduction of import barriers" signals the beginning of the end of supply management boards in Canada. But while one of the basic tools of Canadian government support for agriculture is deemed to be an "unfair trade practice," the agreement does not touch the U.S. system of even greater agricultural subsidies.

Pork and hogs are not covered in the agreement, and the U.S. countervailing duty on Canadian hogs remains in place. The agreement states that the two countries would "exempt each other from their respective meat-import laws," which provide quotas on beef and veal. Canadian cattlemen strongly supported this measure. The agreement provides for the use of import quotas on beef from third countries and attempts to prevent diversion into either Canada or the United States. But the agreement does not exempt Canadian meat processors from U.S. trade actions triggered by federal and provincial government subsidies. In reality, there is no guaranteed access to the U.S. market, even for beef.

Cultural Industries. The main goal of those who work in the area of Canadian culture and communications is to recapture a larger share of the Canadian market from American control and domination (see Chapter 16 for a further discussion of this issue). The Mulroney government has always insisted that Canada's cultural industries would not be covered by the free trade agreement. Nevertheless, the agreement specifically covers retransmission rights by Canadian cable television stations and allows publications printed in the United States to qualify for tax exemption in Canada. U.S. negotiators insist that the Mulroney government also agreed to change the proposed legislation which was designed to give Canadian firms an increased share of film distribution in Canada. In addition, the agreement specifies that all the cultural industries in Canada are to be treated as ordinary commercial industries. Thus, if there are government subsidies in Canada, they are open to remedy action under the U.S. trade laws if American competitors conclude that they give Canadian interests an unfair market advantage. The U.S. preliminary text stated that Canadian cultural policies are not to "constitute a discriminatory and unncessary barrier to U.S. trade," and that certainly reflects the consistent American position.

Financial Sector. The agreement specifies that U.S. nationals and companies controlled in the United States in the financial services sector are to receive national treatment in Canada. Laws which discriminate in favour of Canadian firms would be changed. For example, Canadian banks would no longer be protected from foreign ownership and control. And while U.S. banks would have access to the entire Canadian market, Canadian banks would not have similar access in the United States. Canadian laws which require banks to lend a proportion of their capital to "the middle market," loans between $5 and $20 million, would be removed. U.S. banks may own securities dealers in Canada, but Canadian banks would not have similar rights in the United States.

Service Sector. The most dramatic concessions made by the Mulroney government were in the service sector of the economy. This is the first international trade agreement to provide comprehensive coverage for the service industry. It is the most powerful sector of the American economy. The U.S. negotiators got everything they wanted in this area. The agreement provides for the right of national treatment for each other's enterprises, the legal right to set up shop and do business ("national establishment"), the right of commercial presence, the right to cross-border sales and the right to provincial treatment.

The agreement specifies that this would apply to all future or new measures affecting services. But as the U.S. negotiators have pointed out, the U.S./Canada services market is presently open in most areas. The agreement guarantees that "a liberal regime" would continue in the future. Furthermore, the U.S. preliminary text specifically stated that a major aim in the service sector is to put "disciplines on public monopolies." The final text grants the parties the right to establish monopolies, but they must not engage in policies which gives preference to local firms or discriminate against persons or goods of the other party to the agreement. The annex to the agreement lists an astonishing number of services which are included under the agreement. While the agreement specifically excluded a number of government-provided services (health, education and social services), the agreement also states that the *management* of these services is included. Furthermore, U.S. companies are granted the right to invest and establish in these areas and are to be treated the same as Canadian firms. Many observers have concluded that the concessions made in the service sector would have the greatest economic impact on Canada. The concerns relating to this sector are outlined in Chapter 14.

The Big Sellout

On October 9, 1987, *Inside U.S. Trade*, a Washington publication, reproduced the text of a confidential briefing paper prepared by U.S. negotiators for high-level U.S. administration officials on the Canada/U.S. free trade agreement. The U.S. negotiators concluded that "essentially, in the text we got everything that we wanted." U.S. Secretary of the Treasury, James Baker, has been quoted as telling key U.S. senators that his great fear is that the U.S. negotiators may have achieved "too much," and that this would give ammunition to opponents of the agreement in Canada. Indeed, one has only to read the final text of the agreement to reach such a conclusion. The Canadian negotiators achieved very little. Furthermore, there has been a rather astonishing surrender of Canadian sovereignty in the areas of energy, investment, financial services, agriculture and food, and the service sector.

The agreement is also only a beginning. The objectives are spelled out in the Canadian summary: to "lay the foundation for further bilateral and multilateral cooperation to expand and enhance the benefits of the Agreement." In many areas, sectoral working groups are continuing negotiations. For example, there are working groups in the process of harmonizing all standards related to agricultural and food. What government subsidies are to be allowed in the future is yet to be worked out over the next seven years. The principle has been established that supply-management marketing boards are impediments to free trade; future negotiations will probably see further concessions in this area. The precedents have been set.

Furthermore, it should be pointed out that the continental energy agreement, the policies on investment, and cross-border employment rights for businessmen and professionals represent areas which are not normally included in free trade agreements. Many Canadians, like Mitchell Sharp and Stuart Smith, believe that this agreement is the first, major step towards a North American common market, a goal of the Reagan administration.

Despite the massive campaign by the media in Canada in support of the free trade agreement, most Canadians have not been fooled. In a Decima poll conducted for the Department of External Affairs, and released to the public the first week in November 1987, 62% of Canadians thought the United States got the best of the deal. Another 28% concluded that is was "fair and balanced." Only 7% thought that Canada came out ahead in the negotiations. A Gallup poll conducted November 4-7, 1987 showed that only 29% of the population supported the particular agreement, 42% were opposed and 29% were undecided. In an additional question, 58% expressed concern about the effect that free trade might have on Canada's ability to act as an independent country.

Considering the gross imbalance in the agreement, why is it being pushed by the Mulroney government? Why is it still being strongly supported by business interests, most professional economists, the right-wing "think tanks" and the daily press? First, as Eric Kierans has pointed out, Canadian corporations wanted U.S. citizenship rights, and they got them. But, this is an aspect of the agreement which deals with *investment* rather than trade. As one wag has put it, the free trade agreement is the new "Business Charter of Rights." The key aspects of the agreement remove barriers to investment for both American and Canadian businessmen. That is why the major organizations supporting the Mulroney deal on both sides of the border represent big businesses which operate on a transnational basis.

But there is another very important aspect of the agreement. Despite all the rhetoric, it is not difficult to conclude that exemption from U.S. trade remedy legislation never really was the first priority of the supporters of free trade. There was always a hidden agenda—the New Right program of solving the persistent economic crisis. In Canada, the new agenda was advanced by the Business Council on National Issues, the Canadian Chamber of Commerce and the Canadian Manufacturers Association. The "free market" approach was endorsed by the Macdonald Royal Commission. Unfortunately for these interests, there is strong public support in Canada for the welfare state, greater equality in income and wealth, and the traditional Canadian programs designed to reduce regional disparities. Integration with the United States would greatly facilitate the implementation of the New Right agenda in Canada.

The implications for Canada of the imposition of the New Right agenda is a central focus of this book. It is my belief that the free trade issue is not just a question of the survival of Canada as an independent and sovereign country. Free trade is also polarizing the country along political and class lines, or revealing the polarity that already exists. The reality is that support for free trade comes almost exclusively from big business and its ideological supporters, while opposition comes primarily from the popular sectors: labour, women, farmers, poor people, native Canadians, environmentalists, people in the arts, senior citizens, peace activists, and the established churches. To a very significant degree, free trade with the United States is also a class issue.

This book is divided into three roughly equal parts. Chapters 1 to 6 look at the broad international context of the persistent economic crisis and how free trade with the United States fits into the New Right solution. The middle section, Chapters 7 to 16, examines the special problems associated with Canada/U.S. economic and political integration under free trade, including the support for and opposition to free trade in Canada, and the impacts it may have on the major sectors of the Canadian economy. Chapters 17 to 23 discuss a range of alternative strategies for Canada.

PART I

The New Right Solution
To the International Economic Crisis

CHAPTER 1

The International Economic Crisis

Between 1980 and 1982 the world experienced the most severe economic downturn since the Great Depression of the 1930s. While there has been slow economic recovery since 1983, unemployment in most industrialized Western countries remains very high by historic standards. While stock markets and financial profits escalated until the October 1987 crash, creating the illusion of a "boom" period, production stagnated throughout, and instability and uncertainty were never greater. Outside of a number of Asian countries, the majority of people in the underdeveloped world have experienced declining real standards of living over the past six years. Governments have cut back on social programs in attempts to balance their budgets. Many countries are suffering from serious trade deficits and balance of payments problems. The inevitable next recession looms closer, causing justifiable fear among many, but offering an opportune time to begin the re-examination of the political and economic foundations and alternatives to contemporary capitalist society. In Canada, the long persistence of the international economic crisis has been the main reason why business interests and their political and ideological supporters have chosen an economic strategy based on a bilateral free trade agreement with the United States.

The Postwar Boom

From the end of World War II to about 1971 the world economy grew at a relatively rapid rate, and the real income of most people increased significantly. The major question raised by the recent prolonged economic downturn and persistent high unemployment is whether this long boom was an anomalous period in the history of capitalism or whether the stagnation in the world economy is simply the inevitable result of misguided governmental economic policies and programs.

A great number of people are beginning to realize that the long period of economic good times may be coming to an end. As Cy Gonick has pointed out, there were special factors at work during the period between 1946 and 1971 which sustained the prolonged period of high economic growth. World War II devastated most of the industrial states; Canada and the United States were significant exceptions. An enormous task of reconstruction was necessary, and this rebuilding required heavy capital investment and expanding employment opportunities. The U.S. and Canadian economies greatly benefited, particularly in technology and machinery. As the reconstruction period ended, the civil war in Korea was internationalized, and industrial production was stimulated by massive military expenditures. Even when the Korean War ended, the governments of the Western countries chose to continue expanding their military capacity. This began the era of "military Keynesianism," of governments stimulating economic growth through direct spending on military hardware and technology.

But there were other factors which made important contributions to the long boom. Wages for workers were relatively low. They had been dramatically reduced during the Great Depression, and then they had been frozen during the war. There was no shortage of workers, a fact which had a depressing effect on wages, as people fled the farms and women re-entered the work force.

In addition, trade unions and left-wing political parties were weak. During the rise of fascism in Europe, the trade unions and socialist and communist parties were attacked and their leadership destroyed. After the war there was great concern that the political left would rise to power. But the renewed repression at the onset of the Cold War again devastated the political left and the more militant trade union leadership. This atmosphere encouraged the right wing of the trade union movement to reach an accord with the owners of capital.

The reformist movement in workers' organizations actively promoted the accord with the owners of capital. The capitalist system of production was to persist, and labour gave up the socialist agenda. The owners of capital continued to have the right to dictate investment, and they retained management rights in the workplace. In return, the owners of capital accepted the right of trade unions to exist and to engage in free collective bargaining. The workers were to be protected against a return of the conditions of the Great Depression by the introduction of the welfare state. In contrast to the 1930s, governments would be committed to full employment; in times of economic downturns, they would not sit back and wait for private capital to solve economic problems. Following the policies of the social democratic governments in the Scandinavian countries, the worst aspects of the traditional business cycles would be moderated by government action. In times of economic downturn, the governments would increase spending, borrowing on the capital markets. In theory, in good times governments would increase taxes, run a budget surplus, and retire government debt. Interest rates could also be manipulated by the central banks to ease borrowing during downturns and to raise rates during periods of rapid expansion and inflation.

There were other factors which stimulated economic growth in the industrialized world during the long post-war boom. The prices of raw materials, particularly energy resources, were low. In relation to the prices of manufactured products, they actually declined until about 1971. World War II had also seen the full development of the system of production know as "Fordism," the scientific management of work in large factories. Specialization was the rule, technical innovation was rapid, and new machinery was readily introduced. Labour productivity rose with increased investment. This new industrial revolution brought mass produced consumer goods to most people in the industrial countries.

What made all this possible was a world-wide relative stability created by the dominant (or hegemonic) position of the United States. With the other capitalist states greatly weakened by the war, the United States easily emerged as the economic leader of the West. Politically, the United States exercised this leadership role through its system of military alliances, backed by its massive military force. Its chosen political role was to contain the spread of socialism and communism. The dominant position of the United States was not challenged by the other capitalist states. Until the admission of the newly independent former colonies into the United Nations, the United States and its political allies also dominated that body.

In the economic sphere, the key to stability was the Bretton Woods agreements of 1948 which created the International Monetary Fund and the International Bank for Reconstruction and Development (World Bank). The countries represented agreed to stabilize their currencies by fixed foreign exchange rates, tied to the U.S. dollar (and the U.S. gold standard). The U.S. dollar became the equivalent of gold and served as official reserves, backing the currencies of the other countries. This was a tremendous advantage to the United States as it enhanced U.S. exports.

The United States directed the capitalist reconstruction of Europe through the Marshall Plan. Extensive credits were granted to the European governments to purchase goods in the United States. European recovery was co-ordinated through the organization of developed capitalist states which evolved into the Organization of Economic Co-operation and Development (OECD), under the leadership of the U.S. government.

As the dominant world economic power, the United States became the major proponent of free trade. In 1947 the U.S. government sponsored the General Agreement on Tariffs and Trade (GATT), an international organization of capitalist countries which made a commitment to reduction of tariffs and the promotion of more liberal trading arrangements. During this period of U.S. world economic hegemony, American corporations expanded their influence around the world by means of trade, investment and the manipulation of consumer tastes through advertising, always supported by the U.S. military presence.

The Breakdown of the Golden Age of Capitalism

The stability of the boom period of capitalism was underpinned by the unchallenged political and economic role of the United States. But challenges inevitably began to appear. With reconstruction, Europe and Japan rose in economic importance, and given the system of unequal distribution, "surplus capacity" in production inevitably emerged; U.S. business interests began to face increased competition both at home and abroad.

The driving force of the capitalist system is the accumulation of profits. Those who own capital are always seeking the investments which bring the highest rate of return. However, the inevitable result is constant competition between rival capitalists. When the rate of return in one area of investment declines relative to others, capitalists shift their investment to more profitable sectors of the economy. Capital is national in that it is based in a particular country and relies on that particular state for support. However, the owners of capital also insist on the right to invest abroad when opportunities for profit are better than at home. The current economic crisis had its origins in the decline in the rate of profit (and the decline in investment) in the advanced industrial states. Figure 1 illustrates the downturn in the net rate of return on capital in the European Economic Community (EEC) over a 25-year period from 1960.

Figure 1

Net Rate of Return on Capital
In the European Economic Community

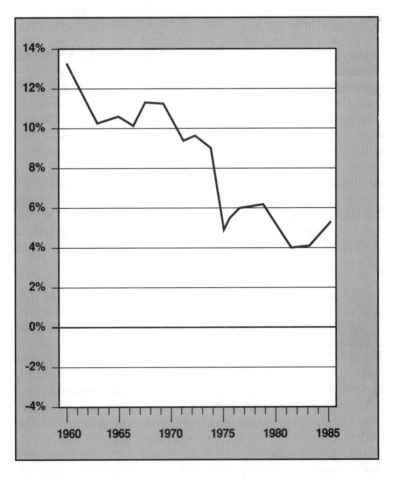

SOURCE: *The Economist,* February 8, 1986; OECD, *Main Economic Indicators,* March 1987.

The 1960s saw an increase in the militancy of labour as strikes for higher wages and benefits were common throughout the industrial countries. While labour costs rose, labour productivity began to decline (real output per hour of labour employed) In response to increased political pressure, the governments of the Western industrial countries also increased the social welfare benefits available, what we now call the "social wage," financed by increased government taxation. After 1972 there was a rise in commodity prices as a result of increased demand for raw materials. Furthermore, by the 1970s it appeared that the market for the major consumer goods in the industrialized countries was becoming saturated, and competition for sales was increasing. All of these factors contributed to the decline in the rate of profit and the rate of investment.

This crisis was revealed in the breakdown of the Bretton Woods monetary system. U.S. dollars were used as foreign exchange reserves by other countries and as hard currency in international trade. In the 1960s, U.S. businesses, governments and individuals were buying goods and services abroad faster than foreign interests were buying goods and services in the United States. The result was a buildup of U.S. dollars abroad. In order to finance the Vietnam War and the domestic social policies of The Great Society, the Johnson adminstration resorted to deficit spending, further increasing the supply of dollars. By the beginning of the 1970s, these "Eurodollars," as they were popularly called, totalled about $100 billion. As a consequence, monetary instability increased as it became evident that the U.S. government could not exchange all of its dollars for gold.

The collapse of the system of fixed foreign exchange rates came in 1971 when speculation in U.S. currency intensified. As the U.S. gold reserves became depleted, President Nixon suspended the convertability of the U.S. dollar into gold. In December 1971 there was an attempt to realign the other major currencies with the U.S. dollar, but in 1973 it was finally agreed to allow all the currencies to float freely on the international market. However, free markets inevitably bring fluctuations, greater instability and financial insecurity.

During the boom period after World War II, economic depressions were unknown, and while there were business cycles, there was no general downturn in the Western economies until 1967. A second general decline occurred in 1969-70. However, the first major postwar recession did not occur until 1974-5. This deep recession should have demonstrated that a major crisis was underway, but it was largely hidden by the inflationary boom of the 1970s.

Table 1

Debt Indicators for Less Developed Countries

Indicator	1980	1981	1982	1983	1984	1985
Ratio of debt to GNP	21.1	22.8	26.8	31.8	32.7	33.0
Ratio of debt to exports	90.1	97.5	116.4	134.3	130.4	135.7
Debt service ratio	16.1	17.7	20.7	19.4	19.8	21.9
Ratio of debt service to GNP	3.8	4.1	4.7	4.6	5.0	5.3
Ratio of interest service to exports	7.0	8.3	10.4	10.0	10.5	11.0
Total debt outstanding and disbursed (billions of dollars)	431.6	492.5	552.4	629.9	674.1	711.2
Private debt as a percentage of total debt	63.3	64.5	64.9	66.1	65.7	64.5

NOTE: Data are based on a sample of ninety less developed countries.
SOURCE: World Bank, *World Development Report, 1986.*

The U.S. dollar had a temporary reprieve with the rapid increase in oil prices; the Organization of Petroleum Exporting Countries (OPEC) accepted payment only in U.S. dollars. To a large extent these petrodollars were recycled into relatively weak investments in Third World countries. With the onset of the great world recession in 1980-2, most of these countries experienced even worse declines in economic growth, the fall of prices of exports, lack of foreign exchange, and a rise in debt payments to foreign lending institutions. This is illustrated in Table 1. The decline in real income and ability to purchase exports from the industrialized West intensified the world recession.

The 1970s also saw a general increase in private and public debt. However, the rates of inflation were higher in the other industrial countries than in the United States. When the United States exported its dollars to cover its mounting trade deficit, it raised the supply of money abroad and increased price levels. The European central banks bought U.S. dollars to try to stop speculation. However, runs on the U.S. dollar intensified in 1977 and 1978. It was at this time that the governments of the Western industrial countries came to the conclusion that inflation was the most serious problem facing world capitalism, and new policies were needed. The result was a general shift to high interest rates and cutbacks in government spending. The new policies culminated in the worst downturn the world economy had seen since the Great Depression of the 1930s.

The Rise of Monetarism

By the middle of the 1970s it was evident that the accord between labour and capital had collapsed. Trade unions in all the Western countries were demanding wage settlements that would keep up with the rapidly escalating rise in inflation. Supporters of moderate government intervention in the economy were unable to come up with alternative policies to deal with "stagflation," the persistence of high levels of unemployment and high rates of inflation. Several governments, including Great Britain and Canada, tried to implement wage and price controls, known as "incomes policies," but in operation these only restricted wage and salary increases and had little effect on price levels or unearned income (dividends, interest, real estate, etc.).

Into this vacuum stepped the supporters of monetarism, led by Milton Friedman and the economists at the University of Chicago. They had been advisers to the Pinochet dictatorship in Chile after 1973. Chile's inflation had been brought under control through strict monetarist policies, but at the price of a rise in unemployment from 7% to 30%. This seemed to be just what the owners of capital had in mind. Monetarism achieved respectability with the release in 1977 of the study done by Paul McCracken and his associates for the OECD. In the best tradition of Ronald Reagan "doublespeak," it was called "Towards Full Employment and Price Stability." The study questioned government policies adopted in the post-war period and advocated a tight money policy (high interest rates), fiscal restraint by governments, cuts in social welfare expenditures, and the deliberate increase in the levels of unemployment. By adopting such a strategy, the study argued, the Western governments could halt the inflationary spiral and restore profitability to the capitalist system through what they called "the democratic disciplinary state."

In the summer of 1979 it looked as if the international monetary system might collapse. The price of gold was soaring and the value of the U.S. dollar was falling. In September the annual joint meetings of the World Bank and the International Monetary Fund were held at Belgrade, Yugoslavia. The European bankers told Paul Volker, chairman of the U.S. Federal Reserve Board, and William Miller, the U.S. Secretary of the Treasury, that if the U.S. government did not do something drastic they would join in the run on the U.S. dollar. On October 6, 1979, the U.S. Federal Reserve Board declared a policy of tight money by raising U.S. interest rates.

The rejection of government stimulation of the economy was reinforced by the election of Margaret Thatcher and the Conservatives in Britain and Ronald Reagan as U.S. President. In West Germany, the Social Democratic government had adopted the new monetarist strategy as early as 1973. The right-wing government in France adopted the Barre Plan in 1976. By late 1980, it was apparent that the world was again sinking into another recession, the deepest in half a century.

The magnitude of the 1980-2 world recession is revealed in the accompanying tables. But the statistics in Table 2 also reveal that there has been a general downturn in the economies of the industrialized capitalist states which has been progressive since the 1970s. The general rate of economic growth in these countries as a

Table 2

Annual Percentage Increase of Real Gross Domestic Product

Country	1966-73	1974-79	1980-5	1986
United States	3.4	2.5	2.5	2.5
Japan	9.4	3.6	4.0	2.5
West Germany	4.1	2.4	1.3	2.4
France	5.5	3.1	1.1	2.0
United Kingdom	3.1	1.5	1.2	2.7
Italy	5.4	2.6	1.4	2.7
Canada	5.3	4.2	2.4	3.1
Group Seven	4.5	2.7	2.3	2.5
EEC Countries	4.6	2.4	1.3	2.4
Smaller European Countries	5.0	2.5	1.9	2.7
OECD Europe	4.5	2.4	1.4	2.5
Total OECD Countries	4.5	2.7	2.3	2.5

SOURCE: *OECD Economic Outlook,* No. 41, June 1987.

Table 3

Percentage of Labour Force Unemployed

Country	1965-73	1974-9	1980-5	1986
United States	4.3	6.6	8.0	7.0
Japan	1.2	1.9	2.4	2.8
West Germany	0.8	3.2	6.4	8.3
France	2.3	4.5	8.3	10.5
United Kingdom	3.2	5.1	11.0	13.1
Italy	3.2	6.6	9.2	11.8
Canada	4.8	7.2	10.0	9.8
Group Seven	3.1	5.0	7.2	7.7
Australia	1.9	5.0	7.6	8.0
Austria	1.6	1.8	3.2	4.0
Belgium	2.4	6.5	12.2	11.2
Finland	2.4	4.6	5.7	7.0
Netherlands	1.3	4.0	11.1	13.5
Norway	1.7	1.8	2.5	2.0
Spain	2.6	5.3	16.6	21.5
Sweden	2.0	1.9	2.8	2.5
OECD Eight	2.1	4.6	11.1	13.4

SOURCE: *OECD Economic Outlook,* various issues.

whole has steadily declined since the heady days of the early 1960s. In the 1980s, growth rates have been only one-half what they were in the 1960s. While our concern in Canada is mainly with the United States, the decline in economic growth has been even more pronounced in Japan and West Germany.

Table 3 illustrates the hard reality that in spite of some indications of economic recovery, the level of unemployment in the Western industrialized countries has been steadily increasing over the 1970s and 1980s. At the end of 1986, there were over 31 million people officially unemployed in these countries. In early 1987, five years into the recovery, official unemployment stood at over 11% in Europe and was as high as 21% in Spain and 20% in Ireland. Youth unemployment was 43% in Spain, 35% in Italy and 25% in France.

The proportion of working people experiencing long-term unemployment (over one year) had doubled since 1979.

The structure of jobs is also changing. First, there has been a
steady increase in the number of people working at part-time jobs. In
Europe, for example, between 1979 and 1985, full-time employment actually declined at an annual rate of 0.1% while part-time employment rose 3.1%. To a large extent this reflects the shift in the
economies of the industrialized countries away from the production
sectors to the service area. Women are more highly represented in the
part-time labour force than men are. Second, there has been an increase in temporary work. A survey of the European Economic
Community (EEC) in 1986 revealed that temporary work accounted
for a low of 4% in Italy to a high of 12% in Greece and Denmark.
Temporary work is concentrated among Europe's youth. A number
of observers, including *Business Week* (March 3, 1986), have noted
that this shift in the economy represents a loss of relatively high paying jobs in the goods-producing sector and their replacement with
rather low-paying jobs in the service sector, which also is
characterized by low opportunities for increasing labour productivity.

Nevertheless, as Table 4 shows, for the industrialized countries as
a whole, hourly wages rose faster than the consumer price index over
the period from 1978 to 1986, indicating that real wages have continued to increase. (This is not true for Canada, as we shall see in
Chapter 2). Yet, over the same period of time, the unit labour costs to
employers declined. This reflects the fact that employers put greater
emphasis on achieving "flexible employment" and reducing fringe
benefits in collective bargaining, and less emphasis on reducing
wages and salaries.

The major gain for employers during the recovery period since
1980 has been in the reduction of the costs of production inputs other
than labour. Since the bottom of the recession, general commodity
prices have fallen on average between 50% and 60%. The most important factor has been the decline in oil prices. This has enabled
profits to begin a recovery. But this also means that to a large extent
the recovery has been paid for by a shift in national incomes. The
major losers have been those countries dependent on the export of
raw materials and food, primarily in the Third World.

Nevertheless, many economists have argued that the major weakness of the recovery from the 1980-2 recession has been a lack of
business investment. This is demonstrated in Table 5. Business confidence has been undermined by the uncertainty of the economy in

Table 4

Percentage Annual Change in Labour Costs, Productivity and Prices

Country	Average 1968-77	1978	1979	1980	1981	1982	1983	1984	1985	1986
Group Seven Countries										
Hourly earnings	10.8	8.8	10.1	11.7	10.6	9.6	5.6	4.6	5.1	3.8
Consumer prices	7.1	6.9	9.2	12.1	9.9	6.9	4.4	4.4	3.8	1.9
Output per manhour	4.1	3.5	3.1	3.1	1.2	2.7	2.2	6.2	3.1	2.2
Unit labour costs	6.5	5.2	6.9	10.4	7.6	7.2	1.1	-1.5	1.9	1.6
Other Industrial Countries										
Hourly earnings	13.5	11.7	11.0	10.88	10.6	10.2	8.4	6.6	6.5	4.1
Consumer prices	8.1	8.5	7.8	10.2	10.4	9.7	7.6	6.3	5.8	4.8
Output per manhour	5.9	3.6	5.6	2.7	3.5	2.7	6.2	5.2	3.7	2.2
Unit labour costs	7.3	7.9	5.0	8.0	7.8	2.1	1.4	1.4	2.7	4.2
European Countries										
Hourly earnings	14.0	11.6	12.3	13.0	13.3	11.3	9.3	6.8	6.7	5.9
Consumer prices	7.8	7.5	8.8	11.8	9.5	7.3	6.1	6.1	5.3	4.8
Output per manhour	5.4	4.0	5.0	2.0	3.7	3.3	5.6	5.1	4.1	2.5
Unit labour costs	8.2	7.3	6.9	10.8	9.2	7.8	3.6	1.6	2.6	3.4
All OECD Countries										
Hourly earnings	11.2	9.2	10.2	11.5	10.8	9.7	6.0	4.9	5.3	4.1
Consumer prices	7.2	7.2	9.0	11.8	9.9	7.3	4.9	4.7	4.1	2.3
Output per manhour	4.3	3.5	3.5	1.4	2.9	2.3	4.7	6.1	3.2	2.2
Unit labour costs	6.6	5.7	6.6	10.0	7.7	7.2	1.2	-1.1	2.0	1.9

SOURCE: International Monetary Fund, *World Economic Outlook*, April 1987.

Table 5

Annual Percentage Increase in Gross Fixed Investment

Country	1968-77	1978	1979	1980	1981	1982	1983	1984	1985	1986
United States	3.6	9.8	3.7	-7.9	1.1	-9.6	7.8	17.6	7.5	1.9
Japan	7.7	8.5	5.3	—	3.1	0	-0.3	4.6	5.8	6.5
West Germany	2.3	4.7	7.2	2.8	-4.8	-5.3	3.2	0.8	-0.3	3.3
France	4.0	1.5	3.7	3.2	-1.1	0.7	-2.3	12.0	-0.5	4.4
United Kingdom	1.2	3.2	2.6	-5.2	-9.3	6.4	4.5	8.2	1.3	0.6
Italy	1.8	-0.1	5.8	9.4	0.6	-5.2	-3.8	4.1	4.3	2.0
Canada	4.4	4.4	-0.1	6.8	3.4	6.4	-9.7	0.7	7.0	2.6
Group Seven	3.7	6.8	4.6	-2.5	-0.1	-4.8	3.6	10.0	5.3	3.0
Other Industrial Countries	3.0	-0.7	0.5	2.2	-1.9	-2.3	-1.1	3.1	4.8	4.2
European Countries	2.6	1.5	3.6	2.2	-3.9	-1.5	0.7	2.4	1.8	3.9
All OECD Countries	3.6	5.6	4.0	-1.8	-0.4	-4.4	2.9	3.1	4.8	3.1

SOURCE: International Monetary Fund, *World Economic Outlook*, April 1987.

general. While business investment has recovered in the United States under the military Keynesianism of the Reagain administration, it has stagnated in other countries, including Japan.

Clearly, what we are witnessing is not just a periodic recession that we have come to expect as part of the normal business cycle, but a general crisis in the world capitalist economy, which began in the latter part of the 1960s. The international economy is fluctuating and unstable. The uncertainty and insecurity experienced by the owners of capital have led to an entire new agenda in the economic and political area. In Canada it has taken the form of the rise of the New Right in politics and economics, the election of the Conservative Party under the leadership of Brian Mulroney, and the promotion of a free trade agreement with the United States.

CHAPTER 2

The Great Recession in Canada

Most Canadians look back on the 1970s as a period of relative prosperity. Thanks to the upturn in prices for raw materials and natural products at the beginning of the decade, the Canadian economy grew at a rate which was higher than the average of the Western industrialized countries and considerably higher than that of the United States (see Table 2). In the first half of the 1970s, Canada's per capita real domestic product rose from 80% to 105% of that of the United States.

The first general recession in the post-war period came in 1974-5. It followed the boost in the price of grains in 1972, the collapse of the Peruvian anchovies which raised the price of feed supplements, the U.S. corn blight in 1973, and the major oil price increases which occurred when the governments of the producing countries began to challenge the international cartel of the Seven Sisters. But the boom in prices for basic raw materials and food helped carry Canada through the recession. While most of the industrialized countries experienced a decline in gross domestic product and industrial production, in Canada there was a drop only in the annual increase. Nevertheless, the general rise in the rate of inflation in the 1970s became a major concern of business interests and the Trudeau government.

The Attack on Inflation

In 1973 and 1974 consumer prices increased by 7.6% and 10.9%. In 1975, Gerald Bouey, Governor of the Bank of Canada, announced the gradual introduction of a policy of monetarism. The Bank of Canada would attempt to control the money supply (and inflation) through increases in the prime interest rate. Between 1975 and 1980 the prime rate rose from 8% to 14%. However, the policy was not very successful; the average annual increase in consumer prices was 10.8% in 1975 and was still 9.1% in 1979.

At the same time as the Bank of Canada was trying to control the supply of money, interest rates and inflation, it was also trying to intervene in money markets in an attempt to prop up the Canadian dollar in relation to the U.S. dollar. This proved to be an impossible task. By 1977 the Bank of Canada was forced to admit that it was unable to implement a monetary policy that was separate from that of the U.S. government. From that time on, the Bank concentrated on slowing the drop of the Canadian dollar against the U.S. dollar.

The Trudeau government also tried to deal with the relatively high rate of inflation by introducing price and wage controls, which were in force from October 1975 through March 1979. Under the controls, which were administered by the Anti-Inflation Board, increases in wages and salaries began to level off; in 1978 and 1979 there was an actual decline in real income for most working people. However, prices continued to rise. The rate of inflation rose to 10.2% in 1980 and 12.5% in 1981. Following the policies of the new right-wing governments in Britain and the United States, the Bank of Canada embarked on a tough monetary policy in 1981. The prime interest rate rose to 17% and commercial interest rates rose to 22%. This had the desired effect—the annual rate of inflation declined to 5.8% in 1983 and 4.4% in 1984. But there was a high price to pay.

The Onset of the Great Recession

The impact is best seen in the rise in unemployment. As Table 6 demonstrates, the number of unemployed reached 1.448 million in 1983. The official rate of unemployment peaked in March of that year at 13.9%. Youth unemployment also peaked in that year at 19.8%. Between 1982 and 1985, the number of people unemployed for more than one year rose by 91%.

According to a special study by the Economic Council of Canada, discouraged workers, those who have given up looking for work believing that none can be found, rose to almost 3% of the labour force. Between 1975 and 1986, part-time employment grew by 83% while full-time employment grew by only 25%. In general, part-time jobs are lower paying jobs with significantly fewer benefits. In 1986 the average part-time job provided only 15.4 hours of work per

Table 6

Unemployment in Canada

Year	Labour Force ('000)	Unemployed ('000)	% Labour Force	Unemployed Youth ('000)	% Labour Force	Part-Time Employed ('000)	% Labour Force	Discouraged Workers ('000)	% Labour Force
1976	9849	726	7.4	348	12.7	1047	10.6	128	1.3
1977	10,030	849	8.5	406	14.4	1128	11.2	138	1.4
1978	10,346	908	8.8	420	14.5	1206	11.7	168	1.6
1979	10,807	836	7.7	388	12.9	1301	12.0	170	1.6
1980	11,181	865	7.7	404	13.2	1392	12.4	225	2.0
1981	11,473	898	7.8	407	13.2	1487	12.9	218	1.9
1982	11,585	1314	11.3	555	18.8	1534	13.2	283	2.4
1983	11,745	1448	12.3	579	19.8	1651	14.0	335	2.9
1984	11,916	1399	11.7	518	17.9	1689	14.2	302	2.5
1985	12,165	1328	10.9	473	16.5	1757	14.4	270	2.2
1986	12,543	1236	9.8	434	15.2	1810	14.4	245	2.0

NOTE: Youth are ages 15 to 24. Discouraged workers are those not actively seeking work because of market conditions, defined as not in the labour force.

SOURCE: Statistics Canada, *The Labour Force*, Cat. No. 71-001.

Table 7

Real Income in Canada

Year	Consumer Price Index (% Change)	Average Weekly Earnings	Real Change (in %)	Average Hourly Earnings	Real Change (in %)	Investment Income ($ Billions)	Real Change (in %)
1978	8.9	269	-2.6	7.04	-2.2	19,805	17.6
1979	9.1	292	-0.5	7.69	0.1	24,136	13.0
1980	10.2	325	1.1	8.59	1.5	28,472	7.5
1981	12.5	363	-0.8	9.70	-1.1	40,472	29.6
1982	10.8	399	-0.9	10.62	-1.3	46,972	5.3
1983	5.8	395	-5.9	9.99	-11.7	44,390	-11.3
1984	4.4	409	-0.9	10.35	-0.8	49,931	8.1
1985	4.0	426	0.2	10.72	-0.4	55,931	7.3
1986	4.1	435	-2.0	10.91	-2.3	57,327	-0.9

NOTE: Average weekly earnings includes average salaries and wages in Canadian industry. Average hourly earnings are for all Canadian industries. Real change is adjusted for inflation.

SOURCE: Statistics Canada. *Employment, Earnings and Hours*. Cat. No. 71-002; Statistics Canada, *National Income and Expenditure Accounts*, Cat. No 13-001. Department of Finance, *Quarterly Economic Review*.

week. From the onset of the recession in 1981 through 1986, the participation rate of males in the labour force declined from 78% to 76%; the participation rate for females increased from 51% to 55%.

A study by Andrew Sharpe of the federal Ministry of Finance reported that since the beginning of the 1974 recession the number of self-employed people had steadily increased in spite of the fact that the average income for this class was declining. This could be explained only by the fact that for many who had lost their jobs, there was no real chance of getting them back. In desperation, as unemployment insurance ran out, they sought any kind of work which would keep them off the welfare rolls. While the "informal economy," or the "black economy," is lauded by many right-wing economists, it actually means longer working hours, lower income per hour worked, and lower overall income for participants in it.

The recession and the moderate recovery after 1984 has brought a decline in real income (adjusted for inflation) and in the standard of living for most people on wages and salaries. This is illustrated in Table 7. Over the period between 1978 and 1986, average real weekly earnings for those on wages and salaries in Canadian industries dropped by 8.1%. For those working in Canadian industries on an hourly wage, the average loss was 14.9%. And of course, those trying to exist on unemployment insurance or welfare had much greater declines in their standard of living.

In contrast, income from dividends from corporate stocks, interest and other miscellaneous investments rose substantially (see Table 7). Over the 1978-86 period, real income from these investment sources increased by 119%.

There was also a steady increase in the number of people living on some form of provincial social assistance during the great recession and the recovery period. Actually, the number of people on social assistance did not peak in 1983, as did unemployment, but continued to rise through 1985. In 1985 the number of cases of people receiving social assistance reached 1,046,000, and with dependants accounted for 1.9 million Canadians. In addition, around 60% of Canada's status Indians were forced to live on federal social assistance because of lack of jobs; in Saskatchewan and Manitoba, over 80% were on assistance.

Using a relative income approach, the poverty line in Canada is estimated to be about 50% of the average Canadian family income, adjusted for size. However, the social assistance rates established by the provincial governments are based on what they believe to be a subsistence level, or the minimum required to provide food, shelter and clothing. In 1984 the provincial levels of assistance for families ranged between 45% and 76% of the poverty line established by Statistics Canada. For single employable people, the rate of assistance fell to as low as 14% of the poverty line. Lineups at food banks and at charities which served hot lunches became a regular fact of life in Canada.

Furthermore, since the mid-1970s the provinces have been cutting back on social assistance and deliberately refusing to raise levels of assistance to keep up with inflation. These cutbacks intensified with the onset of the great recession of the 1980s. Actual reductions in the amount of assistance available to welfare clients were introduced in some provinces. With the Canada Assistance Plan of 1966, the federal government assumed 50% of the costs of social assistance. In return, the federal government required certain common standards for all provinces. But while the CAP legislation requires that provinces provide "adequate assistance to and in respect of persons in need," there had been no attempt to define or to enforce standards of adequacy, even when major cutbacks were made in the 1980s.

These statistics give an overall picture of the impact of the great recession. But they tell only part of the story. Harvey Brenner, an American economist, has calculated that a 1% increase in the unemployment rate leads to a 4.1% increase in suicides, a 3.4% increase in mental hospital admissions, a 4% increase in prison admission, a 1.9% increase in cirrhosis of the liver and a 1.9% increase in deaths from cardiovascular disease.

In its brief to the Macdonald Royal Commission in 1984, the Canadian Mental Health Association presented similar figures for Canada. An economic crisis erodes the mental and physical well being of the victims. Chronic stress is the norm; the unemployed lose self-respect and suffer from frustration, anguish and insecurity. Marriages break up. Violence within the family becomes much more common. People lose their independence and are forced to rely on government support. The shutdown of plants results in loss of a sense of community. It is impossible to fully measure these costs.

Business was also hard hit by the collapse of the economy. Bankruptcies among business firms rose dramatically from 5,474 in 1979 to 10,913 in 1983. Net losses in these bankruptcies rose from $342 million in 1979 to $1,885 million in 1984. Smaller businesses, of course, were the hardest hit.

The extent of the economic collapse has been reflected in the decline in figures on capacity utilization rates in Canadian manufacturing. Capacity utilization peaked in the first quarter of 1974 at 95.2%

and then declined to a low of 66.3% in the fourth quarter of 1982. The hardest hit industries were transportation equipment, chemicals, primary metals, non-metallic minerals and wood products. But recovery has been relatively slow, with capacity utilization reaching only 77.7% in 1986, well below the average rate for the latter half of the 1970s, which was about 85%.

Corporation profits fell by 35% in 1982, but since then they have recovered. However, the rate of profit still remains substantially below the levels of the 1960s and 1970s. The most notable change in the economy in the late 1970s and 1980s has been the rather dramatic decline in corporation profits in relation to interest and other financial income. This is consistent with the trends in the other advanced capitalist countries.

Finally, there is the impact of the great recession on the financial structure of the federal and provincial governments. Beginning in 1975, the federal and provincial governments began to run budget deficits. These increased during the periods of high inflation in the latter half of the 1970s. By 1985 the federal budget deficit exceeded $26 billion. The provincial governments were also running deficits, but they were of a much smaller magnitude.

By 1986 the federal government's total unmatured debt had risen to $201 trillion, representing 41% of the country's gross national product, up from 22% in 1978. The annual interest on the public debt consumed 23% of all federal revenues. The Canadian taxation system is very regressive, with taxes falling hardest on those least able to pay. Federal government bonds are held primarily by those in the upper income brackets. Therefore, the high interest payments on government debt represent a major transfer of income from those in the lower income brackets to those in the higher.

Richard Deaton, a researcher for the Canadian Union of Public Employees, has estimated the cost of the great recession for the year 1982 at about $75 billion. This includes $7.4 billion for physical and mental stress-related factors, $8.9 billion in lost earnings, $8.1 billion in unemployment insurance payments, $2.7 billion for educational investment in unemployed youth, and $41 billion in lost production. These personal and economic costs are a very high price to pay for the continuation of the boom and bust society where all the key decisions are made by a small handful of powerful people.

The Answer: The Macdonald Royal Commission

In the great Canadian tradition, the federal government responded to the persistent economic crisis by appointing another Royal Commission. Headed by Donald S. Macdonald, a former Liberal finance minister, the new Royal Commission on the Economic Union was asked to report on "the appropriate national goals and policies for economic development." The Commission held hearings across Canada, but as Daniel Drache and Duncan Cameron have stressed, they ignored the briefs presented by the groups representing labour, farmers, women, the unemployed, native peoples, the churches, youth and the poor. They listened to the voice of big business. About 300 academics were paid to produce background studies for the Commission; almost without exception, they spoke the language of neo-conservatism and the New Right.

The message of the Macdonald Royal Commission was clear. Canada needs to "significantly increase our reliance on market forces" in solving economic problems. A major effect was made to show that most people who were unemployed were there because of their own choosing—"voluntary unemployment." Government intervention in the economy to try to mitigate the impact of recessions was "unrealistic" and "unnecessary." If the government would only free business from the maze of regulations and restrictions, the economy would recover on its own. Foreign investment should be encouraged. The welfare state should be streamlined. But the Commission's central proposal was a comprehensive bilateral free trade agreement with the United States.

CHAPTER 3

The New International Economy

During the 1960s and 1970s there were major changes in the international economy, many of them stimulated by the general reduction of tariffs effected by multilateral negotiations under the General Agreement on Tariffs and Trade (GATT). With the reduced tariffs, a number of underdeveloped countries embarked on programs of economic development which stressed the expansion of exports of manufactured goods. Their much lower labour costs enabled them to compete successfully in the markets of the more advanced industrialized countries. The other major change in the world economy was the relative decline in the economic power of the United States. In addition, the world recessions of 1974-5 and 1981-2 brought growing concern in the industrialized nations about the loss of jobs and industries to offshore competition. Under pressure from domestic political sources, many governments, including that of the United States, began to invoke non-tariff barriers to trade in an attempt to protect threatened domestic industries. With relatively low growth rates in their own economies, the industrialized capitalist countries put greater efforts into production for export. The result has been much more economic competition at the international level and much greater industrial instability.

The Development of the GATT

With the onset of the Great Depression in the 1930s, most governments responded by raising their tariffs to protect their national economies. From that time on, orthodox economists blamed the severity of the depression on high tariffs which restricted international trade. For the small countries more heavily dependent on international trade, the impact was disastrous. This was particularly true of those countries, like Canada, which depended on the export of agricultural products and raw materials.

However, the main problem with the strategy of the 1930s was that governments raised tariffs and then sat back and waited for private capitalists to invest and restart the economy. This did not happen. But where governments helped to mobilize capital and stimulate investment, recovery from the recession was fairly rapid. The most noted example was in Germany, where the Nazi government was the first to practice "military Keynesianism." In Sweden, the Social Democratic Party was elected in September 1932. While they continued to emphasize exports, extensive government intervention in the economy resulted in a rapid increase in economic growth between 1932 and 1939, and unemployment fell from 30% to 11%.

For most of the major industrialized states, including Canada, recovery from the Great Depression did not really occur until the onset of World War II. Orthodox economists conveniently forget that for all of these countries, recovery came quickly once the governments adopted policies of direct investment, government borrowing and spending, controls on imports, and strict foreign exchange controls to prevent capital from moving abroad. International trade was managed to a high degree. Because of the international crisis, private capital was in no position to oppose these measures, but, also, there was no reason to object. The policies of these governments during World War II were very favourable to capitalist development and profitability.

The planning for post-war management of international trade was almost completely under the control of the governments of the United States and Britain. British policy was dominated by John Maynard Keynes, the internationally renowned economist. His *General Theory*, published in 1936, had revolutionized economic thought, and the escape from the Great Depression during World War II had vindicated his position.

In a widely read article published in 1933, Keynes argued that growing international economic dependence had increased the severity of the Great Depression and had extended its impact worldwide. He concluded that governments required greater national self-sufficiency if they were to pursue a policy of full employment. The key was to control "capital flight," that is, private corporations moving their capital abroad to gain higher returns and to blackmail governments by threatening to relocate if given unfavourable treatment. In 1943 he suggested that governments needed to control and direct between two-thirds and three-quarters of total national investment to guarantee a policy of full employment and peace. A government policy of full employment would require much greater state management of trade, including the continuation of import controls, according to Keynes.

Thus his plan for the post-war international economy centred on the creation of an International Clearing Union which would attempt to deal with balance of payment problems by stimulating the expansion of international trade instead of curtailing it. Penalties would be imposed on countries which maintained large balance of payments surpluses. The penalties were designed to stimulate imports in the countries holding a surplus, and exports in the deficit countries. The goal, again, was the maintenance of full employment, in all countries.

However, Keynes' proposals for an International Clearing Union were opposed by the U.S. government. World War II had been a blessing for the American economy. They had recovered from ten years of depression, and, except for the attack on Pearl Harbor, their physical capacity had been untouched. In contrast, their major competitors had been devastated by the war. As the most powerful economy in the world, they naturally backed policies of free trade. Britain and Lord Keynes were in no position to challenge the United States. The U.S. position was reflected in the Bretton Woods agreements of 1946 which created the International Monetary Fund (IMF) and the International Bank for Reconstruction and World Development (World Bank). Voting power in these two institutions was weighted according to financial contributions, and from the beginning they were both under the domination of the U.S. government.

During World War II the Roosevelt administration had used its position of power to include principles of trade liberalization in the Atlantic Charter and the lend-lease agreements with its European allies. In 1946 the U.S. government produced a draft charter for an International Trade Organization (ITO). The aims of the organization were to reduce and eventually prohibit high tariffs and non-tariff barriers to trade, such as import controls and quotas. In early 1948 most of the capitalist countries who were members of the United Nations met in Havana and drafted a charter for the ITO, based on the U.S. proposal. However, the ITO never did come into operation because the treaty was blocked in the U.S. Congress.

In 1947, 23 countries, including Canada, signed the General Agreement on Tariffs and Trade (GATT), which pledged their governments to tariff reductions and the mutual adoption of most-favoured-nation policies. Under the principle of most-favoured-nation, a country reducing tariffs on a commodity for one trading partner automatically extends that reduction to its other trading partners. Every few years the members of the GATT meet for extended periods of time to negotiate multilateral agreements on trade issues. Today, only a few countries are outside of GATT; even China and several Eastern European state socialist countries are members.

While the basic principles of the GATT are non-discrimination in trade and the expansion of most-favoured-nation treatment, there are major exceptions in the Agreement and in the special codes which have been adopted over the years. Governments are permitted to discriminate against foreign products in their own procurement policies. Agriculture and the service industries are excluded from coverage. Protectionist policies are permitted for the purposes of health, safety and national security.

From the beginning, the United States, as the dominant world economic power, has pushed for reduction in tariff protection. Major across-the-board reductions were made after the 1964-7 Kennedy Round of GATT negotiations. Most recently, the Tokyo Round (1973-9) resulted in an average reduction of around 35%; by the end of 1987, tariffs were reduced to the 5% to 8% level. Since the end of 1987, around 80% of all Canada's exports enter the United States duty free, and over 90% of our exports face tariffs of less than 5%. In return, 65% of U.S. exports to Canada enter duty-free, but existing tariffs are scheduled to remain somewhat higher. For the most part, tariff barriers have been removed. As Glen Williams has stressed, the GATT negotiations have already produced *de facto* free trade between Canada and the United States.

In recent years public attention has been focused on non-tariff barriers to trade. Most of these are permitted either under the GATT itself or the special codes which have been agreed to through special multilateral negotiations. These, in turn, are enforced primarily by national legislation. The major non-tariff barriers are as follows:

Anti-Dumping Duties. Special duties may be invoked, under Article VI, if an imported product is priced at "less than normal value" and causes "material injury" to existing domestic producers or retards the development of a local industry.

Countervailing Duties. These can be applied under Article VI when government subsidies to an industry result in an increase in the export of any product. The countervailing duty is not to exceed the amount of the government subsidy. At the Tokyo Round of the

GATT negotiations, a new code on these duties specified that they may not be applied unless there is "material injury" to a domestic industry."

Safeguards. Article XIX of the GATT permits governments to impose special duties or quantitative restrictions on imports if they pose a "serious injury" to domestic producers. At the Tokyo Round of negotiations an attempt was made to limit this final "safeguard" for industries, but it was not possible to reach an agreement.

Adjustment Policies. In the 1970s and 1980s, with the expansion of the world-wide market for production and distribution, many mature industries experienced considerable competition from imports and found it necessary to adopt expensive new technologies. Most governments have adopted programs to help these industries adjust to change—to help capital and labour rationalize or shift to other sectors. In many cases, however, the adjustment programs appear to be defensive efforts designed to protect existing jobs and local communities.

In recent years, these non-tariff barriers have been used by the U.S. government against a number of imports from Canada. The U.S. Congress, which has never ratified the GATT, vigorously defends its powers under the Constitution in the area of trade policy. Since the recessions of 1974-5 and 1981-2, it has been pressing the executive branch of the U.S. government to take stronger actions against what it calls "unfair trade." The U.S. government has invoked these non-tariff barriers more than any other government. But in addition, much U.S. trade legislation goes well beyond the GATT principles. For example, both the GATT and the OECD accept subsidies as valid when they are used to try to redress regional inequalities. But since 1979 the U.S. government has unilaterally declared Canada's regional development programs to be "unfair subsidies." The GATT provisions are also available to the Canadian government under the *Special Import Measures Act* (1984), and they have been used.

The New International Division of Labour

The rise in protectionist sentiment in the United States and the Congress is the result of the penetration of the U.S. market by imported manufactured goods. Imports as a share of total sales of industrial goods in the U.S. rose from 14% in 1980 to 21% in 1984. By 1984, employment in manufacturing in the United States was 1.8 million below the 1979 peak.

While the trend was apparent during the 1970s, the trading world's dependence on the U.S. market increased after the 1981-2 great recession. Despite the rhetoric of economic conservatism, the Reagan administration was practising a form of "military Keynesianism." First, there were the massive federal tax cuts in 1981. The main cuts in personal income tax were in the upper economic brackets. Corporations received tax reductions and increased capital cost allowances. While this did not produce the rate of investment hoped for, it did provide a stimulus to the economy, and in particular, to the financial sector.

More important, however, was the Reagan administration's significant increase in military expenditures. Because the Congress resisted major cutbacks in social programs which might have offset these increases, the federal budget deficit quickly rose to over $200 billion per year. This deficit spending provided a major boost to the U.S. economy. Except for Japan, all the other industrialized capitalist countries were struggling with weak growth in their domestic markets, and they all looked to the more vigorous U.S. market. In order to finance the tax cuts, the increased military spending, and the deficit in the balance of trade in goods, the U.S. Federal Reserve Board kept U.S. interest rates high and the dollar strong, drawing foreign capital to the U.S. economy, in both direct investment and the financial market. Moreover, the reduction in tariffs brought about by the Kennedy and Tokyo rounds of the GATT negotiations had encouraged the development of manufacturing for export in the less developed countries (LDCs). Between 1979 and 1984, the share of manufactured goods in the Western industrialized countries (the OECD) provided by the LDCs rose from 10% to 14.5%, and the U.S. market accounted for 80% of this increase.

Most of these manufactured exports to the OECD countries originate in only ten LDC countries, as the 1984 figures on the following page show.

The East Asian "Gang of Four" (Taiwan, South Korea, Hong Kong and Singapore), with only 2% of the population in the LDCs, accounted for over 55% of the total.

In their search for higher rates of profit, the owners of capital shifted investment and production to low-wage areas at home and abroad. In the case of the United States, offshore processing and assembling has played an important role in manufacturing, encouraged by changes in the U.S. *Tariff Act* which provides incentives to offshore subcontracting. Import duties under sections 806 and 807 of

Country	% of total
Taiwan	21
South Korea	16
Hong Kong	14
Mexico	8
Brazil	6
Singapore	5.5
China	5
Malaysia	3
Philippines	2.5
India	2
Total of top ten	83

the Act are levied only on the value-added of manufacturing done abroad.

Thus, for many types of manufacture in the United States, it has been advantageous to shift labour-intensive assembly functions overseas in order to take advantage of the significantly lower labour costs. This has become normal practice in the areas of clothing, leather goods, electronics, electrical appliances, electrical machinery and automotive parts. The Mexican free trade zones on the U.S. border were developed to take advantage of this situation.

The "international comparative advantage" of the less developed countries has little to do with ecological conditions or the distribution of natural resources. It has everything to do with the social structure of production. The advantages to the capitalist, whether local or foreign, are the result of the history of uneven development and social and political control. The key factors are as follows:

There are direct and indirect subsidies to foreign investment, including tax holidays, free repatriation of profits, exemption from customs duties, free movement of exports and imports, and plants and land provided by the state at minimal costs.

Export processing zones were created to take advantage of the U.S. tariff rules on offshore processing and assembly.

Production costs in the LDCs are low due to much lower wages, the absence of fringe benefits, the lack of business contributions to social services, non-enforcement of health and safety regulations, and exemption from regulations such as environmental controls.

The high level of hidden unemployment in the "informal economy" and agriculture creates a large reserve army of labour, including children, which keeps wages low.

Relative docility in the labour force has been enforced by very authoritarian governments which outlaw strikes, ban labour unions and repress left-wing political parties and liberation movements.

There is a vast pool of women workers with few employment opportunities. A 1978 survey by the United Nations Industrial Development Organizaton found that plant managers in Singapore and Malaysia preferred women workers because they were more obedient, less likely to organize unions, more prepared to accept low wages on a piece-work basis, and more willing to work long hours and evening shifts.

The primary response in the United States has been pressure on the Congress to enact legislation which would raise tariffs or impose quotas on imports from these countries. A second response has been the formation of the International Labor Rights Working Group, an alliance of trade unions, churches, human rights organizations and community groups. The goals of this alliance are to make violations of basic human and labour rights an unfair trade practice under U.S. law, and to have the GATT declare it unjustifiable for a country to use repression and gross exploitation of workers to gain "international comparative advantage" in trade.

The Decline of American Hegemony

For 25 years after the end of World War II the United States was clearly the dominant country in the capitalist and non-capitalist world. This hegemonic position rested on the American military preponderance, achieved through nuclear weapons and their delivery systems, a large and mobile military force, the newest and best of weapons-systems technologies, a series of military alliances which allowed the United States to dominate foreign and defence policies of subordinate capitalist states, and an impressive list of overseas military bases throughout the world. While ostensibly justified on the basis of containing military expansion by the Soviet Union, the underlying reason for the American-led military alliance system was the preservation of the capitalist market economy and the containment of the spread of various forms of socialism. In the post-war period, the American government, backed by its powerful military machine, could now directly support the historic foreign policy of the "Open Door" to U.S. investment and trade.

During this period the U.S. government assumed the role of chief protector of the system over which its hegemony existed. Through political pressure and the economic power of the Marshall Plan, the U.S. government successfully rolled back the trend towards socialism in the Western European countries at the end of World War II. In the United Nations, the United States and its military allies represented over two-thirds of the member-states and could easily win any vote. Through military and economic assistance, the U.S. government was able to buy considerable influence in the authoritarian governments in the Third World. On occasion, direct political and military intervention was necessary to carry the day. There was the intervention in the Korean civil war between 1950-4 to prop up the right-wing dictatorship in the southern half of the country. American policy even included the overthrow of social democratic governments, as in Iran and Guatemala in 1954, the Dominican Republic in 1965 and Chile in 1973.

The long rule of American hegemony was also made possible by the strength of the U.S. economy. In 1950 the gross national product of the United States represented over 50% of the total for all capitalist countries. As late as 1960 U.S. military spending represented 50% of the world's spending on the military. While depleting its own natural resources, the United States was able to control access to all the major sources of raw materials in the non-communist world. Most important, they controlled the world's energy sources. U.S. technology, capital and world marketing gave its producers a tremendous advantage over competitors. Exports were not that important, as the United States itself was by far the world's most valued market. Yet with trade only 6% of the American gross national product, the United States in 1950 still accounted for over 16% of total world exports.

It was inevitable that this position of dominance was to erode. First, there was the economic recovery of Western Europe. By the mid-1950s the European Common Market was growing at a rapid rate and beginning to provide economic competition. In the 1960s Japan's economy began a period of spectacular growth, and their exports challenged those of the United States in every market. As Table 2 demonstrates, betwenn 1966 and 1973 the economy of the United States grew at an average annual rate of 3.4%, considerably below the average of 4.5% for all the OECD countries, and well below that of its major industrial competitors.

In the 1970s the United States lost 23% of its share of the world trade in manufactured goods, in spite of a 40% devaluation of the American dollar. In 1960, U.S. manufacturing supplied 98% of the American market; by 1985 this had declined to 79%. In 1980 a special report by *Business Week* attributed the decline to an erosion of savings, lack of investment in new plants and technologies, the decline in labour productivity, as well as inflation, labour conflicts, excessive expectations by the poor, the proliferation of social welfare programs, and a business class more interested in financial profits than production. They called for a "new social contract," teamwork between capital, labour and the government.

Five years later *Business Week* found that despite President Reagan's policies, little had really changed. America was abandoning its status as an industrial power as its corporations were shifting production to low-wage countries and relying more heavily on parts and assembled products from abroad. The result was the development of the "hollow corporation," basically a marketing organization for other producers. The rapid development of the service sector of the economy was "a false paradise" because of the preponderance of low-paying, non-union jobs, and the lower capacity to increase productivity. But even in the service sector, the U.S. share of world trade had fallen from 15% in 1973 to 8% in 1983.

Many have attributed the decline of the U.S. economy to the preponderant role of military spending. Research and development is heavily oriented to the military sector in the U.S., in dramatic contrast to its major competitor, Japan. Others have noted the decline in U.S. direct (equity) investment overseas and a pronounced shift to finance capital, primarily through banking interests.

In the political arena, U.S. hegemony was also eroding. With decolonization, the newly independent states entered the United Nations, and the Western alliance system could no longer dominate that institution. U.S. government frustration with its inability to manipulate the United Nations to serve its own interests was dramatized by its withdrawal from UNESCO. The Soviet Union began producing nuclear weapons and quickly achieved rough parity in what the experts call "mutually assured destruction."

But the major political disaster for the United States was the decision to enter the Vietnam civil war in an attempt to prevent a victory by left-wing revolutionary forces. After twelve years of war, trillions of dollars, American troop commitments of over 500,000 and 50,000 dead, the U.S. government was forced to admit defeat and withdraw. The unpopular war brought massive opposition at home. The defeat by a poor underdeveloped country, which received only limited economic and weapons assistance from the state socialist countries, resulted in a profoundly humiliating international loss of face.

Ronald Reagan took office in January 1981 with a pledge to restore America's standing in the world. However, not a great deal has changed, as his policies appear to be based on a continuation of the assumption that proved so disastrous in the Vietnam experience, that military power can produce political credibility and effectiveness. Military spending escalated. The invasion of tiny Grenada may have seemed to some Americans to restore pride and confidence, but to the rest of the world it was the (not very competent) act of an international bully. American support for the right-wing forces in Central America, Angola, Mozambique and South Africa has contributed to instability (and suffering) in those areas. The U.S. government has also given substantial support to Muslim fundamentalists in the Afghanistan civil war, causing major problems for the government backed by the Soviet Union and for the Soviet troops themselves.

The U.S. economy is not yet experiencing the absolute decline seen in the United Kingdom during its fall from the position of world leader. U.S. manufacturing and industry are still the strongest in the capitalist world in terms of output and employment. The United States is still the world's most lucrative market. In the period between 1984 and 1986 the U.S. economy outperformed most of the industrialized countries. National income is rising. Unemployment is declining. And the rich have been getting richer.

But as we complete the fifth year of the economic recovery from the 1981-2 great recession, we are getting ever closer to the inevitable next downturn in the business cycle. The world's overinflated stock markets experienced a dramatic drop in October 1987, and only general state intervention to cut interest rates prevented a major collapse. In an effort to prop up the American economy, the U.S. government then unilaterally repudiated the agreement by the Group Seven and decided to let the dollar fall against other currencies. This has only created further instability in the international economy. With unemployment already higher than in any previous recovery period, with social programs cut everywhere, and with governments struggling with budget deficits, many believe that the next recession will be even harsher than the last. Ironically, through the bilateral free trade agreement the Mulroney government has decided on a policy of "Fortress North America," tying our future to the United States just before the next recession and at a time when the general decline of the U.S. economy is becoming most noticeable.

CHAPTER 4

The Development of the
New Business Agenda

The 1970s saw the onset of economic stagnation, growing unemployment, high inflation, worker discontent and the decline in the rate of profit in the advanced industrialized countries. The owners of capital began to search for the means to restore the high profit levels that had persisted since the end of World War II. They redirected investment to low-wage areas at home and abroad. New technologies were introduced to reduce the amount of labour required in the production process. Pressure was put on governments to provide tax relief and direct assistance. And they sought the implementation of policies which would reduce the power and influence of labour.

At first, the capitalists and their governments looked to incomes policies (or corporatism), systems of labour/management co-operation which would limit wage increases. These policies had been successful in several of the very small Western European countries, and the experiment in West Germany showed some promise. But all attempts to introduce incomes policies in the major industrial countries failed. At this point the capitalist class shifted emphasis and declared war on trade unions and labour in general. They set forth a new business agenda, which was actively promoted by the Thatcher government in Britain (elected in 1979) and the Reagan administration in the United States (elected in 1980). Furthermore, the essential aspects of this policy package were adopted by many other governments, including Canada. Using the threat of capital flight, the now united capitalist class was even successful in forcing similar policies on social democratic governments in West Germany, France, Australia and New Zealand.

Moderately Successful Experiments in Corporatism

There are three counties always cited as the key examples of successful incomes policies: Sweden, Norway and Austria. Their reputation has increased in recent years; while unemployment rates in most of the Western industrialized countries have been rising during the 1970s and 1980s, these three countries have been able to keep their unemployment rates down to between 2% and 3% of the labour force. But all three are quite small countries—their combined population and gross national product is about equal to that of Canada. Many observers have concluded that they are special cases which cannot be repeated in the larger countries with different historical traditions.

All three of these countries have elaborate institutional arrangements for implementing a policy of corporatism. In essence, corporatism is the ideology of social partnership or class collaboration between labour and capital. In these countries the leaders of the trade union movement and the dominant social democratic parties have rejected class conflict for social partnership. (In Canada the term "tripartism" is used instead of corporatism, signifying co-operation between labour, capital and government.) Private capital has done well in these three countries. The capitalist class is strong in all three. Economic growth rates and profits have been relatively high. In addition, the use of the strike by organized labour has greatly diminished over the years.

There are some basic common characteristics which set these three states off from others in Western Europe. First, the major interest groups are highly centralized and concentrated. The labour unions and business organizations operate through national federations. These federations represent their groups in centralized collective bargaining. The results of these negotiations are then extended to all workers in the country, regardless of whether or not they are covered by agreements reached through collective bargaining.

All three countries have traditionally had very high participation by workers in trade unions; with the adoption of centralized collective bargaining, membership has risen even higher. They have also had strong social democratic political parties representing organized workers. Furthermore, the social democratic parties are the dominant parties in all three countries, and they have all held office for long periods of time. They are the traditional administrators of the corporatist policy.

The other major characteristic of the three is political compromise.

The tradition of political compromise was strengthened by the introduction of an electoral system based on proportional representation. Proportional representation ensures the persistence of the smaller liberal, radical, and agrarian parties. It also makes it impossible for the governing party to represent only a minority of the electorate. Because of the tradition of political compromise, the occasional minority governments have been able to function adequately.

Incomes Policies in Major Capitalist Countries

The most significant experiment in incomes policies in a major capitalist country is that of West Germany. Throughout the 1970s, the per-capita loss of work days due to industrial disputes was by far the lowest of the seven major capitalist countries and was only one-fortieth that of Canada, which ranked first. There were two basic reasons for the low level of strikes. First, legislation prohibits strikes unless 75% of the membership vote for a strike. Political strikes are illegal. Second, there is a long tradition of "co-determination," or joint worker/management consultation processes at the plant level. There is no process of country-wide negotiations, but there are industry-wide negotiations. Furthermore, trade unions are larger and far less fragmented than they are in the United States and Canada. Under this system, the negotiation process is highly bureaucratized, with little rank-and-file participation.

In Canada and elsewhere there has been considerable interest in the German system of co-determination. Factory works councils were first legalized in 1916, and they were required under legislation passed by the Social Democratic government in 1920. Since World War II they have been strengthened by additional legislation. In general, elected trade union representatives sit on the plant supervisory board, a second-tier "board of directors" which makes all the major operating decisions. However, only in the iron and steel industries have the workers achieved parity with management. Major corporate decisions are still made by the traditional board of directors, which represents the interests of capital. But companies with as few as five employees are required by law to have works councils. Thus, workers have representation under the system, but ultimate control of major decisions still rests in the hands of the owners of capital.

The major criticism of the system is its bureaucratic nature, its tendency to develop oligarchic structures, the lack of contact with the rank and file, and the lack of direct membership participation. The West German system is clearly not one of workers' control; it is a system of workers' representation, allowing for more institutionalized expression of grievances.

The trade union movement is fairly strong in West Germany, with around 40% of employees holding membership in unions affiliated with one of the four federations. The Social Democratic Party (SPD) has been one of the two dominant parties; with an electoral system based on proportional representation, and with the party's leadership chosing the candidates on the voters' list, trade union members actually constitute the overwhelming majority of SPD representatives in the federal legislature.

There is no centralized collective bargaining in West Germany, and thus it would be much more difficult to impose an incomes policy. Beginning in 1967, the federal government instituted a policy of "Concerted Action," tripartite consultations designed to encourage wage negotiations to fall within the range of government economic objectives. The process was formally ended by the trade unions in 1977.

Following World War II, the country was dominated by federal governments led by the conservative, pro-business Christian Democratic Party (CDU/CSU). The SPD finally gained a share of office between 1966 and 1969, when they formed part of the Grand Coalition with the CDU/CSU. Between 1969 and 1983 the SPD was the major partner in a series of coalition governments with the much smaller Free Democratic Party (FDP), a liberal party.

During the early period when the SPD was sharing political office, the rate of economic growth was respectable, though slightly below the average for Western Europe (see Table 2). The record in job creation was quite good, with unemployment between 1965 and 1973 being the lowest of all the major Western industrial countries. The crisis came with the breakdown of the monetary system in 1971-3 and the increase in oil prices in 1973. The resulting cost-price squeeze seriously threatened profit margins, and capital reverted to its traditional means of controlling input costs, the limitation or reduction of labour costs. Big business and the political right thus rejected the accord with labour, and turned to the third member of the tripartite relationship, government, demanding the "disciplining" of labour. Government responded by accepting the new alignment, and in 1973 the SPD government under Willy Brandt began to abandon their commitment to full employment. In 1974 Helmut Schmidt became the new leader of the SPD, and the party accepted a policy of crisis management.

Ironically, then, the West German Social Democratic government was the first in the West to accept a policy of tight money and fiscal restraint. In 1974-5, the Federal Bank instituted a monetarist policy, and the SPD government supported this effort with fiscal restraint. Thus, from 1974 through 1981 West Germany had the lowest inflation rate of any of the major industrial countries. Over the same period they maintained a favourable balance of international trade. However, the rate of job creation was among the lowest in the OECD. A large percentage of foreign "guest workers" were sent home. Even so, unemployment rose from less than 1% to over 6%. The SPD government strongly supported the tough monetarist solution adopted by the major industrial countries after 1979. With the subsequent onset of the 1981-2 great recession, economic growth rates dropped to levels below those of most of the OECD countries. Having lost its support among its trade union constituency, the SPD was soundly defeated in the 1983 federal election and was succeeded by the even more pro-business CDU/CSU government headed by Helmut Kohl.

In West Germany today, big business and the political right claim that the relative economic decline of the 1970s and 1980s is due to the extensive welfare state, the large public sector and its borrowing requirements, high wages and excessive fringe benefits, and the long paid holidays enforced by federal legislation. It is argued that these policies and programs led to the decline of exports and made the economy vulnerable to cheap imports.

While outside business interests have been impressed by the success of the West German effort in controlling inflation and strikes, and providing assistance to capital, they want no part of any program of workers' representation which might infringe on some management rights and perogatives.

France has a long history of price controls, but intervention to control wages has been on an ad hoc basis. The rise in oil prices in 1973 also created a crisis for France. In December 1973 the right-wing government and business interests attempted to implement an incomes policy to fight inflation, but it proved to be a failure. Trade unions were unwilling to accept policies of restraint. Following the narrow defeat of the Socialist-Communist candidate, Francois Mitterand, in the 1974 presidential election, the two major trade union federations, the CGT and the CFDT, signed an "agreement of offensive" on objectives and strategies. The number of days lost due to strikes increased. The Barre Plan of 1976 was an attempt to control inflation through fiscal and monetary restraint, as there seemed little hope for a voluntary incomes policy.

Britain has a high percentage of workers in trade unions combined with a decentalized system of collective bargaining. But over the 1970s, on a per capita basis there were fewer working days lost to strikes than in Canada, Australia, Italy or the United States. Yet with low rates of economic growth, and deindustrialization, there were pressures from business interests and the political right to bring labour under control.

The Labour Party, under the leadership of Harold Wilson, was elected in 1974. Prior to the election, the Labour Party had produced a new "social contract" which became an important part of its platform. The Trades Union Congress agreed to voluntary wage restraints in return for government programs to move towards full employment and modifications in legislation hostile to trade unions. The Labour government also created the Advisory, Conciliation and Arbitration Service, a tripartite council designed to settle industrial disputes. Despite the onset of the 1974-5 recession, the trade unions, for the most part, accepted wage controls from "their" government.

However, the British economy had been hard hit by the introduction of floating exchange rates for currencies after 1973 and the steep increase in the price of oil. The Labour government began to cut back government spending and social programs. Limits were put on government borrowing. High interest rates were used to limit the growth of money. All policies moving towards full employment were abandoned in an attempt to prop up the international value of the pound sterling. This effort failed, culminating in the humiliating capitulation to the International Monetary Fund in 1976. Britain became the first (and to date the only) industrialized country to allow itself to be dictated to by this agency of international finance capital.

Incomes policies had been pursued by British governments since at least 1961. The Labour government which took office in 1964 set as its first commitment the maintenance of the high international value of the pound sterling; full employment policies took a back seat. After 1976 the last Labour government adopted monetarist policies, and the result was an increase in unemployment from 2.5% in 1974 to 6% in 1978. The Labour government's political standing, and its incomes policy, was finally undermined by the strikes during the "winter of discontent" and the election of Margaret Thatcher's Tories in 1979.

The Japanese Model

While capitalists in Europe and North America were searching for solutions to the decline in the rate of profit, high inflation and weak economic growth, attention centred on the successes in Japan. Growth rates were spectacular in the period from 1960 down to the oil crisis of 1973. Although growth began to level off during the 1970s, it was still considerably higher than the OECD average. The rate of unemployment was by far the lowest of the larger capitalist countries. Furthermore, increased competition from Japanese exports was not based solely on lower prices; Japanese goods had established a reputation of high quality. Profits were high and the Tokyo stock market was booming. Overseas investment was rapidly expanding. How did they manage to do this?

Many pointed to the very low spending on the military. Instead, there are strong state supports for the private sector, and in particular research and development. But it was the system of Japanese industrial relations that was most attractive to Western capitalists.

First, the trade union movement in Japan is particularly weak. In the immediate period after World War II, the U.S. military forces gave trade unions legal status and encouraged membership. Trade union participation peaked at 56% of the labour force in 1949; but by 1985 this had dropped to 28%. The weakness of trade unions is directly traced to the system of "enterprise" unions. The employees of each business form a single union; there are no industry-wide unions. Thus there are an enormous number of trade unions—around 74,000 in 1983. These individual company unions do join federations; in 1983 there were about 100. While the federations try to deal with industry-wide problems, negotiations and contracts are in reality on a company basis.

Enterprise unionism readily leads to labour-management co-operation. Workers are more easily persuaded by management's argument that it is "our plant" in competition with others. In addition, in Japan the difference in pay between blue-collar and white-collar workers is small. Workers receive wages, but there is a definite shift to remuneration based on incentives. There are large bonus payments equivalent to one-third or more of their annual wages. The size of the bonus depends on the plant's profits and the worker's performance.

The well-known system of company paternalism is popularly identified with a guarantee of "lifetime employment" for all loyal employees. The pay for an individual worker has traditionally increased with the length of service with the firm. However, this system, which began in the 1920s, had been modified by management to suit the needs of capital in the 1970s and 1980s.

One of the key management advantages of the Japanese system is flexibility in the hiring of labour. Individuals are regularly shifted around the plant; unlike stipulations in labour contracts in North America, job descriptions and work rules are vague. Today, only around one-third of company employees are truly lifetime employees. Significantly, they tend to be the trade union members. Today, Japanese employers depend heavily on part-time and temporary workers. Much work is done by contracting out to smaller, non-unionized firms. This has resulted in a "dual economy," as the differences in wages, fringe benefits and working conditions between the permanent, unionized employees and the temporary, non-unionized employees are significant. When there are downturns in a firm's economic performance or when adjustments are made, permanent unionized workers are rarely affected. The cutbacks are absorbed by the more marginal workers.

This has been one of the major keys to the success of Japanese capitalism. Firms have a much greater ability to adjust to change. Labour flexibility greatly enhances management rights. Furthermore, union contracts are short-term, making adjustments easier. They are negotiated on an annual basis, taking place during the Spring Labour Offensive in April and May.

The weakness of the trade union movement is a result of the historic development of Japanese capitalism. From the beginning, the capitalist class has worked in close partnership with the state. Furthermore, there was no democracy in Japan until after World War II. Prior to the military coup in 1932, only a tiny handful of property owners had the right to vote. The conservative, pro-business Liberal Democratic Party has ruled Japan continually since the end of the war. Governments have always been authoritarian. The last major wave of industrial strikes was in the 1940s, and many of these were over general issues like the shortage of food. It is easy to see why businessmen in the West have looked with envy on the Japanese system. And many of the basic characteristics of the Japanese labour/management system are found in the new business agenda.

The New Business Agenda

The economic crisis of the 1970s and 1980s put the progressive liberal political agenda of the capital/labour accord on the defensive. The political right, previously looked on as a fringe element, increased their influence as the supporters of the post-war accord failed to come up with any solutions. The New Right that developed in Canada was a blend of three influences. First, there was big business, primarily old capital. It is most commonly associated with the Trilateral Commission, an international organization of big business interests and conservative politicians. In the 1970s these self-appointed world leaders began to attribute the persistence of the economic crisis to the increased demands of the common people and the "excesses" of democracy. Their publications called for a return to the traditional values of authority, obedience and management rights in business operations. Trade unions had become much too powerful, they argued. Governments needed to bring spending under control and to reduce the expectations of the poor.

The second major element in the developing creed of the New Right was the revival of support for individual over collective rights. According to this view, the free market was the best method of deciding all economic issues. The work of Milton Friedman and F.A. Hayek, previously dismissed as the ranting of cranks, now became most influential. Friedman and Hayek openly reject state intervention to moderate the business cycle. Their advocacy of a greatly reduced role of the state through privatization, deregulation, contracting out and reduced government spending on social services was widely accepted by business interests. In Canada, this element of the New Right is best represented by the Fraser Institute in Vancouver; originally the preserve of local right-wingers afraid of the New Democratic Party, its list of current financial supporters reads like a Who's Who of Canadian big business.

Finally, there is the fundamentalist religious right. They are committed to preserving the traditional nuclear family, and to combatting the rise of feminism, permissiveness, sexual freedom and abortion, the environmental movement and the growing acceptance of rights for lesbians and gays. They are virulently anti-socialist. The religious right has been quite influential in the United States but much less so in Canada.

The election victories of Margaret Thatcher's Conservatives in Britain in 1979 and Ronald Reagan in the United States in 1980 issued in the era of New Right politics. The policies they and their supporters have advocated are, in general, the new business agenda. Following the collapse of incomes policies, big business abandoned the concept of the New Social Contract as advocated by *Business*

Week and others in favour of an all out attack on labour. The new agenda includes a number of basic policies:

Monetary Policy. A tight money policy was introduced to bring down the rate of inflation. High interest rates have constrained economic growth, and the resulting higher levels of unemployment have served to discipline the labour force. Wage demands have been countered by demands from employers for wage cuts and concessions.

Taxation Policy. Taxation systems have been adjusted to better serve the interests of capital accumulation. Corporate taxes have been even further reduced. Businesses have also received other tax concessions, such as accelerated rates of depreciation. Taxes have been reduced for those in the upper income brackets. The principle of taxation according to ability to pay is being abandoned. Everywhere, direct taxes are on the increase, especially value added taxes, a major sales tax. As may be expected, these actions have increased inequalities in income and wealth.

Reduction in Social Services. All social programs established during the period of the capital/labour accord are under attack. Only the concerted resistance of popular groups has prevented a far-reaching dismantling of the welfare state. In the face of this resistance the New Right is seeking to have users' fees instituted for all social and government services.

Increase in Military Spending. While right-wing governments try to cut historic social programs, at the same time they are increasing spending on political and police forces, penal systems and internal intelligence agencies. These increases are justified by the revival of the new Cold War against "foreign communism," both at home and abroad.

Support for the "Free Market." The new business agenda puts a high priority on the restoration of the "free market" to solve all social and economic problems. As Margaret Thatcher plainly put it, she regards part of her job to be "killing Socialism in Britain." Thus, special emphasis is placed on the "rights of the individual" in contrast to collective rights. The revival of 18th century liberal rights is being used to undermine the collective rights of trade unions, women, farmers, minority groups and the poor.

Deregulation. As part of the revival of 18th century economics, business is demanding the deregulation of the economy. "Getting the government off the back of business" will reduce costs and increase profits. Thus, there is a broad attack on government regulations on business and finance, transportation and communications, environmental controls, health and safety standards, and community standards in general.

Privatization. Privatization is also high on the new business agenda. Margaret Thatcher found it difficult to break the trade unions in the state-owned corporations and in the public service in general. The way around this was to sell the crown corporations to private interests and to contract out traditional public services. In the 1987 election she even promised to privatize the system of water supply! Many governments have joined the bandwagon.

Opposition to Trade Unions. The New Right in government has led an open attack on trade unions. Historic trade union rights are being dismantled in Britain, the United States and Canada. Combined with other policies, the breaking of unions increases "labour flexibility" and reduces labour costs for business.

Centralization of Political Power. In addition, the New Right has led an attack on political democracy. Centralization of power is part of the agenda. The prime examples in Britain were the abolition of the metropolitan county councils, the undermining of local school boards and increased control from Whitehall, and centralized control over local public housing. Centralization was carried out to impose national priorities on spending and social policies and also to undermine local government bodies controlled by the Labour Party and left-wing interests. A similar pattern developed in British Columbia under the Social Credit governments after the May 1983 election, particularly in the area of education. If an NDP government had tried to implement such a centralization of power there would have been a massive outcry from the media and right-wing political forces.

Direct Political Action. Capitalists as a class are now more united than ever before. Major new organizations have been formed and political activity by business interests is on the rise. For example, in the United States the proliferation of Political Action Committees (now numbering in the thousands), which provide funds for favoured candidates, is changing the party system. All legislators, both Democrats and Republicans, have become far more dependent on these special interests for campaign funds than on their political parties. In this period of economic crisis, business interests have buried their differences in order to act as a united front against labour and its political allies.

Free Trade. Free trade is very much a part of the business agenda. This is the era of the large conglomerate corporation, operating on a transnational basis. Big business wants the right to export and invest wherever a profit can be made. The key to this goal is the elimination of tariffs and non-tariff barriers to trade and to the free mobility of capital. It is no surprise that big business and the New Right in general are the main supporters of the Canada/U.S. bilateral free trade agreement.

CHAPTER 5

The Ideology of Free Trade

The economic concept of the advantages of the free market and free trade go back to the rise of capitalism and the industrial revolution in Great Britain in the 18th century. There it was identified with the new class of industrial capitalists who opposed the restrictive government policies of mercantilism. It was also associated with the rise of political liberalism and the development of parliamentary government, based on representatives elected by men who had substantial property qualifications. Free trade was initially supported by the growing class of merchant capitalists who wished to seek a profit wherever it could be found, not just within the British Empire.

The Dream World of Adam Smith

The general principles of 18th century economics are most appropriately identified with Adam Smith, the University of Glasgow professor who published *The Wealth of Nations* in 1776. The general principles outlined in this historic text remain to this day the basis for the new school of classical economics and the political right, popularly know as "neo-conservatives."

The key belief of classical liberal economics is that all persons operate in a rational manner, in all activities, and always pursue their own self-interest. Egoism was deemed to be the fundamental characteristic of all human beings. Thus, the new liberal view represented a direct rejection of the dominant Christian ideology of the time which held that everyone had an obligation to others, to be "his brother's keeper." There was a special obligation to the poor which grew out of this general rule. For the Christian church, charity and almsgiving were to be praised, and greed, acquisitiveness and covetousness were evils to be condemned. Equally important to institutional Christianity was the ideal of co-operation and obligation to the community. These values, of course, ran contrary to the fundamentals of capitalism.

Smith believed that when all pursued their own self-interest, the "invisible hand" which guided the free market would bring about a peaceful society. When individuals sought their own self-interest, the general interest of the society would also be served. The free market would lead to the most rational use of capital and labour, and the society as a whole would benefit. Thus, there was little need for government to intervene in the natural market. Governments would be responsible for national defence, law and order, and creating favourable conditions for the capitalist system, including protecting private property, enforcing contracts, and bearing responsibility for necessary public works.

The regulator of the free market society would not be the government but competition. Conflicting self-interests, and the freedom of consumers to buy whatever they wished, would produce social harmony. The market would guarantee that no sector could gain monopoly power.

What drove the capitalist system, according to Smith, was the Law of Accumulation. The object of investment was the accumulation of additional capital. Those who failed to follow Smith's law, who did not invest, realize a profit, and reinvest, would fall by the wayside. The fear of some that there would be a shortage of labour, resulting in higher wages, was countered by the Law of Population: if wages were higher, it was assumed workers would have more children.

These basic, very simplified principles carried over to the area of international trade. Much of *The Wealth of Nations* was devoted to an attack on the mercantilist policies of the day. For Smith, the general welfare of the world would be greatly increased by free international movement of goods and capital.

However, Adam Smith's model of the perfect world of competitive capitalism was a far cry from the reality of Great Britain in the 18th century. As Robert Heilbroner points out, the general condition was one of "rapacity, cruelty, and degradation." There were large bands of poor people, dispossessed from agriculture, wandering the cities and countryside on the verge of starvation, seeking any kind of work. This was pre-industrial England, but the factories which did exist revealed the horrors that were to come. Manchester was described as "a dog's hole." Women and children were already working in the factories and mines for twelve or fourteen hours a day; in the

free market, wages for a man were already too low to support a
family.

But as Cy Gonick points out, there is another side of Adam Smith
which has been ignored by his present-day supporters. Smith
believed that whenever capitalists got together they would naturally
conspire to create monopolies so as to increase the rate of profit.
They were always seeking government protections and subsidies. He
believed that urban, factory life was debilitating to labour. He
recognized that there was an inevitable conflict between capital and
labour, and that in this battle capital was stronger. Furthermore,
whenever labour showed any signs of strength, the capitalists would
call on the government and state force to act on their behalf. Smith
noted that the state was an "indispensable" instrument to protect the
"rich against the poor, the property owners as against those who
owned nothing at all."

Ricardo and International Comparative Advantage

The advantages of international trade are obvious. Countries can
obtain goods which they may be unable to produce or may be able to
produce only at greater cost. Ecological differences between one part
of the world and another create natural comparative advantages and
disadvantages. Canada grows hard wheat with a high protein content
on the prairies which cannot be grown in humid tropical areas. In
turn, we import many tropical fruits, vegetables and condiments
which would be most costly to grow in Canada. Natural resources are
unevenly distributed around the world, and there is a natural
comparative advantage in trading resources which are abundant for
those which a country does not have or which would be more costly
to extract.

The classical theory of international trade is identified with David
Ricardo, the wealthy English stockbroker who publised *Principles of
Political Economy* in 1817. In Britain at this time there was a
vigorous struggle going on between the rising industrial capitalist
class, and the merchant capitalist class aligned with the interests of
the old landed aristocracy. Ricardo was a major defender of the interests of the new industrial capitalist class.

The struggle for "free trade" in Britain at this time centred around
the Corn Laws, which provided protection for agricultural products.
Ricardo argued that these protections resulted in higher-than-
necessary food prices. In the free market for labour at this time (trade

unions were non-existent and there was a large reserve army of unemployed labour), the capitalist had only to pay the labourer a wage
that provided the subsistence level of existence, their "dry crust" as it
was termed. However, the high price for bread forced the capitalist to
pay a higher-than-necessary wage, and this prevented him from ex-
tracting an even higher rate of profit. Free trade would permit the
importation of cheap grain, lower food prices for workers, and result
in lower wages and higher profits for industrial capitalists.

Like Adam Smith before him, Ricardo was a supporter of the
labour theory of value: the value of any commodity was determined
by the labour time that was required for its production. Therefore, in
the perfect competitive model, each country will specialize in the
production and export of those products that use the lowest amount of
labour time relative to the competition. As well, a country will import those products which require the highest amount of labour time.
For Britain, he argued, this meant concentrating on the export of
manufactured goods like textiles and importing food and other raw
materials.

The example used by Ricardo to justify his theory of international
comparative advantage was British exports of textiles to Portugal and
the importation of wine. With the technological lead in manufacturing, Britain could produce textiles using less labour time than could
Portugal. But Britain also could grow most agricultural products at a
lower cost than Portugal. Ricardo argued that Britain should concentrate on the export of manufactured goods, for this is where it had
the greatest advantage.

But why should Portugal trade with Britain when Britain had a
cost advantage in both manufacturing and agriculture? Ricardo
reasoned that Portugal should concentrate on the export of agricultural products like wine because the cost disadvantages were
greater in manufactured goods. The alternative for Portugal, autono-
mous development of both agriculture and manufacturing behind
tariff barriers, was simply ruled out by Ricardo.

In reality, Ricardo's theory of international comparative advantage was little more than a defence of British/Portuguese trading
relations which were based on a grossly unequal power relationship.
Historically, this trading arrangement was a disaster for Portugal.
When Portugal regained independence from Spain in 1640, the
Portuguese were desperate for international recognition and support.
Their government signed a series of commercial treaties with Britain
culminating in the Treaty of Methuen in 1703. In return for political
support, Portugal exempted Britain from the 1684 prohibition on

textile imports; British textiles were allowed to enter Portugal upon paying a 23% duty. In return, Portugal was given a 33% discount on the British tariff on wines.

The result of these unequal treaties was the collapse of the Portuguese textile industry, which had grown and prospered after 1681, the destruction of the infant bourgeois class, and reinforcement of the political power of the rural aristocracy which depended on the wine industry. The unequal exchange between textiles and wine (net barter terms of trade) left Portugal with a huge balance of payments deficit which was paid in gold and silver from their Brazilian colony. By 1820 Portugal had been reduced from a major imperial power to a relatively weak secondary power, totally dependent on Britain, a "dependency" or a "semi-colony."

Free Trade and Industrialization

In the 20th century, the classical theory of free trade was modified by two Swedish economists, Eli Hecksher and Bertil Ohlin. Their simple neoclassical model is often called the "factor endowment theory." In addition to labour and resources, the newer theory adds the other major factor of production, capital. Under this theory, countries will export products that make more use of their abundant factor. That is, advanced industrial countries, with a storehouse of capital, will export capital-intensive products. Those countries with a surplus in labour will export labour-intensive products. And those with an abundance of natural resources will specialize in those commodities.

As in the Ricardo model, all countries are said to gain from this specialization in trade, and total world output is increased. But there is another advantage claimed for this model. With free trade, and free movement of technology and capital, world labour and capital costs would theoretically gradually move towards equalization.

In reality, all of the major world political and economic powers today originally developed behind the barriers of high tariffs. In the 17th and 18th centuries, Indian textiles were of the highest quality in the world. To protect its infant textile industry, Britain imposed a series of tariffs against imported textiles beginning in 1690; they rose progressively to 85% in 1813. In 1700 the British government completely banned all Indian cottons and silks, but importing for re-export to Europe was encouraged. In addition, British colonial policy destroyed the Indian textile industry by prohibiting duties on

British textile imports and by imposing an excise tax on all Indian production. Although from the beginning Britain was the world leader in technology and production of iron and steel, this industry was protected by high tariffs until 1825.

A similar story can be found in all the other industrialized countries. In 1798 the United States instituted tariffs and progressively raised them in order to protect infant industries. The American Civil War was primarily a war between northern manufacturing interests and southern agricultural free trade interests. In the period of rapid industrial expansion after the Civil War, the U.S. government raised tariffs even higher. France, Germany and Belgium followed the same policy, as did the other European states. After the Meiji restoration in 1868, Japan followed an isolationist policy, rejected the free market and began a tradition of strong state support for industry. The Soviet Union rose from a primarily peasant society in 1917 to the second greatest world economic power, and certainly not by following a policy of free trade. Most recently, the governments of Taiwan and South Korea have industrialized along the lines of the Japanese model, rejecting free trade and embracing strong state support for industrial development.

In contrast, after their independence in the 1820s, the new Latin American governments rejected protectionist policies and adopted free trade. Their ruling classes were dominated by agricultural, mining and merchant interests concentrating on exporting primary products. They imported manufactured goods from Europe. The Latin American states never reached the level of development of their European counterparts.

Free Trade as an Ideology

If the advantages of free trade are so self-evident, as the orthodox economists claim, why is it that all governments today reject it as a state policy? First, there are some obvious problems with the assumptions upon which free trade is based which should be evident to anyone at first glance. Both the classical and neoclassical models assume that resources are fixed and internationally immobile—but mobile within the domestic market. They both assume that industrial capacity is fully utilized. Perfect competition is assumed (no monopolies or cartels). Both economic models even assume that there is full employment! They do not take into account cost advantages of scale of production, the different levels of technology, and the major differences in education and labour skills.

Both the classical and neoclassical models of free trade are ahistorical: they do not consider historical developments or political factors. They assume that adjustments are made through supply and demand, and problems are evened out through the floating exchange rate for currencies. Yet we know that a great many countries, particularly those that are less industrialized and developed, have severe balance of payments problems.

One of the earliest critics of the theory of international comparative advantage was Frederick List, a German political economist. He pointed out that Britain adopted a policy of free trade only after 1846, when it was the most advanced manufacturing country in the world. He advised countries wishing to industrialize to follow the British practice and adopt high tariffs to protect infant industries. Clearly, government policy makers listened to List rather than Smith, Ricardo and their disciples.

In the period after World War II, the theory of international comparative advantage began to come under criticism. Hans Singer pointed out that specializing in the export of food and raw materials was "unfortunate" because it removed secondary processing to the more industrialized countries and denied primary producing countries technological progress. He also demonstrated that the long-term trend in prices was against the sellers of food and raw materials. This latter point was also stressed by Gunnar Myrdal, the noted Swedish economist, in his major study of underdeveloped countries. Myrdal argued that history shows that the play of the free market "tends to increase, rather than decrease, the inequalities between regions."

The British economist Joan Robinson argued that the classical economists were in favour of free trade "because it was good for Great Britain, not because it was good for the world." Free trade was the natural economic policy for the most powerful capitalist countries.

Karl Marx presented a radical critique of free trade during the British debate over the repeal of the Corn Laws. What was so natural about the West Indies producing sugar and coffee? he asked. Before colonialism, Marx pointed out, they had neither. What was so natural about British textile workers using machines and those in Dacca being destined to weave by hand? In Marx's view, free trade could not be separated from imperialism and the power of capital.

Most interesting is the debate in the British parliament at that time and how similar it is to the debate going on in Canada today over free trade with the United States. The industrialists and their supporters in Britain noted that "the national good" unfortunately could not be purchased without some cost, and this was the displacement of workers. Marx argued that free trade really means the freedom of capital to do what it wants and to invest wherever it can obtain the highest profit. The victims are the workers, thrown out of work or forced to accept lower wages in order to compete with workers elsewhere who, because of historical conditions over which they have no control, are forced to work for even less.

There obviously is a wide gap between the simple models of free trade and the real world. Then why do the vast majority of economists have such a deep faith in the benefits of free trade? The answer is obvious to anyone who has taken a course in economics at one of Canada's universities. Students are taught orthodox economics as if it were the Truth handed down by God to an earthly prophet, most recently the U.S. economist Paul Samuelson. Central to this Truth is faith in the free market and free trade. Joan Robinson bluntly called it a process of brainwashing.

Free trade and the free market are therefore part of the ideology of orthodox economics. They are part of the system of beliefs or ideas that tries to explain and justify the economic and social divisions of capitalism.

But among the capitalists in any country, the degree of commitment to the free market and free trade varies over time. Although Adam Smith was critical of capitalists as potential monopolists, British industrial capitalists used his arguments to oppose government spending and intervention in the market to aid the poor. However, capitalists have usually supported tariff protections for themselves; they have always supported government financial and taxation assistance for themselves. At other times they will support the free market and free trade. As we will see, most business organizations in Canada today support bilateral free trade with the United States. Yet in 1911 they strongly opposed it. To understand that about-face we must look at the history of commerce in Canada.

CHAPTER 6

Continental Integration

The history of Canada is the history of a constant struggle to create and maintain an independent country. This has been a most difficult task, given the hostile climate, size and distances, the east/west barriers, the diversity of natural resources and regional differences. It has been made more difficult by the fact that we share the North American continent with the richest and most powerful country in the world. The economic market naturally pulls to the south, rather than east/west. A common language with the United States had made it extremely difficult for English Canada to maintain a distinct national culture. In addition, there have always been strong political and economic interests in the United States which have insisted that it is the "manifest destiny" of that country to rule the whole continent. Maintaining an independent country under these circumstances has required a strong commitment from Canadian governments and Canadian citizens. However, in times of economic crisis, the dominant business classes in Canada, and their political supporters, have always turned towards integration with the United States.

Early Canadian Commercial Policy

From 1763 until Confederation, Canadian commercial policy was largely determined by the colonial power, Great Britain. Mercantilist policies prevailed until around 1849, although with steadily diminishing force after Britain emerged the victor in the Napoleonic wars. Trade was directed to the mother country. Duties were imposed on imports from non-imperial sources. Under the terms of the *Navigation Acts*, goods were to be transported in British ships. In return, colonial exports were given preferential treatment in British markets. Canadian exports to the United States were hindered by progressively increasing tariffs.

However, the rise to power of industrial capitalism in Britain led to the adoption of a general policy of free trade. Between 1815 and 1849 British mercantilist policies were slowly repealed, and Canada lost its preferential markets. Furthermore, in 1846 and 1848 the U.S. government imposed heavy tariffs on imports of Canadian wheat and timber, contributing to an economic depression. In an attempt to counteract these adverse economic developments, free trade in natural products was established between all the British colonies in North America, which were finally granted "responsible government" in 1848. The legislature of the Canadas (what is now Quebec and Ontario) reduced tariffs on U.S. products and raised them on British products. In 1849 they sent representatives to Washington and proposed a free trade agreement. The U.S. Congress refused. At the same time the Canadian business elite, who formed the Montreal Annexation Association, proposed that the United States annex the British North American colonies.

Fearing the complete loss of its empire in North America, the British government responded by supporting the Canadas in securing the Reciprocity Treaty with the United States in 1854. Many Canadian natural products were given tariff-free entry to the United States in return for U.S. access to the Canadian east coast fishery and the St. Lawrence canal system. During this period, the Canadas raised tariffs to try to pay for the development of the St. Lawrence canal system and the connecting railways.

Confederation and the National Policy

The next crisis for the Canadian economy came in 1866, when the U.S. government unilaterally terminated the Reciprocity Agreement, partly as penalty for British support of the South in the U.S. Civil War. The annexationist movement in the United States also believed that if reciprocity were cut off the Canadian colonies would be forced to seek admission to the American union. But the most important reason for termination was the decision, renewed by successive U.S. governments, to pursue an industrial policy behind tariffs.

The loss of the U.S. markets created a crisis for the Canadian colonies. It was undoubtedly the most important factor behind Confederation and what is now known as the National Policy. Cut off from its main markets abroad, Canadians would instead try to create an independent country with a major internal market. The Intercolonial Railway would link the Maritime provinces to the Canadas. The purchase of Rupert's Land from the Hudson's Bay Company and the building of the Canadian Pacific Railway would link the prairies and British Columbia to the Canadas.

The creation of Canada was hampered by the onset of a major world depression in 1873. Aside from a few brief periods of recovery, this general depression lasted until 1896. How did Canadian governments respond? The Liberal government under Alexander Mackenzie sent George Brown to Washington to seek a new reciprocity agreement; however, the draft treaty was blocked in the U.S. Senate.

In 1878 Sir John A. Macdonald was returned to office as prime minister. While in opposition he had advocated a new National Policy for Canada, behind tariff barriers. The result was the 1879 tariff, generally referred to as the National Policy Tariff. It was designed to stimulate industrial development and employment. But the American link was certainly not dead. Even Macdonald sought new trading agreements with the United States. In the 1880s the Liberal Party seriously considered a complete commercial union with the United States.

In the election of 1891, the Liberal Party under Wilfrid Laurier advocated unrestricted reciprocity with the United States and was soundly defeated. By the 1896 election, Laurier had revised Liberal tariff policy so that it was hardly different from that of the Conservatives. However, the Liberals were very dependent on the west, and farmers were calling for free trade. In 1910 the U.S. government proposed a new reciprocity agreement, and the Laurier government agreed. Industrial interests in Canada strongly opposed the agreement. The Trades and Labour Congress, becoming more class conscious, refused overtures from the Canadian Manufacturers' Association to form an alliance against reciprocity with the United States. At the same time, they refused to endorse the reciprocity agreement and free trade; most of the trade union locals believed that these agreements would undermine industrial jobs and bring a reduction in wages. In the 1911 federal election the central issue was the reciprocity agreement. The Laurier government was soundly defeated. The Conservatives were even able to win eight of ten seats in Manitoba.

This was the era of American economic and political expansion into Latin America and the Pacific. "Dollar Diplomacy" and "The

Open Door" meant that U.S. business interests were moving overseas. That expansionist mood brought a revival of the old doctrine of Manifest Destiny, first enunciated by President Monroe in 1820. President Theodore Roosevelt stole the Alaska panhandle territory from Canada. During the 1911 election campaign, U.S. President William Howard Taft, Senator Henry Cabot Lodge and the Speaker of the House of Representatives, Champ Clark, all publicly stated that they saw reciprocity as the first step towards bringing Canada into the U.S. federal union. The rejection of reciprocity was not just a victory of Canadian business interests over western farmers; it demonstrated that there was a popular Canadian nationalism, a will to remain independent of the United States.

World War I and the Decline
of the Commonwealth Option

Canada is a resource-rich country with a relatively small population. The export of surplus natural resources, or "staples," was a logical development, but it required securing overseas markets. As an alternative to trade with the United States, commercial interests first looked to the British Commonwealth. When the U.S. government raised tariffs again in 1897, the Laurier government had unilaterally introduced a system of British preferential duties, hoping to encourage reciprocal action. However, the general system of Commonwealth preference was not established until 1932.

The onset of World War I led to a dramatic decline in British interests in Canada. Canadian business was forced to shift from London to New York for outside capital. British investment in Canada fell, and American investment steadily increased. After the United States entered the war, President Woodrow Wilson proposed that the resources of the two countries be pooled as if there were no political border. The U.S. government began the practice of granting Canada a special status among its trading partners; the War Department was given permission to place orders for military equipment with Canadian firms.

Following the war, the U.S. Republican administrations continued the historic American policy of high tariffs. Throughout the 1920s, the value of Canadian exports to the United States fell. The Great Depression arrived in October 1929, and the following year the U.S. Congress passed the even more protectionist Smoot-Hawley tariff. The Mackenzie King government responded by raising

Canadian tariffs on imports from the United States and by lowering them on imports from the Commonwealth. In addition, duties were lowered on many items from other countries covered under the most-favoured-nation treaties. In 1930 R.B. Bennett's government took office in Ottawa, and soon afterwards Canadian tariffs were raised an average of 30%.

Change came with the election of Franklin Roosevelt in 1933. The new president repudiated the historic American policy of high tariffs. The United States was now the most powerful country in the world, and a policy of free trade had become more attractive to them. The Roosevelt administration began negotiations with all its major trading partners, seeking reductions in tariffs. They met with an eager response from Mackenzie King, who had returned to office in 1935. There were two roads open to Canada at the time: an emphasis on continental trade with the United States, or a continuation of the policy of the 1920s, seeking more trade with the Commonwealth and other countries. King made it plain that he wanted to choose "the American road." The result was the 1936 and 1938 trade agreements with the United States which dramatically cut tariffs. The latter required Canada to abandon British preference on a number of items.

As Vernon Fowke has pointed out, the National Policy ended around 1930, symbolized by the transfer of control over natural resources to the three prairie provinces. The west had been settled and the wheat economy was in place. The infrastructure was completed, the final links being the creation of the Canadian National Railways and the western grain terminals. Hydroelectric power was being developed for the pulp and paper and base-metal industries. But there was no policy in place to deal with the Great Depression and World War II.

World War II and the Cold War

World War II provided the pretext for a new round of continental integration. In 1940 President Roosevelt and Mackenzie King signed the Ogdensberg Declaration, committing both countries to joint defence of the North American continent. The Permanent Joint Board on Defence began the process of joint military integration under the direction of the dominant country, the United States. The U.S. undertook Lend Lease for the Allied countries, and Canada again sought special status on these contracts. In 1941 the Hyde Park Declaration called for a "rationalization" of the military effort on a

North American basis. With great enthusiasm, the Mackenzie King government was accepting a level of economic integration which proscribed independent action by Canada. By the end of World War II, Commonwealth interests in Canada were negligible, and we were definitely on "the American road."

In the years following the war, Canada's Liberal governments doggedly supported U.S. political, economic and military leadership. They embraced the trade liberalization policies of the GATT. They welcomed American investment. They again sought special status in Washington and were allowed to benefit from Marshall Plan assistance to Europe. Economic policy was formulated by C.D. Howe and his agents in the Department of Trade and Commerce. In 1947 they negotiated a bilateral free trade agreement with the U.S. government. Despite strong support from Lester Pearson, at the last minute Mackenzie King refused to sign the treaty. In 1953 President Eisenhower sought a free trade agreement with Canada, but it was rejected by Prime Minister Louis St. Laurent. However, they did create the Joint Committee on Trade and Economic Affairs, which became inactive in 1970.

The Truman Doctrine in 1947 formally declared the Cold War against the Soviet Union. In February of that year, the United States and Canada issued a joint Declaration of Defence Co-operation, announcing that wartime military collaboration would be continued. The Mackenzie King government gave the United States permission to fly bombers carrying nuclear weapons over Canadian territory on "fail-safe" missions. In 1949 the United States, Canada and most of the Western European countries created the North Atlantic Treaty Organization. In practice, this military organization has been under the direct control of the U.S. President and his military staff.

With the onset of the Korean civil war in 1950, and general Western intervention, the Canadian and American governments signed the New Hyde Park Agreement. It was a formal break with Britain and the Commonwealth and a commitment to complete economic and military co-ordination with the United States. In 1951 construction began on the radar system in Canada designed to warn the United States of any possible air attack from the Soviet Union. In 1957 the radar system, and the Canadian air defence system, was integrated into the North American Air Defence System (NORAD), again under U.S. military and political control. Shortly thereafter, the two countries signed the Defence Production Sharing Agreement to allow Canadian firms to bid on U.S. military contracts. From the point of view of the Canadian government, the treaty was designed to try to offset the purchase of major military systems in the United States.

There have been two basic U.S. government objectives in their policy towards Canada during the period of the Cold War. The first is to assure that Canada is closely tied to the United States through a series of military treaties, with the Canadian armed forces under the general direction of the U.S. military command system. The other objective is to gain access to Canada's storehouse of strategic raw materials, including energy sources.

The latter policy was outlined in the *Report of the President's Materials Policy Commission* (1952), commonly referred to as the Paley Report. The Paley Report first declared that the United States, as the leader of the "free world," was everywhere combatting "a new Dark Age," the spread of socialism and nationalism. The chief concern of the U.S. government was the depletion of its domestic stocks of strategic raw materials and the growing need to rely on imports. Canada was identified as the "friendly" and "non-nationalist" best source of these resources. Canada, and underdeveloped countries, were advised to concentrate on their natural "competitive advantage." They were encouraged to borrow capital to develop an infrastructure necessary to extract and to export their resources. In the development of these resources, they were to rely on foreign, particularly American, investment. This basic objective has been a regular part of U.S. policy towards Canada since the onset of the Cold War and is central to proposals for trade liberalization, whether through the GATT or on a Canada/U.S. bilateral basis.

Canada: The Rich Dependency

In 1987, around 78% of Canada's trade was with one country, the United States. The dependence on trade with the United States has been steadily growing over the years, but it has accelerated since the onset of the great recession of 1981-2. As we can see from Table 8, Canada is more dependent than any other country on trade with one country. In fact, since the end of World War II only Canada and Mexico have increased their trade dependence on one country (Cuba shifted dependency from the United States to the Soviet Union). All other countries are in the process of trying to diversify their trade, most notably those in Central America and Eastern Europe. It is a poor economic strategy for any country to become heavily dependent on trade with one country. As Mel Hurtig points out, any business-

Table 8

Trade Dependence on One Country: 1979-83 Average

Country	Exports & Imports (US$ Millions)	Per Capita GDP (US$)	% Trade with Largest Partner	Largest Trading Partner
Canada	123,171	11,673	68.9	United States
Cuba	7014	1537	64.5	Soviet Union
Mexico	32,682	3356	60.7	United States
Haiti	450	312	54.2	United States
Bulgaria	19,397	4108	54.0	Soviet Union
Central African Rep.	143	690	53.8	France
Dominican Republic	2036	1187	50.1	United States
Afghanistan	1094	187	49.1	Soviet Union
Honduras	1534	626	47.9	United States
Ireland	18,107	4879	45.3	United Kingdom
Trinidad Tobago	6114	5766	45.2	United States
East Germany	36,900	7048	41.2	Soviet Union
Indonesia	33,419	568	40.1	Japan
Czechoslovakia	30,203	5733	39.4	Soviet Union
Ecuador	3911	1562	37.5	United States
Peru	5008	1368	36.9	United States
Panama	1749	1837	36.6	United States

SOURCE: United Nations. *Statistical Yearbook on Trade*, 1983; World Bank, *World Development Report*, 1983.

man would avoid becoming too dependent on one customer. For a relatively small country, to become dependent on a much larger country is to guarantee a loss of political freedom of action, or sovereignty.

But Canada's military subordination and trade dependence is enhanced by other factors of Canadian dependence in general. Canadian governments and corporations are heavily dependent on U.S. capital sources. Canada has by far the highest percentage of its industry controlled by foreign investors of any high income country.

In 1986 there was a net outflow of $19 billion in the form of interest, dividends, fees and service charges in order to pay for foreign investment.

Continental integration is reinforced by the impact of American cultural imperialism on Canada. Our television screens are overwhelmingly dominated by American programs. Canadian programs are hard to find. Furthermore, our Canadian-owned stations see little value in buying programs from Britain, Australia, New Zealand or European countries. We never see productions from less developed countries. Our records, tapes, videos, movies and books are American. Our magazine racks are crammed with U.S. periodicals. Our international news, whether on television, radio or in the newspapers, comes primarily from U.S. sources.

Our schools are dominated by American culture. About 70% of all English-language books sold in Canada are of U.S. origin. Our textbook industry is mainly U.S.-controlled. Our school curricula have precious little Canadian content, as any parent knows. In stark contrast to the United States and European countries, almost 50% of our university professors are non-Canadians, with the highest percentage of these from the United States. It is no wonder that public opinion polls indicate that more Canadian children know the capital of the United States than the capital of their own country.

One incident in 1985 dramatized the political reality of continental integration. In May the U.S. government notified the Canadian government that a U.S. Coast Guard icebreaker would travel through Canadian Arctic waters over the summer. The U.S. government did not ask permission because it does not recognize Canadian sovereignty in the area. In contrast, the Soviet Union does recognize Canadian sovereignty. The Mulroney government's response was to "grant permission," even though the U.S. government had made no request, to restate Canada's historic claim to the area, and to announce that they would build one Canadian icebreaker capable of patrolling the North some time in the future.

A second example emerged in 1987. The Mulroney government has substantially increased spending on the military. The decision was due in part to pressure from the U.S. government, but Tory Members of Parliament are also still trapped in the old Cold War thinking of the 1950s. They are also strong believers in continental military integration. This inevitably leads to some confused policy positions.

It is widely known that American submarines regularly enter Canadian waters in the Arctic Ocean. As noted above, the U.S. government does not recognize Canadian sovereignty in this area but the Soviet Union does. There is no evidence that Soviet submarines enter Canadian waters. In June 1987 the Mulroney government announced that they would spend $10 billion to purchase ten or twelve nuclear submarines—not to defend Canadian waters against U.S. submarines but against Soviet intrusions! Since Canada had no experience in building nuclear submarines, the Mulroney government is planning to purchase them from either Britain or France. But first they had to obtain U.S. government approval, because the U.S. government owns the technology for the power plant aboard this class of submarines. In November 1987 U.S. military officials announced that Canada would have to agree to a closely integrated Canada-U.S. maritime strategy to get approval for the technology transfer from the U.S. Congress. On the other hand, in early October the Soviet Union proposed an agreement with Canada to jointly ban nuclear weapons and demilitarize the Arctic Ocean. Many Canadians believe that this would be a positive step towards peace and disarmament. The Mulroney government simply ignored the proposal.

The Canada/U.S. free trade agreement carries on the tradition of continental integration. If implemented, it would tie Canada even closer to the United States, drawing us irrevocably into Fortress North America. It has already been noted in the introduction that many of the provisions of the agreement go beyond traditional free trade agreements—they are major steps towards the creation of a common market.

One of the most astonishing parts of the agreement deals with Canadian energy resources. For years the U.S. government has sought a continental energy agreement with Canada. They have finally sneaked it in through the back door. The United States has a shortage of energy resources, and energy firms and crown corporations in Canada have been eagerly filling that market. But the agreement would give the United States guaranteed access to all of Canada's energy sources: oil, natural gas, coal and its products, as well as electricity and uranium. The Canadian government would be denied the right to impose minimum export or import prices or to set quotas. A national energy policy would no longer be possible. Furthermore, in times of scarcity, Canada would be obliged to grant the United States a proportion of our energy sources, based on the percentage they have consumed over a recent three-year period. Canada already has a national shortage of conventional crude oil and rapidly depleting reserves. Under the free trade agreement, the private oil corporations would be able to export this oil to the United

States as fast as they could sell it. Then, in the near future, Canadians would have the privilege of paying the higher cost for frontier oil and syncrude. Only an impotent satellite government would agree to such a surrender of national sovereignty.

PART II

Canada/U.S. Economic Integration:
The Dangers

CHAPTER 7

U.S. Trade Objectives

It is widely believed in Canada that the initiative for the bilateral free trade agreement with the United States came from Brian Mulroney. But this is not the case. It originated with Ronald Reagan, during his campaign to win the Republican presidential nomination in 1980. Reagan proposed a "North American Accord," a new system of economic co-operation between the United States, Canada and Mexico. In May of that year Prime Minister Pierre Trudeau and President Lopez Portillo of Mexico issued a joint statement rejecting the proposal. But that had little impact on Ronald Reagan. He has continued to advocate the proposal for comprehensive trilateral co-operation. Most recently, the concept was included in the Senate version of the 1987 U.S. trade legislation.

The U.S. government placed a high priority on extending the trade liberalization process under the GATT to include the service sector. When the GATT ministerial meeting in 1982 failed to make any major moves beyond the scope of the Tokyo Round of Tariff reductions, the U.S. government began to direct its efforts to bilateral agreements. Special talks were held with Japan, the Caribbean countries, Israel, Canada and the right-wing southeast Asian countries.

In 1983 the Trudeau government responded to the U.S. government initiative by proposing to extend trade through a series of sectoral free trade agreements, based on the precedent of the 1965 Canada/U.S. Auto Pact. The areas advanced by the Canadian government were urban mass transport equipment, textiles and petro-chemicals. In February 1984, the two countries agreed to a "work program" covering four areas: urban mass transport equipment, informatics, agricultural equipment, and steel. A follow-up meeting was held in Ottawa in June. However, the process was interrupted by the Canadian federal election.

But, as Carol Goar of *The Toronto Star* has documented, the idea of a comprehensive bilateral free trade agreement was still very much part of the U.S. trade agenda. In 1983 the U.S. Ambassador to Canada, Paul Robinson, held special talks with the president of the Canadian Chamber of Commerce, Sam Hughes. The Reagan administration would first sign a comprehensive treaty with Israel. Why couldn't Canada be the second country? This strategy was later formalized in the U.S. *Trade and Tariff Act* of 1984, which specifically granted the president the power to negotiate trade agreements with Israel and Canada under the special "fast track" procedures. Robinson's meetings with Hughes on the trade proposal were extended to include Tom d'Aquino, president of the Business Council on National Issues, and Roy Phillips, executive director of the Canadian Manufacturers Association. The U.S. trade representative, then William Brock, insisted that the initiative would formally have to come from Canada in order to try to avoid a repeat of 1911.

Throughout 1983 and 1984 Sam Hughes undertook to mobilize business interests to support a comprehensive free trade agreement with the United States. A key forum was the 1983 hearings held by the Royal Commission on the Economic Union and Development Prospects for Canada, commonly known after its chairman, Donald Macdonald. The new business agenda in Canada included a comprehensive bilateral free trade agreement with the United States, the use of the "free market" to make key decisions (which require deregulation and privatization), and cuts in government programs to effect a major reduction in the federal budget deficit. It was the Reagan/Thatcher agenda. Donald Macdonald was quickly won over and became one of the strongest supporters of the free trade proposal—even before the Royal Commission had made its request.

In her history of the origin of the free trade initiative, Carol Goar points to the key role played by the Canada/U.S. Committee of the Canadian Chamber of Commerce. Chaired by David Braide of CIL Inc., its 40 members, representing the largest corporations in Canada, pushed the newly elected Mulroney government. In January 1985, James Kelleher, then Minister of Trade, issued his discussion paper advocating a comprehensive bilateral free trade agreement with the United States. When Kelleher decided to set up an advisory committee on the issue, he simply appointed the Canadian Chamber of Commerce committee!

At the "Shamrock Summit" in Quebec City in March 1985, Prime Minister Mulroney and President Reagan agreed to work on trade liberalization through the GATT and bilaterally. In September the Trade Minister presented his background paper to the House of Commons advocating negotiations to secure and enhance access to the U.S. market. On December 10, 1985, President Reagan formally notified the U.S. Congress that he was taking advantage of the 1984 U.S. *Trade and Tariff Act* and was beginning negotiations with Canada to reach a comprehensive bilateral free trade agreement under the "fast track" procedure.

Long-Term Objectives of the U.S. Government

U.S. objectives in negotiating a comprehensive bilateral free trade agreement with Canada must be seen in the context of major American geopolitical goals and the major problems currently facing that country. The United States is desperately trying to hold on to its position as the dominant capitalist country. It also continues to see itself as the primary defender of the "free world" against the spread of socialism and anti-imperialist nationalism. The Reagan administration has revived the old Cold War rhetoric of the 1950s. Unfortunately, this has come right at the time when the Soviet Union is seriously pushing for disarmament and moving towards more Western-style democracy.

Since the onset of the Korean War, the U.S. government has viewed Canada as the most secure source of strategic raw materials. Under American tariffs, Canadian raw materials enter the United States duty-free. A comprehensive bilateral free trade agreement would obviously enhance U.S. access to Canadian resources.

At the Shamrock Summit in March 1985, Brian Mulroney and Ronald Reagan agreed to a modernization of the North American Aerospace Defence System, reaffirmed the 1959 Defence Production Sharing Agreement, and supported the American attempt to create the Strategic Defence Initiative ("Star Wars"). The two leaders signed a statement which argued that "the security of Canada and the United States is inextricably linked." The prime minister also agreed to the U.S. request that Canada increase spending on its military commitment to NATO. Subsequently, the new Canadian government agreed to continue to permit the United States to test the Cruise missile over Canadian territory. In the United Nations, Canada joined the tiny group of ten countries supporting U.S. policy in voting against a resolution calling for a freeze on the development of nuclear weapons by the two superpowers. In geopolitical terms, it was clear that the new Mulroney government would cause American policymakers even fewer problems than had the Trudeau government.

The major immediate problems faced by the United States in 1986-7 included the general deficit in the trade balance, the dramatic decline in U.S. agricultural exports, and the instability in international currencies. The protectionist bills coming out of the U.S. Congress were a direct result of the continuing large deficit in U.S. trade. In 1985 the overall deficit was $148.5 billion, and it rose to $156.2 billion in 1986. In spite of the steady devaluation of the U.S. dollar against the other major currencies, through the first three-quarters of 1987 the U.S. trade deficit was running at an annual rate of $168.5 billion. Despite the fall of the U.S. dollar against other currencies, in October 1987 the U.S. monthly trade deficit soared to a record high of $17.6 billion.

In 1985, the United States had a trade deficit of $21.5 billion with Canada, the second largest deficit after that with Japan. While this deficit declined to $13.3 billion in 1986, the U.S. government has determined to reduce it even further. That was one of their primary objectives in pursuing the free trade agreement with Canada.

The decline in the export of U.S. agricultural products has been a major political concern in that country. Over a five-year period from 1980 to 1985, U.S. agricultural exports declined from $47 billion to $31 billion, a decline of 34%. In the period since World War II, the United States has normally enjoyed a substantial surplus in the trade of agricultural products with Canada. Over the 1978-82 five-year period, the annual average exceeded $1 billion. But the 25% devaluation of the Canadian dollar vis à vis the U.S. dollar led to the disappearance of the surplus by 1985. The U.S. government expects that the free trade agreement with Canada will restore the favourable trade balance in agricultural products.

There were two major programs that the U.S. government and U.S. business interests wanted eliminated: the Foreign Investment Review Agency (FIRA) and the National Energy Program (NEP). In June 1984, while leader of the opposition, Mulroney promised the Reagan administration, on a visit to Washington, that if elected he would abolish FIRA and NEP. Immediately after his election, he flew to New York City to make his first speech as prime minister. He told the Economic Club that FIRA and NEP were dead and declared to the beaming businessmen that "Canada is open for business—again." Unfortunately, in this game of friendly poker with the U.S. government, Mulroney had given Ronald Reagan Canada's two aces in the hole and had gotten absolutely nothing in return.

During the free trade negotiations in 1986 and 1987, the U.S. government consistently supported the following objectives:

The Inclusion of Services in the Agreement. On numerous occasions the U.S. adminstration made it known that it wanted at least part of the service area included in the agreement. For years different U.S. administrations have been pressing to expand the jurisdiction of the GATT to include services, and a treaty with Canada would set a useful precedent. The U.S./Israel agreement pledged the two governments to expand trade in the service area. The United States has a distinct international advantage in services, which is reflected in a positive balance of payments in that area. Expansion of the U.S. service industry into Canada would help reduce the trade deficit.

The service sector includes banking and finance, insurance, advertising, real estate, professional services, tourism, transportation, communications, wholesale and retail trade, franchising, construction, design and engineering, utilities, and the cultural industries. For U.S. companies, Canada is the first logical market for expansion abroad because of its close proximity and similar language. Private economic interests in these areas in the United States are pushing hard for the agreement.

The Inclusion of Agriculture in the Treaty. The Reagan administration wanted to include agriculture as a predecent for the current GATT negotiations and to facilitate increased exports to Canada. U.S. agricultural exports to Canada have not only suffered because of the devalued Canadian dollar, they have been restrained by federal and provincial barriers to trade. Most of these policies were established to support regional development. The U.S. Department of Agriculture and U.S. farm interests have been consistently pushing for a list of concessions from Canada. These included the end to all supply management programs for agricultural products (Canadian Wheat Board, Canadian Dairy Commission and boards in the feather industries), the removal of seasonal tariffs on fruits and vegetables as well as those on corn and rapeseed, the end to the *Western Grains Transportation Act,* the *Feed Freight Assistance Act,* and the *Western Grain Stabilization Act,* the removal of interprovincial barriers to trade, including discrimination by provincial liquor boards, and an end to provincial government agricultural support programs.

The American and Canadian governments agreed to negotiate harmonization of standards for agricultural products, including health and safety regulations, testing, certification, labelling and packaging. On several occasions the chief U.S. negotiator, Peter Murphy, argued that major concessions in this area were "essential" in order to get support from the U.S. administration and the Congress.

Elimination of federal and provincial government subsidies. Achieving what the U.S. government calls a "level playing field" means the elimination of the full range of subsidies to industry that have traditionally been supplied by both federal and provincial governments under regional development programs. These include joint ventures, capital grants, research and development assistance, loans at low interest rates, guaranteed loans, tax holidays, support for employee training programs, preferential purchasing, and infrastructure subsidies, such as low power rates. All the Canadian provinces use them extensively.

The U.S. federal and state governments have some similar programs, but they are not nearly as comprehensive as those in Canada. In addition, provincial support for agriculture is much more extensive than support by the U.S. states. But if we include U.S. military spending, which is almost exclusively in the form of contracts to private enterprise, the extent of U.S. government support dwarfs that of Canadian governments. However, U.S. politicians typically do not see reduction of this form of American government subsidization as a factor in obtaining a "level playing field."

In the area of procurement policy, both levels of government in both countries give preferential treatment to promote local production. In 1986 U.S. federal procurement was around $21 billion; in Canada in that year it was around $1 billion. While U.S. business interests have pushed for the elimination of procurement discrimination in Canada, the U.S. Congress took the position that it would not agree to mutual concessions in this area.

A More Stable Exchange Rate. In September 1985 the Reagan administration announced a change in policy on the question of the American dollar. In order to eliminate the mounting U.S. balance of payments deficit, the U.S. dollar would have to fall in relation to the currencies of the other major industrial countries. The Group Five (United States, Japan, West Germany, France and the United Kingdom) agreed at its meeting in Tokyo that the American dollar was too high and should come down. However, the fall of the dollar did not cause the U.S. balance of trade to improve noticeably, partly because four of its major trading partners tie their currency to the U.S. dollar: South Korea, Taiwan, Hong Kong and Canada. Since September 1985 the U.S. dollar has been steadily dropping—but not against the

Canadian dollar. On occasion, the Bank of Canada has intervened in the international money market to try to keep the Canadian dollar at around US$.75. However, most economists agree that under the present circumstances it is impossible for the Bank of Canada to fix the value of the Canadian dollar. Many U.S. Congressmen, led by Texas Senator Lloyd Bensten, argue that there is a need for currency stabilization between Canada and the United States, including a move towards parity.

The devaluation of the Canadian dollar has been a concern of major American exporters. In March 1986 the U.S. National Association of Manufacturers argued in a major brief that a trade agreement with Canada would be "impractical" without an agreement to narrow and stabilize the gap between the two currencies. In May 1986 the U.S. Secretary of the Treasury, James Baker, told the U.S. Senate Foreign Relations Committee that the price of Canadian admission to the Group Five would be to boost the value of the Canadian dollar. The solution would be a co-ordinated rate.

The Reagan administration cites the large federal budget deficit in Canada, second only to that of Italy on a per capita basis, as the reason for the weak Canadian dollar. They have suggested that the two currencies move back towards a fixed exchange rate through the use of "target zones."

Because of the diametrically opposed positions of the two countries on this issue, it was not included in the free trade negotiations. It has been put off until the agreement is ratified and comes into effect. But it is very likely that the implementation of a comprehensive bilateral free trade agreement with the United States would force the two countries to reach an agreement on stabilizing exchange rates. When corporations invest, they take into account the cost of production. However, these costs can be artificially altered by the manipulation of the official rates of exchange. For investors in industrial production, this is an unacceptable solution.

The 25% devaluation in the Canadian dollar has reduced the cost of production below that in the United States in several industries. For example, in 1987 General Motors laid off 29,000 employees in the United States but none in Canada. It is currently cheaper for the Big Three to manufacture cars and trucks in Canada. But that would change if there was a rise in the value of the Canadian dollar.

In the future, U.S. corporations may decide to close their branch plants in Canada and pull back their manufacturing to the United States. In an effort to reverse such a trend, the Bank of Canada and the Canadian government could decide to further devaluate the

Canadian dollar, thus lowering labour and other production costs in Canada. Most likely, business interests would demand exchange stabilization. This is what happened in the European Economic Community.

In early November 1987, Saskatchewan's Trade Minister met with a group of Saskatchewan manufacturers as part of the provincial government's program of promoting free trade. They all stressed the absolute necessity of maintaining the Canadian dollar at a 25% discount. As a Regina manufacturer of agricultural machinery noted, "the exchange rate has kept American manufacturers out of our markets and helped us break into their markets."

Figure 2, by Katie Macmillan, an economist with the Canada West Foundation, illustrates the effect of the lower Canadian dollar on trade between Canada and the United States. The favourable balance of trade for Canada began when the Canadian dollar dropped to US$.80. Professor Urie Zohar of York University compared the productivity of seventeen manufacturing industries in both countries and concluded that a US$.72 Canadian dollar would be good for Canada under a free trade agreement, but if it rose to US$.84 it would "spell almost certain disaster."

National Treatment for U.S. Investors. As the negotiations progressed in 1987, attention focused on a demand by American business interests to achieve "the right of establishment" and "national treatment" in Canada. The objective is to obtain for American firms operating in Canada equal status to Canadian firms. If this is achieved, neither the federal nor provincial governments could apply any policies which give preference to Canadian or local firms.

U.S. Business Support for an Agreement

As the negotiations progressed throughout 1986 and 1987, other issues rose to the surface as they were promoted by special interests in the United States. For example, the Northeast-Midwest Congressional Coalition, and the governors from a number of these states, were demanding that the 1965 Auto Pact be significantly revised. It was also revealed that the U.S. government wanted Canada to remove all remaining barriers to trade in energy.

The U.S. government was also insisting on greater protection for "intellectual property rights." This issue became very embarrassing for the Mulroney government. In 1987 an Act was pushed through

Figure 2

Foreign Exchange Rate and the Balance of Trade

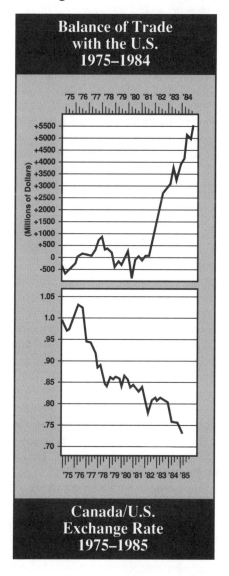

SOURCE: Katie Macmillan. "International Trade: Problems and Prospects." *Western Perspectives,* Canada West Foundation, November 1985, p. 13.

the House of Commons to undermine the production of low-cost generic drugs, manufactured by Canadian firms. This was widely seen as another concession to the United States to get a trade agreement; in fact, such a provision was specified in an early text of the agreement. In addition, heavy pressure was being applied by the transnational drug companies, many of them American. The large agribusiness corporations were pressing the Conservative government to pass "plant breeders rights" legislation, which would give private corporations patent controls over basic food items.

In the United States, the only visible private sector support for the trade agreement with Canada has come from business interests, and, in particular, large transnational corporations already doing business in Canada. When approval for the negotiations seemed to be stalled in the U.S. Senate Finance Committee in April 1986, a group of very powerful business organizations sent a letter to the committee urging support for the agreement. They argued that free trade with Canada "could offer significant benefits to U.S. business" and that the U.S. government should not miss out on "this historic opportunity to improve the American economy and American trade." The eighteen organizations which signed the letter included the Business Roundtable, the National Association of Manufacturers, the Chamber of Commerce, the National Foreign Trade Council and the U.S. Council for International Business.

In May 1987, over 175 major U.S. corporations launched the American Coalition for Trade Expansion with Canada. In order to build a broad geographical base, the Coalition sent invitations to 1500 corporations and trade associations. By August the membership list had risen to over 400. The Coalition planned to spend millions of dollars on advertising, and it hired four public relations firms to engage in a major lobbying campaign in Washington. These corporations are the main contributors to the many Political Action Committees (PACs) which provide the campaign funds for members of Congress and Senators.

The Coalition was initiated by American Express Co., which was pushing hard for free trade in services between the two countries. A spokesman for the Coalition told the press that they did not want trade with Canada to fall into the same category as trade with Taiwan, South Korea and Japan. "In fact, we don't want people to focus on the trade word at all. Instead, we want them to think in terms of what Canada means to the U.S."

An examination of the final text of the free trade agreement indicates that the Reagan administration got almost everything they wanted. The continental energy policy ties Canada firmly to the United States, and it maintains Canada's role as America's resource stockpile. Brian Mulroney, Quebec Premier Robert Bourassa and the chief Canadian negotiator, Simon Reisman, are all major supporters of the GRAND (Great Recycling and Northern Development) Canal scheme which would pipe water from James Bay to the American sunbelt. The Americans got far more than they dared to hope for in the service sector. They achieved the right of establishment, the right of national treatment, the right of provincial treatment and the right to do across-the-border business for all American firms. Agriculture is included in the agreement; Canadian tariffs will be removed, and the precedent has been set for the further erosion of the powers of supply management marketing boards. The deal on access to government procurement contracts is more favourable to U.S. firms. The only major issue that remains to be settled is the exchange rate.

One month later, on November 6, 1987, the United States also signed a major trade agreement with Mexico. Around 60% of Mexico's trade is with the United States. U.S. business interests have assets of $10.1 billion in Mexico, representing around 60% of all foreign investment. The two countries spent six years in negotiations.

Mexican officials and the political opposition were stunned by the Canada/U.S. free trade agreement. First, it strengthened their fears that the United States also had designs on their national resources, and there was strong opposition to anything like the proposed Canada/U.S. continental energy deal. Second, they had no intention of giving up their controls over foreign ownership. Spokesmen for the Mexican government stressed that they would not be drawn into a North American common market, as proposed by President Reagan.

The U.S./Mexican agreement is quite different from the Canada/U.S. agreement: they have only agreed to consult within 30 days on any trade dispute. In the difficult areas of investment, intellectual property rights, services, electronics, textiles and agriculture they have agreed to further consultations beginning within 90 days. Looking at the Canada/U.S. agreement, Mexican officials noted that "all the U.S. powers of protectionism are still there."

Nevertheless, Ronald Reagan concluded that the two agreements were the basis of his new North American Accord. On October 5 he proclaimed that "now it's time to dream bigger dreams of an entire hemispere from the Arctic Circle to the Tiera del Fuego united by the bonds of democracy and trade." It was "time we stopped thinking of our nearest neighbors as foreigners. Let us instead think of them as partners, independent and sovereign, but united in a common purpose." In a speech to the New Jersey Chamber of Commerce on October 13, President Reagan declared that the "U.S./Canada free trade agreement is a new economic constitution for North America." A few days later in Washington he proclaimed that "ours is a dream of an open world where all are free to trade and do business together." The Canada/U.S. agreement would serve as a model for others. "We are demonstrating to all humanity that there are indeed no limits to what people can accomplish when they are free to follow their dreams. We're making that dream a reality. It is the American dream." On a more practical note, he told the U.S. Congress that the Canada/U.S. free trade agreement would be "a key to tackling America's $170 billion world trade deficit." That is what worries many Canadians.

CHAPTER 8

Canadian Support for Free Trade

Canada has always had groups of citizens who have advocated free trade with the United States. However, in the post-World War II period the main advocates have been academic economists, and they have been largely ignored by policymakers and other interest groups. The notion of free trade and of allowing the free market to determine economic decisions is not part of the Canadian tradition. Canada did not follow the United States and break with the imperial connection and mercantilism. The 18th century liberal approach to economics has always been weak and secondary in this country. As Canada moved towards nationhood and independence, a strong tradition of state intervention in the economy developed. Many believe this to be both pragmatic and natural, given the enormous distances of the country and its persistent regional disparities. The tradition of the state playing a positive role in economic development was reinforced with the adoption of the modern welfare state.

But orthodox economists have never been happy with the Canadian experience. They regularly attacked the National Policy and tariff protection. The classic liberal position was set forth in John H. Young, *Canadian Commercial Policy* (1957), Harry G. Johnson, *The Canadian Quandry* (1963), and John H. Dales, *The Protective Wall in Canadian Development* (1966). To the orthodox economist following the 18th century ideal model of Adam Smith, a society is nothing more than a collection of individuals, each pursuing his or her own self-interest, primarily concerned with buying and selling in the marketplace. Government economic development policies create barriers to the consumer's right to buy the cheapest product, wherever it is produced. In 1967 John and Paul Wonnocott published *Free Trade Between the United States and Canada*. Tariff protection, they argued, had created inefficiencies in production and had

105

caused consumers to pay higher-than-necessary prices. As an alternative policy they advocated unilateral free trade with the United States.

For the most part, these liberal economists were ignored. But that began to change with the onset of the economic crisis, dramatized by the four-fold rise in oil prices in 1973. In 1975 the annual report of the Economic Council of Canada, *Looking Outward*, advocated a policy of multilateral free trade, or, if this were not possible, bilateral free trade with the United States.

Greater acceptance of the free market and free trade developed because of major changes in the world economy in the 1970s and 1980s. First, with the onset of "stagflation" in the 1970s (high unemployment and high inflation), the post-war policies of government fiscal and monetary intervention in the economy came under increased attack from the advocates of the free market alternative. Second, with the election of the Thatcher and Reagan governments, the neo-conservative agenda took root; in Canada, the political right increased its influence. Third, as the American economy began to recover from the 1981-2 great recession, Canada became even more dependent on that market. For some Canadian exporters, the United States became an uncertain market. As we have seen, with the loss of the position of unchallenged hegemony, U.S. protectionist sentiment increased, and Canada was no longer exempt from government actions.

Canadian Free Trade Objectives

The main objectives of a comprehensive bilateral free trade agreement with the United States, in addition to the complete phasing out of all remaining tariffs, are as follows.

Assured Access to the U.S. Market. The strongest argument put forth has been a negative one. Even as the negotiations were underway, the U.S. International Trade Commission and the U.S. Department of Congress took actions which had an unfavourable impact on some Canadian exports. These included safeguard actions in the shakes and shingles industry and countervailing tariffs imposed on softwood lumber and potash. The steel industry was also forced to "voluntarily" restrict exports to the United States. In September 1987 a U.S. Court of Appeal backed U.S. uranium interests which sought a ban on Canadian imports. The U.S. *Atomic Energy Act* of 1956 states that the United States must have a viable uranium industry for

national security reasons. Thus, it is argued, unless Canada negotiated a free trade agreement with the United States, we would continue to experience restrictions on our exports.

There is no question that the United States, more than any other
country, has resorted to GATT-supported protectionist actions.
Between 1980 and 1986, the U.S. International Trade Commission
(ITC) examined 281 countervailing duty and 348 anti-dumping
cases. Over the same period of time there were eight countervailing
duty cases and 30 anti-dumping cases brought against Canadians by
U.S. interests. Over the same period there were only six countervailing duty cases in the entire European Economic Community, and
Japan initiated only one.

The extent of the threat to Canadian exports has been magnified by
the supporters of free trade. Bruce Wilkinson, an economist at the
University of Alberta, has pointed out that Canadians have done fairly well in arguing their case before the U.S. International Trade
Commission. The ITC ruled against Canadian interests in one of nine
countervail cases, eight of fourteen "unfair trade practices" cases,
and four of twenty anti-dumping cases. In 1985, for example, the
cases against Canada represented less than 2% of Canada's exports to
.ie United States.

The main concern for Canada has been the unilateral interpretation
of export subsidies by the U.S. government. Government programs
which are designed for regional development purposes are legitimate
under the GATT. But the U.S. government has repeatedly listed
them as "unfair trade practices" in trade disputes with Canadian industries. The Mulroney government insisted that Canada had to
obtain from the United States a clear definition of what was a legitimate government subsidy and what was an "unfair trade practice."
The provincial governments were adamant. Everyone wanted this.
But the U.S. negotiators would not give an inch. No agreement could
be reached. The final text proposes that a working group of
Canadians and Americans sit down over the next seven years to try to
work this out. In the meantime, U.S. trade laws would remain in
force. However, Canada has already given away most of its bargaining chips and has gotten virtually nothing in return.

The Mulroney government, provincial premiers, and many businessmen long argued that a treaty with the United States would be
unacceptable unless it contained a special disputes settlement
tribunal, with the power of binding arbitration, which would replace
the present system. It would need to be a *court of first resort* to
eliminate the long and costly existing process. This was the recom-

mendation of the Macdonald Royal Commission. Thus, it was hoped, trade disputes could be settled in a legalistic manner, quickly, without the influence of politics and economic interests. However, just how this tribunal and process were to operate was never spelled out to the general public. It is not surprising that the final result was a sham.

The proposal for binding arbitration was incredibly naive. It overlooked the historic role of the Congress in trade. There was no indication that the Congress was willing to give up its powers in this area. It ignored the fact that most of U.S. trade laws are based on the GATT codes and are perfectly legal under international trade rules. It also ignored the fact that President Reagan had promised the U.S. Senate Finance Committee in April 1986 that the U.S. negotiators would "retain full access to multilaterally sanctioned U.S. trade remedies." Finally, it ignored the precedent of the U.S./Israel bilateral free trade agreement, which limited the dispute settling tribunal to non-binding conciliation.

But what is most curious is the assumption that it is possible to set up some sort of arbitration system that would be unbiased and immune from politics and economic issues. Since the beginning of the 1974 economic crisis, there has been nothing more political than trade issues. Furthermore, there can be no guarantee that the parties will live up to the terms of the agreement or even its spirit. Let us look at two examples. Under the Canada/U.S. Defence Production Sharing Agreement (1959) Canadian firms were supposed to have "national treatment" in bidding on U.S. military contracts. Yet, at least since 1973, the U.S. Congress has passed acts, amended others, and included clauses in appropriate bills which have effectively excluded bids by Canadian businesses in a growing number of areas. Under international law, when one country mines the harbours of another country, that is by definition an act of war. When the U.S. government mined the harbours of Nicaragua, that country took the case to the World Court. But when the World Court ruled unanimously against the U.S. government, and ordered them to cease their actions, the Reagan administration simply dismissed the decision out of hand.

Access to a Market of over 100 Million. At least since the 1975 Economic Council of Canada report, it has been argued that Canada cannot survive in the world market without assured access to a market of over 100 million people. The United States, Japan and the European Economic Community have such market access.

Yet access to a market of over 100 million is certainly no guarantee of economic success. The 1981-2 great recession was as severe in the United States and the European Economic Community as it was in Canada, New Zealand or Australia. Indeed, in 1987, Belgium, the Netherlands and Denmark, all members of the European Economic Community, had unemployment rates well over 10%, considerably higher than Canada's.

In 1987 the economy of Denmark continued to stagnate; it had become "the sick man of Scandinavia." It was the only Scandinavian country in the European Common Market. In 1986 it had a US$7.1 billion trade deficit. In 1987 it was experiencing negative economic growth. Unemployment continued to rise. Economists concluded that under the rationalization imposed by membership in the European Economic Community, the country's industrial base had become too narrow. The production sector of the economy had declined too rapidly. In order to compensate for the loss of these jobs, the service sector of the state had increased. But the narrow tax base provided by such an economy was producing persistent budget problems.

What happened to Ireland when it joined the European Economic Community? At first, the results looked encouraging. But this was during the phase-in period of adjustment. There was increased investment in Ireland due to its lower labour costs. But with the end of the adjustment period, and the onset of the great recession, Ireland was devastated. In 1987 its official unemployment level reached 20%, and, once again, the export of people became its primary economic activity.

Before Spain joined the European Economic Community in 1986, it had a US$1 billion trade surplus with its northern neighbours. But by November 1987 this had changed to a US$3 billion deficit, as exports moderated while imports soared, even though Spain's tariffs are being phased out over six years. In addition, Portugal has a special free trade agreement with Spain which permits exports from third countries; this loophole has provided a "back door" for imports of manufactured goods from Japan, Taiwan, Hong Kong and South Korea. Unemployment has soared to over 20%. As the head of the Spanish business association put it, "Spain did not enter the community, but the community has made a massive entry into Spain."

One can also look at the impact of joining the European Common Market on Britain. There was a strong division of opinion within the UK over joining the EEC, with financial capital in favour and industrial capital generally opposed. Organized labour was also generally opposed. In the five years before joining the EEC (1968-72), the UK ran an average annual deficit in trade with the EEC of £214 million. In the six-year period after joining (1974-79), the average annual deficit rose ten-fold to £2112 million.

When the new Conservative government under Margaret Thatcher abolished foreign exchange controls in 1979, the outflow of foreign capital from Britain rose from £909 million to £4100 million in just three years. The largest proportion of this overseas investment was within the EEC. In recent years, British investment has boomed in the United States and Canada; but investment in production has stagnated at home. London and finance capital have done well since the UK joined the EEC. But the rest of the UK is suffering from a prolonged depression, manufacturing continues to decline, and unemployment remains unusually high, no matter how it is defined. Clearly, access to a market of 100 million is no guarantee of any improvement in an economy.

The supporters of free trade with the United States continually refer to Canada as a "small, open economy." In terms of population alone, Canada ranks 30th in the world. But as Table 9 demonstrates, in terms of its economy Canada is the ninth most important single market in the world, just behind that of China, and more important than that of Mexico, Brazil or India.

Obtain "National Treatment" for Canadian Goods and Services Within the United States. Most businesses expected that a comprehensive bilateral free trade agreement would do more than just gain assured access to the U.S. market. At the "Shamrock Summit" in March 1985 Brian Mulroney and Ronald Reagan signed a declaration which called for the removal of procurement and funding policies which restrict companies from bidding on government contracts. However, because of the massive impact of military spending in the U.S. economy, a mutual agreement to suspend "buy local" rules would clearly be to the advantage of Canada. The figures cited in the text of the free trade agreement fall far short of actual government spending on the procurement of goods. While the agreement seems to give Canada a proportionately higher access than the United States, U.S. officials have pointed out that 80% of the $3 billion of potential contracts for Canadian exporters were already covered in the 1959 Defence Production Sharing Agreement.

There is also the question of the "right of establishment." This is particularly important in the area of services. For example, in finance and the cultural industries there are extensive national restrictions on both sides of the border. There is also the problem of existing state,

Table 9

Gross Domestic Product, 1986

Country	Population (Millions, 1983)	Gross Domestic Product ($ Billions)
United States	234.5	3117
USSR	272.5	1540
Japan	119.3	1310
West Germany	61.4	890
France	54.7	707
Britain	56.3	600
Italy	56.8	424
China	1191.1	352
Canada	24.9	308
Brazil	129.7	280
India	733.2	202
Poland	36.6	188
Mexico	75.0	185
Netherlands	14.4	178
Australia	15.4	170
East Germany	16.7	154
Sweden	8.3	139
Switzerland	6.5	110
Czechoslovakia	15.4	110
South Korea	40.4	97

SOURCE: World Bank, *World Development Report,* various issues.

provincial and local government restrictions. Individual Canadian firms wanted the right to establish in the United States. But many Canadian interests are concerned that any mutual lifting of such restrictions would hurt Canada much more than the United States.

Canadian Firms Would Achieve Economies of Scale. It has long been argued that Canadian tariffs (now almost non-existent under the GATT reductions) have created inefficient businesses and plants. Exposing these manufacturers to competition from the admittedly larger American firms would force them to "rationalize."

Larger, more modern plants, with a greater specialization of products, would result in more efficient firms with lower costs to consumers. These rationalized firms would then be better able to compete in international markets.

Orthodox economists regularly cite this restructuring of manufacturing as a key objective in a comprehensive bilateral free trade agreement. This new industrial policy would also require the elimination of trade barriers between provinces. Two economists, Richard Harris and David Cox, developed a simulation model of the Canadian economy under free trade, widely cited by orthodox economists as the best computer model ever created. From this model they conclude that bilateral free trade with the United States would result in a 4% increase in real gross national product, a 10% increase in real wages and a 20% increase in labour productivity.

The model predicts that the major beneficiaries from free trade would be in transportation equipment, paper and allied products, textiles, clothing and agriculture. But others have pointed out that the automotive industry, by far the largest part of the transportation equipment industry, already has rationalized on a continental basis under the Auto Pact. Little gain can be expected in this sector. Paper and allied products are among Canada's most efficient industries, and their products enter the United States almost duty free. Very few people expect free trade to result in a net benefit to Canadian agriculture; climatic factors alone give American producers a major advantage over Canadian producers. And almost everyone thinks free trade will have a negative effect on the more protected Canadian textile and clothing industries. Clearly, this famous econometric model does not conform to the real world. Unfortunately, many politicians have singled out some of the conclusions to use for propaganda purposes.

The Hidden Agenda: The Expansion of Neo-Conservatism. Finally, free trade with the United States is seen as a means of facilitating the restructuring of the Canadian economy along the lines of the Reagan/Thatcher agenda. The United States is a much more market-orientated society than is Canada. Social welfare programs are quite primitive by Canadian standards. Trade unions are much weaker. There is no political left in the United States—not even a social democratic party. The business elite and the political right in Canada expect that through the inevitable pressures for harmonization of policies, a comprehensive bilateral free trade agreement will ultimately force Canada to conform to American practices.

The Macdonald Royal Commission concluded that "closer free

trade relations will increase the force of U.S. political influence at both levels of Canadian government." They feared the alternative: "a status quo trade policy might lead very quickly, over the next few years, to calls for a planned economy." Thomas Courchene, an economist who played a key role with the Royal Commission, argues that "forced harmonization" will lead to a more market-driven Canadian economy. Richard G. Lipsey and Murray G. Smith, writing for the C.D. Howe Institute, argue that most of the advocates of the comprehensive bilateral free trade agreement with the United States see it "as part of a larger package of economic policies designed to increase the importance of the free market in determining investment and output decisions." This package also included privatization and deregulation. Herbert Grubel, an economist at Simon Fraser University in B.C. and an associate of the Fraser Institute, argues that "free trade will slow the creep of socialism in Canada." The case for the free market and free trade is best put forth by Katie Macmillan, research economist for the Canada West Foundation:

> It is highly unlikely that the Americans will explicitly ask that [our social programs] be dismantled. Indirectly, however, they could be at some risk. This risk will arise because free trade between our two countries will inevitably lead to wages being equalized between Canada and the United States. This will occur since a high cost producer will not be able to compete against a lower cost producer if goods are traded freely. The higher cost producer will have to lower his costs or lose his market. Canada's generous social programs such as U.I.C., baby bonus, etc., tend to raise labour costs in this country, and ultimately Canadian production costs. There could therefore be *market* pressure for a reduction in these programs or their elimination.

This view was echoed by Laurent Thibault, now president of the Canadian Manufacturers Association, in testimony before the Canadian Senate in 1980:

> It is simply a fact that, as we ask our industries to compete toe to toe with American industry . . . we in Canada are obviously forced to create the same conditions in Canada that exist in the United States, whether it is the unemployment insurance scheme, Workmen's Compensation, the cost of gov-

ernment, the level of taxation, or whatever.

Business Support for the Free Trade Agreement

The political debate around free trade with the United States has centred on the question of the survival of Canada as an independent country. Canadians are well aware of the extent to which our country is dominated by U.S. political, economic and cultural influences. It is not surprising that we have concentrated on this aspect of the trend towards further dependence on continental trade. But there is another equally important aspect of bilateral free trade: it is also very clearly a class issue. Support for a comprehensive bilateral free trade agreement with the United States has come almost exclusively from organizations representing big business and their neo-conservative ideological supporters. In contrast, opposition has come from trade unions, teachers' organizations, women's organizations, farm organizations, church groups and a wide variety of popular community groups. This fundamental class division is illustrated in Table 10, which lists the main supporting and opposing groups.

As we have seen, the major business organizations in Canada played a key role in getting the free trade negotiations underway. They were also the driving force behind the formation of the Canadian Alliance for Trade and Job Opportunities; this lobby group developed out of the 40-member International Trade Advisory Committee appointed by the Department of External Affairs. Financed by contributions from 112 Canadian-based corporations, the Alliance has been boosting free trade through advertisements in newspapers and on television. While they have been very secretive about their financial sources, a list of 32 contributors released in May 1987 revealed that all were members of the exclusive Business Council on National Issues. In September 1987 David Crane of *The Toronto Star* revealed a list of the major financial backers for the organization. Alcan, the Royal Bank and Noranda alone had provided $400,000 of a $1.4 million advertising campaign. The Alliance planned to raise $4 million for the pro-free trade campaign, but reneged on their prior commitment to open its books to the public.

The major business organizations supporting free trade include the following:

Business Council on National Issues (BCNI). Formed as a political pressure group in 1976, this organization represents the chief executive officers of the top 155 business enterprises in Canada.

They have been the most consistent promoters of a comprehensive bilateral agreement with the United States.

Canadian Manufacturing Association (CMA). This historic organization represents around 3300 manufacturers across Canada. However, its board of directors in dominated by large corporations. A 1984 survey found that only one-third of its members felt that free trade with the United States would be of benefit to themselves. Yet the organization has been a strong supporter. They have also demanded extensive federal government financial and tax support during a ten-year adjustment period. On April 13, 1987, the CMA and its American counterpart, the National Association of Manufacturers, issued a joint statement from Washington, D.C., supporting the agreement and pledging a joint effort on lobbying.

Canadian Chamber of Commerce (CCC). While representing 150,000 businesses and local groups across Canada, the board of directors is dominated by large corporations and financial institutions. Although strongly supporting free trade with the United States, they have expressed concern that the agreement might lead to the loss of numerous government subsidies and incentive programs. In general, they support the New Right agenda.

Canadian Bankers Association (CBA). It is not surprising that the CBA is a strong supporter of free trade with the United States. For years the banks have been the key institutions fostering American corporate takeovers of Canadian business firms. They have consistently opposed any government-directed industrial policy. In their view, Canada must be "open for business" for the financial interests.

Canadian Federation of Independent Business (CFIB). The CFIB represents thousands of small businesses across Canada. A 1985 membership survey found that 66% of respondents were for a bilateral free trade agreement, 20% opposed and 14% undecided. They have been the most vociferous supporters of the New Right attack on trade unions and social welfare programs.

Many other trade associations support a comprehensive agreement, including the Retail Council of Canada, the Canadian Export Association, the Canadian Importers Association, the Mining Association of Canada, the Aerospace Industries Association, the Canadian Chemical Producers Association, the Machinery and Equipment Manufacturers Association of Canada, the Canadian Electrical Association, the Canadian Pulp and Paper Association, the Canadian Business Equipment Manufacturers Association, the Independent Petroleum Association of Canada, the Canadian Life and Health Insurance Association, the Investment Dealers Association

Table 10

Political Alignments on the Free Trade Issue

Groups Supporting Free Trade
(Partial List)

Business Council on National Issues
Canadian Chamber of Commerce
Canadian Manufacturers Association
Canadian Bankers Association
Canadian Federation of Independent Business

Retail Council of Canada
Mining Association of Canada
Independent Petroleum Association
Canadian Pulp and Paper Association
Canadian Chemical Producers Association

Pharmaceutical Manufacturers Association
Canadian Life and Health Assurance Association
Investment Dealers Association of Canada
Aerospace Industries Association of Canada
Canadian Chemical Producers Association

Canadian Exporters Association
Association of Consulting Engineers
Canadian Importers Association
Institute of Corporate Directors in Canada
International Business Council of Canada

Economic Council of Canada
The Institute for Research on Public Policy
The C.D. Howe Institute
Conference Board of Canada
Canadian-American Committee
Canada West Foundation
The Fraser Institute

Western Canadian Wheat Growers Association
Canadian Cattlemen's Association
Canadian Pork Producers' Association

The Financial Post
The Financial Times
The Globe and Mail (Toronto)
The Southam Press
The Thomson Newspapers

**Groups Opposing Free Trade
(Partial List)**

Canadian Labour Congress
Council of Canadian Unions
Quebec Federation of Labour (FTQ)
Confederation of National Trade Unions (CSN)

Quebec Teachers' Federation (CEQ)
Canadian Teachers' Federation
National Farmers Union
Quebec Farmers Union (UPA)
Ontario Federation of Agriculture
Dairy Farmers of Canada
Canadian Turkey, Broiler and Egg Producers Associations

National Action Committee on the Status of Women
Voice of Women
Congress of Canadian Women
Ontario Working Women
Women Working with Immigrant Women

National Anti-Poverty Organization
Council of Canadians
GATT-Fly
United Church of Canada
Jesuit Centre for Social Faith and Justice

Assembly of First Nations
Consumers Against Rising Prices
Toronto Disarmament Network
Toronto Union of Unemployed Workers
Law Union of Canada

Coalition of Senior Citizens' Organizations
Canadian Council of Retirees
Pollution Probe
Playwrights' Union of Canada
Canadian Conference of the Arts
ACTRA
Writers' Union of Canada
The Artists Union

and the Pharmaceutical Manufacturers Association.

But not all business organizations are in favour of free trade. Many clearly see that they will be badly hurt by more competition from the United States. Some of these include the Canadian Textiles Institute, the Canadian Carpet Institute, the Brewer's Association of Canada, the Wine Institute of Canada, the Automotive Parts Manufacturers Association, the Canadian Council of Furniture Manufacturers, the Motor Vehicle Manufacturers Association, the Rubber Association of Canada, the Society of the Plastics Industry of Canada, and the Graphic Arts Industry Association. Others such as the Grocery Products Manufacturers Association of Canada and the Canadian Meat Council are in favour of a free trade agreement only if the Canadian dollar is pegged at between US$.70 and US$.75. They realize that the strong growth of Canadian exports to the United States is dependent on the perpetuation of the devaluation of the Canadian dollar.

The Political Alignment on the Free Trade Question

Many Canadians were surprised when they learned that the Con-sumers Association of Canada (CAC) joined the alliance of business groups in March 1987. Earlier, the CAC had been expelled from the International Organization of Consumer Unions for accepting advertising in its magazine, *Canadian Consumer*. They had also drawn the wrath of Canadian consumers by breaking with the inter-national organization and endorsing the irradiation of food. The CAC, espousing the 18th century ideology of Adam Smith, has con-sistently supported free trade and free markets. They have a long history of opposing protection of Canadian industries and govern-ment support for the agricultural community. But the decision to join the alliance, made by the executive, was strongly challenged at the CAC annual convention later in 1987. Delegates continued to sup-port free trade in general, but they rejected the Fortress North America approach reflected in the Canada/U.S. bilateral agreement.

Support has also come from the various "think tanks" supported by corporate and financial interests across Canada. The most prestigious of these is the Institute for Reseach on Public Policy, a liberal organization co-sponsored by business interests and Canada's universities. It has consistently advocated policies of trade liberal-ization and closer ties with the United States.

The Economic Council of Canada (ECC) was created by the

federal government in 1963, and for years it had some standing as a fairly independent, though orthodox, economic research organization. However, in November 1985 Judith Maxwell of the C.D. Howe Institute was appointed to chair the Council, and it was transformed into a propaganda arm for the Mulroney government. It became a high-profile supporter of the New Right agenda. Citing its computer model, the ECC has issued reports claiming an enormous number of jobs would be created by a free trade agreement with the United States. It has also issued reports supporting deregulation, privatization and tax "reform." In August 1987 it went so far as to support a sales tax on food.

Other support has come from the Conference Board of Canada, an influential branch of the U.S. organization which does economic forecasting. The Canadian-American Committee, with links to the U.S. National Planning Association, has a long commitment to increased political and economic integration between the two countries. Closely tied to these is the conservative C.D. Howe Institute, which has been one of the chief sources of pro-free trade propaganda. The chief agents of these organizations have been Richard G. Lipsey, Murray G. Smith, Ronald J. Wonnacott and Paul Wonnacott. Strong support has also come from the Canada West Foundation, the Alberta pro-business research organization.

The chief voice of big business in Canada is the Fraser Institute, formed in Vancouver in 1974 by Michael Walker, a right-wing economist, John Raybould of the B.C. Employers Council, and Sally Pipes of the Council of Forest Industries. Since then it has been transformed from a B.C. business organization to a Who's Who in Canadian big business. Corporations and financial institutions pay membership fees based on the size of their assets. The Fraser Institute has close links with the Bilderberg Club in the Netherlands, the Trilateral Commission set up in New York by the Rockefellers, the Mont Pelerin Society, the Institute for Economic Analysis in Britain, and the American Enterprise Institute in Washington. All of these are far-right political organizations and supporters of the Reagan-Thatcher agenda.

The major spokesmen for the Fraser Institute, including Michael Walker, Walter Block and Herbert Grubel, are strong advocates of free trade with the United States. They see it as the best way to promote the New Right agenda in Canada. They recognize that there is a strong majority of the population who support the welfare state, trade unions and the expansion of human rights. Fearful that powerful political forces in Canada might block a free trade agreement with the United States, the spokesmen for the Fraser Institute have urged the Mulroney government to make a unilateral declaration of free trade.

The Fraser Institute shares a common ideology with Canada's National Citizens Coalition, formed in 1967 by millionaire Colin Brown. Over the years this secretive organization has attacked trade unions, peace groups, bilingualism, universal medicare, indexed pensions, public servants, unemployment insurance, welfare programs, Asian immigration, equal rights for homosexuals, and restrictions on extra-billing for doctors. Aside from the usual corporate supporters, the Coalition claims support from individuals like Professor Thomas Courchene, who was a member of the research team for the Macdonald Royal Commission.

Finally, free trade has had overwhelming support from the mass media in Canada. The business press and publications have been sources of unending propaganda. The Thomson and Southam daily newspaper chains, both of which support the Fraser Institute, have backed free trade. A survey of publishers attending the annual meetings of the Canadian Press and the Canadian Daily Newspaper Publishers Association in April 1987 revealed that almost all of them supported free trade with the United States and saw newspapers as having a major role in "explaining" the advantages to their readers. Only *The Toronto Star* had opposed the agreement. Given the one-dimensional portrayal of free trade in the mass media, it is not surprising that the Canadian Alliance for Trade and Job Opportunities turned down the proposal by the Ontario Anti-Free Trade Coalition for a public debate on television.

The opposition to free trade with the United States is much more broadly based (see Table 10). They are grouped together in the national Pro-Canada Network, based in Ottawa. Every province also has its own coalition, and those in Ontario and Quebec have been very active for well over a year.

The Mulroney government certainly had no political mandate to negotiate and ratify a bilateral free trade agreement with the United States. During the 1983 campaign for the leadership of the Conservative Party, Mulroney strongly opposed any free trade agreement. On several occasions during the 1984 federal election he said he would consider carrying on with a few sectoral agreements as proposed by the Trudeau government. But there was absolutely no public discussion of a comprehensive bilateral free trade agreement.

Over 1986 and 1987, the Mulroney government's standing with the Canadian electorate declined dramatically. During the intense

Over 1986 and 1987, the Mulroney government's standing with the Canadian electorate declined dramatically. During the intense period of negotiations for an agreement in 1987, public support for the Conservative government fell in all public opinion polls to only 24%—well behind both the Liberal Party and the New Democratic Party. This was the lowest standing of any governing party in Canadian history. The rout of the Conservatives in the September 1987 election in their historic stronghold of Ontario was to a large extent a reflection of the loss of public support everywhere. Free trade with the United States was clearly the central issue in the Ontario election. Under these circumstances, the Mulroney government could not possibly claim to have any mandate for pushing the free trade agreement through Parliament.

Unfortunately, the Canadian political system is very un-democratic. With the British system of election of representatives to Parliament from single-member constituencies, and the tradition of strict party discipline in the Parliamentary caucus, there is no way that the popular majority can change a government which has lost the public confidence. As I write this, there is a growing demand that the Mulroney government call an election on the free trade issue. An Angus Reid poll taken the week of October 7-14, 1987, revealed that 59% felt an election was needed on the free trade agreement while 37% said no election was needed. Many organizations were also asking their provincial governments to veto the free trade agreement. However, the Mulroney government was taking the position that the federal government had the legal authority to force the agreement on the provinces, even where it overrode constitutional provincial authority.

CHAPTER 9

Foreign Ownership and the Branch Plant Problem

One of the basic characteristics of Canada is the high degree of foreign ownership and control of the economy. In 1984 foreign non-financial corporations accounted for 24.2% of assets, 19.5% of sales and 43.3% of profits. In the key area of manufacturing, foreign-owned corporations accounted for 44.3% of assets, 50.4% of sales and 63.3% of profits (see Table 11). Furthermore, this degree of control is considerably understated, as Statistics Canada arbitrarily defines control as 50% of shareholding. But we know that control can come at a much lower level of stock ownerhsip. For example, Argus Corporation took control of the Massey Ferguson corporation with only 8% of the shares of common stock.

Ownership patterns in Canada stand in direct contrast to other advanced, industrialized capitalist countries. In the United States, Britain and France, foreign ownership of the assets of non-financial corporations is between 3% and 5%. In Japan, it is less than 1%. In the smaller countries within the European Common Market, it ranges up to a high of 15% in Belgium. This reflects the differences in approaches to economic development. In Canada, the National Policy tariff was designed to attract foreign (and in particular, American) investment. It also aided domestic manufacturers; a number of key industries in the manufacturing sector, like steel and agricultural machinery, were Canadian owned. But this "Canadian model of development," as it is commonly called elsewhere, differed from that of the major industrial countries in Europe and Japan. There, high tariffs and other protections were established to promote industrial development by the domestic capitalist class. In Canada, there was no effort to use protectionist measures to particularly develop a dominant local capitalist class. The result is the high degree of foreign ownership.

Table 11

Foreign Ownership of Canadian Industry, 1984

Industry	% Assets	% Sales	% Profits
Mining	35.1	50.2	72.9
Mineral Fuels	39.1	39.1	69.3
Manufacturing	44.3	50.4	63.3
Food Manufacturing	31.5	26.3	47.7
Wood Products	13.0	12.8	18.9
Paper & Allied Products	25.8	25.0	33.8
Machinery	44.0	48.8	56.5
Transport Equipment	73.8	88.4	94.0
Electrical Products	48.0	59.3	63.1
Petroleum & Coal	71.0	59.4	64.9
Chemicals	69.9	75.4	89.3
Construction	9.9	7.7	13.3
Utilities	3.3	5.4	7.3
Wholesale/Retail Trade	18.0	18.8	13.9
Services	15.4	15.8	27.0

SOURCE: Corporations and Labour Unions Returns Acts, *Annual Report*, 1984.

The other factor associated with foreign ownership is the dominant role in Canada of American capital. Originally, Canada depended heavily on capital from Great Britain. In 1900, around 85% of all foreign capital invested in Canada was controlled from Britain. The decline of British capital intensified during World War I, and by 1926 the majority of foreign capital in Canada was controlled from the United States. In 1984, the latest year for which data is complete, U.S. non-financial corporations accounted for 71.8% of assets, 76.8% of sales, and 85.4% of profits of foreign-controlled corporations. Again, this contrasts with other countries, where foreign ownership is much more diversified.

Originally, most foreign investment in Canada was in the form of portfolio debt, which includes bonds, debentures and non-voting shares of stock equities. Portfolio debts are for a fixed period of time, carry a fixed rate of return, and are automatically retired. In 1900, around 75% of Canada's external debt was portfolio debt; after World War II it declined rapidly in relation to equity debt. Direct foreign (or equity) investment occurs with the establishment of business operations in Canada. Normally it takes the form of share ownership. Unlike portfolio debt, it continues to expand and to pay returns out of the country until it is either bought by Canadians or ceases operation. Unlike portfolio debt, rates of return are not fixed, and payments take the form of dividends, interest and other service payments to the foreign owners. For branch plants of foreign corporations, the transfer of capital back to the head office also takes the form of intra-corporate pricing. It is a well-documented fact that transnational corporations manipulate "profit" levels in branch plants to suit overall corporate strategies. Foreign equity investment in Canada increased dramatically after 1950.

Problems of Foreign Ownership in Canada

For a country which is relatively undeveloped, and has a very limited ability to raise capital for investment, foreign investment can offer significant advantages. Whether is it a good strategy for countries like Canada, which have the capability of raising all the capital they need from domestic sources, is another question. There is inevitably a loss of sovereignty with extensive foreign ownership, particularly if it comes in key sectors of the economy, like energy.

All orthodox economists in Canada strongly support the capitalist system of ownership and production. They have traditionally opposed tariffs, and have been strong supporters of foreign, and in particular American, investment in Canada. They claim that foreign ownership brings Canada advanced technologies, entrepreneurship, and jobs and income for Canadian workers. With the aid of Canadian financial institutions, U.S. corporations mobilize Canadian capital for profitable investment. Basically, the arguments rest on the belief that these efforts could not be replaced by Canadian private and government initiatives. Nevertheless, a number of problems have been identified with foreign ownership. These were documented in the Watkins Report (1968), the Wahn Report (1970), the Gray Report (1972), and various studies by Statistics Canada, the Department of Industry and Trade, the Science Council of Canada, and private scholars. In general, these are as follows:

The Resource Economy. Historically, Canada has placed heavy emphasis on the development of natural resources for export. Resources commonly leave Canada in an unprocessed or semi-processed form. The manufacturing end of the production process provides the greatest value added and number of jobs. Resource extraction is highly capital intensive, requires extensive investment in supporting infrastructure, and provides relatively few jobs. Emphasis on resource extraction for export has rapidly depleted Canada's conventional oil reserves. Furthermore, resource extraction has brought significant environmental problems which then require public expenditures to correct.

High Levels of Imports. Canada has the highest level of import penetration of any of the advanced industrialized countries in the Organization of Economic Co-operation and Development (OECD). Canada imports a higher percentage of its manufactured end products than any of the industrialized countries. As the Science Council of Canada demonstrated in the late 1970s, the high level of import penetration is linked to the high degree of foreign ownership of Canadian industry. This is particularly true in manufacturing. A 1981 study by Statistics Canada of the import of 211 products found that 79% of imports were by firms with over 50% foreign ownership. The study found that foreign-controlled firms were four times more likely to import component parts and inputs in manufacturing than were Canadian firms. This, of course, results in the loss of production and jobs in Canada.

Limited Research and Development. As a general rule, transnational corporations do their research, development and product promotion at the central plant, or at least in the home country. Canada has historically devoted the lowest percentage of gross domestic product to R&D of any of the advanced industrialized countries. This fact is attributed to the relatively high degree of foreign ownership in Canadian history. This has an adverse impact on Canada. In the present era of rapid technological change and restructuring of manufacturing, the "core jobs" in industry are in the area of R&D, management, product design, and product promotion. Skilled Canadians are thus denied these key jobs. For example, in the automotive industry, which is almost 100% foreign owned, only 0.5% of all R&D is carried out in Canada. A study by the Economic Council of Canada in 1980 found that Canadian firms of similar size and in similar sectors of the economy spent close to five times more on R&D than did foreign-owned firms. As a percentage of sales, Canadian firms' expenditures on R&D were three times that of foreign firms.

Control of Exports. Foreign firms export primarily to their head offices. The Gray Report (1972) found that 58% of U.S.-based and 43% of other foreign-owned subsidiaries in Canada admitted to having restrictions on exports placed by the parent corporation. The Royal Commission on Economic Concentration (1978) reported that while foreign-owned firms tend to export slightly more than Canadian firms, a very large percentage of their exports go to the parent firms. It is here that we again get into the problems of intra-corporate transfer pricing.

Increased Market Control. Historically, there has been a higher level of corporate concentration in the sectors of the Canadian economy which have a high degree of foreign ownership. The Royal Commission on Economic Concentration found a strong correlation in manufacturing between foreign ownership and oligopoly, market control by a few firms. This has been attributed to the greater marketing power of American branch plants. They have a tremendous advantage over Canadian firms through brand identi-fication, enhanced by American overflow advertising through tele-vision and magazines.

Control of Trade. Foreign ownership can result in loss of sovereignty in the area of trading. The U.S. *Trading with the Enemy Act* prohibits all subsidiaries of U.S. corporations from trading with countries identified as "enemies" by the U.S. government. When a U.S. parent has adopted a particular sales strategy which complies with this law, Canadian subsidiaries may also neglect to pursue sales in these outlawed countries, or be subject to U.S. government or head office attempts to prevent seeking these markets. We know that economic embargoes placed by the United States on China, Cuba and Nicaragua have had carry-over effects in Canada. Most recently, attention has focused on the attempt by the U.S. government to restrict sales of electronic equipment to the Soviet Union.

Branch plant corporations do not always act independently in general policy matters. The Canadian business community was shocked in 1965 when President Lyndon Johnson tried to ease the U.S. balance of payments problem by issuing guidelines to American corporations which instructed them to increase the re-patriation of overseas earnings as well as part of their liquid assets. They were also ordered to increase their borrowing in the host country. The data available suggests that U.S. subsidiaries in Canada complied with the guidelines to a surprising degree.

Balance of Payments Inequities. Foreign ownership has also created an unending balance of payments problem for Canada. As the amount of foreign ownership expands in Canada, so does the outflow of earnings in the form of interest, dividends, management fees and services. For example, in 1986 the net outflow of investment income was $16.8 billion, with another $2.2 billion in net outflow due to business services. In order to balance off this net outflow of capital each year from Canada, we have to maintain a large balance in the area of merchandise trade. In 1984, Canada's surplus in exports over imports more than offset this outflow of capital, and we had a $3.3 billion surplus in the balance of payments (the current account). But Canada's favourable balance in merchandise trade then declined, and the result was an $8.8 billion deficit in the balance of payments for 1986.

Canada requires a large favourable balance of trade with the United States in order to offset the heavy net outflow of investment payments to that country, which totalled $10.5 billion in 1986. The net outflow of business service payments was an additional $2.3 billion. However, the favourable balance of merchandise trade more than offset the capital outflow in 1984 through 1986. Given the present circumstances and the policies of the recent Liberal and Conservative governments, we know that it is essential that the Canadian dollar stay at around US$.75 in order to assist Canadian exports to the United States and to keep foreign branch plants in Canada.

In 1986, foreign direct and portfolio investment in Canada totalled $259.4 billion. In contrast, Canadian direct and portfolio investment abroad totalled $74.2 billion. But between 1980 and 1986, Canadian capitalists rapidly expanded their direct (equity) investment abroad. Over that period of time, the outflow totalled $27.4 billion.

One important aspect of foreign investment in Canada has been subject to a rather intensive debate over the years—the use of domestic Canadian capital to expand foreign ownership of the economy. When most people think of foreign investment they think of capitalists bringing their own money into Canada. But actual new foreign capital is a minor percentage of new foreign ownership. For example, the U.S. Department of Commerce's *Survey of Current Business* reports that around 80% of all new American investment in Canada is actually raised locally, through retained earnings by U.S. branch plants, depreciation and depletion allowances granted by Revenue Canada, or just capital raised in the Canadian market, primarily through financial institutions. When the U.S. investors take legal ownership of this domestic Canadian capital, it immediately becomes classified as "foreign investment." Thus, the amount of capital repatriated to the U.S. (and elsewhere) regularly exceeds the amount of new capital which actually comes into Canada. This illustrates that Canadians, through their own savings, could easily provide all the capital needs of the country.

Free Trade and Foreign Ownership

When Brian Mulroney and the Conservatives were elected in 1984, they announced that Canada was once again "open for business." The newly named Investment Canada began actively to support new foreign investment and foreign takeovers of Canadian firms. *The Financial Post* (March 13, 1987) reports that since the Tories took office, around 1400 Canadian firms have been taken over by foreign capitalists. The official data in Table 12 demonstrates that this indeed is the case. The dollar value of takeovers has risen since 1984. Furthermore, the trend in ownership has changed, and the percentage of takeovers by U.S. interests is again on the increase. The most notable fact is that foreign capitalists are much more interested in acquiring existing Canadian businesses than in establishing new enterprises in Canada. U.S. capitalists have shown relatively little in-

Table 12

New Foreign Investment in Canada

Category	1980-1	1981-2	1982-3	1983-4	1984-5	1985-6
Number of Business Takeovers	330	338	427	461	474	475
Total Asset Value ($ millions)	4076	8456	5325	4488	11,900	9800
% of Takeovers by U.S. Capital	74.2	65.3	47.7	62.2	70.9	73.8
New Business Cases	401	401	460	512	455	318
Planned New Investment ($ millions)	1271	705	3448	2749	810	467
% of New Investment by U.S. Capital	29.9	19.6	7.6	17.8	53.7	56.1

SOURCE: Investment Canada. *Annual Report*, 1985 and 1986. Foreign Investment Review Act. *Annual Report*, 1981-1984.

terest in founding new business entities in this country.

The great fear of a bilateral free trade agreement with the United States is that American corporations will close down their branch plants in Canada. Most of them were established here to get over tariff barriers which have either disappeared or will soon be gone. Of course, they would not necessarily do this overnight; but when it comes to investing in new plants or machinery, they may well choose to centralize at the home office. What is keeping many of them going in Canada is the fact that the Canadian dollar has been devalued to around US$.75. This has resulted in lower costs for labour and other inputs in Canada which has made continuation or even expansion of capacity in Canada profitable. But even with this probably temporary advantage, the industrial restructuring that has been triggered by greater world competition for relatively declining markets has produced some disturbing examples of what might become the norm.

In January 1987 *The Report on Business Magazine* reported that Goodyear Canada was to close its Toronto plant, laying off 1557 workers. Canadian General Electric, under orders from its head office, introduced restructuring which eliminated 11,500 jobs. Celanese Canada was also restructuring and laid off 2100 employees. Campbell Soup shut down its Quebec plant and consolidated administration at Chatham, Ontario; many jobs were lost. In July of that year political furor erupted when Firestone announced it was closing its Hamilton plant, laying off 1300 employees, consolidating production in the United States. Firestone received large federal and provincial government grants to keep operating in Canada.

Most of the Canadian branch plants were established as "miniature replicas" of their American parents, charged with producing the full product line of the parent. In the much smaller Canadian market, this resulted in relatively inefficient plants, producing many products on short runs. The alternative proposed by economists in Canada and the Department of Industry, Trade and Commerce was to have the parent corporation grant the subsidiary a "world product mandate" for one or a few of the company's products. It was assumed that the Canadian branch plant would have control over research and development and marketing as well as production.

But this strategy has not worked well. The U.S. parent corporations are reluctant to give up their control over R&D and international marketing. With the introduction of computer technology, Canadian branch plants now find that they have even less independence from U.S. management control than in the past. Furthermore, world product mandating still has to operate in the

climate of global sourcing. John Ralston Saul, in his excellent survey
of branch plant managers in Canada which appeared in the *Report on
Business Magazine* in January 1988, reports that the norm is for the
head office to control the best product lines and grant the Canadian
subsidiary those that are weaker or for which they have no
experience.

One example which received considerable press attention in-
volved the plant owned by Canadian General Electric at Barrie,
Ontario. In 1984 it was sold to another U.S. corporation, Black &
Decker, which received a large interest-free loan from the Ontario
government and approval from the Foreign Investment Review
Board. It reduced its product lines from 27 to seven. But it began to
move production to the United States and then to low-wage areas in
Asia. When the Canadian workers refused to abandon their union,
Black & Decker simply shut the plant down, permanently.

The 22 top executives interviewed by Saul all reported how little
power they had over their Canadian branch plants. All major
decisions were made by the parent corporations. They were most
concerned over the lack of control over capital and profits, product
lines and marketing strategies. Many Canadians will be surprised to
learn that, privately, almost every executive Saul interviewed concluded that a free trade agreement with the United States would not
be in the best interests of Canada. But they could not state this publicly.

In the free trade agreement, the Mulroney government has made
an unprecedented surrender of sovereignty in the area of investment
policy. Furthermore, it has attempted to bind all future Canadian
governments; this is a direct challenge to the Parliamentary system of
government. If the agreement goes into effect, Canadian governments would no longer be able to establish performance criteria by
U.S. investors in Canada. They would no longer be able to require
that foreign corporations allow Canadians to purchase a percentage
of their shares in common stock. They would no longer be able to
give preferences to local firms in government-supported projects.
They would be prevented from introducing legislation or guidelines
restricting the repatriation of profits. Barriers would be imposed
which would make it difficult for future governments to nationalize
U.S. firms. Finally, they agreed that after three years Investment
Canada would review U.S. takeovers of only those Canadian firms
which have assets of over $750 million; this would limit the review
process to only the top 150 corporations in Canada! And they agreed
that after three years Investment Canada would not review indirect

acquisitions, purchases of Canadian subsidiaries that occur when the parent corporation in the United States is taken over. Most of these were unilateral concessions.

The main argument advanced by orthodox economists to support bilateral free trade with the United States is the efficiencies of production which are expected to occur with industrial restructuring. With the elimination of interprovincial barriers to trade, and barriers to trade with the Untied States, increased competition will force Canadian manufacturers to rationalize production. Plants will centralize into much larger operations, narrow their product lines and lengthen the remaining production lines. This supposedly will increase their ability to compete in the U.S. and international markets. But this rationalization process, if it occurs, will inevitably lead to a net loss of jobs. John L. Orr, of the Council of Canadians, citing figures from Statistics Canada, has shown that during the period from 1978 to 1985 small firms with less than 20 employees created 96% of all new jobs (see Figure 3). In contrast, large firms (with over 100 employees) actually reduced employment by 31,900 jobs. Over this same period of time, Canadian-owned firms created 876,200 jobs. Employment by U.S. subsidiaries reduced their employment by 14,200 jobs.

Ironically, what free trade is supposed to do is to prepare Canadian manufacturers for the last industrial revolution, mass production of consumer goods for a mass market. Unfortunately, the production process is rapidly changing—away from this model of the 1950s. The new generation in industrial production is computer-integrated manufacturing (CIM). Its application to Canada has been projected in a study done for the Ontario Government by Jack Baranson, who teaches at the Illinois Institute of Technology. CIM is linked to scope rather than scale. New plants are able to produce a very large volume of products, in direct contrast to the old high-volume, fixed purpose plant. The new trend is to flexible manufacturing systems (FMS) which can quickly and cheaply adapt to new design changes. The plants are operated mainly by robots, operating three shifts, every day of the week. Furthermore, the plants are relatively small. This new technology cannot be split into two segments—with ten percent of production being reserved for the Canadian market. As Professor Baranson notes, the new plants are being located in the Sunbelt regions and the depressed Midwest of the United States, where labour costs are low and non-union workers are willing to easily adapt to automation, new work rules and new factory discipline. Some examples are cited in Professor Baranson's study:

Figure 3

Job Creation in Canadian Industry:
Net Change vs. Country of Control, 1978-85

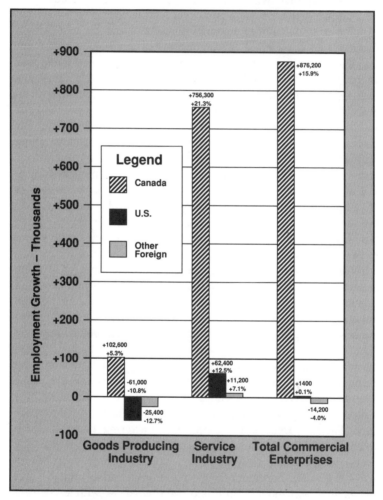

SOURCE: Statistics Canada, compiled by John L. Orr, Council of Canadians, Victoria, B.C., November 21, 1987.

• Hughes Aircraft has replaced 25 plants with nine FMS centres, reducing machine time by 90% and labour costs by 87%.

• Vought installed one plant that can turn out 600 different designs, and they reduced labour costs by two-thirds.

• Ingersoll Milling Machine has installed a CIM system in a new plant which can produce 25,000 different prismatic parts. Unit costs are about the same as the previous long production lines.

• Mazak (Yamazaki) has opened a CIM machine tool plant in Kentucky which produces 180 different parts ranging from a few pounds to three tons. Production time for machine tools has been reduced from six months to 30 days.

• General Electric has installed an FMS system for the manufacture of diesel locomotive engines. They have reduced complete production time from sixteen days to sixteen hours.

The new industrial technologies require a drop in factory employment, varying from 30% to 90% below present levels. New CIM and FMS technologies require more highly trained people in the areas of design and engineering, technical marketing, customer servicing and communication office automation. Canada is far behind the United States, Japan and Sweden in adapting this new technology. Furthermore, we run far behind these countries in the percentage of high school graduates going on to university and other higher education.

The new era of production is suited for a world without tariffs and with limited non-tariff barriers. But what will it mean for Canada? In order to survive in a highly competitive international market, the large U.S. transnational corporations that operate in Canada are moving to adopt the new production techniques. It seems unlikely as they plan for change and new investment they will be inclined to continue operations in Canada. A bilateral free trade agreement will further encourage them to locate in the United States, near the head office, and in the low-wage areas.

CHAPTER 10

Regional Disparities and Free Trade

Everyone is aware of the existence of profound regional disparities in Canada. They are certainly not new. At least since the Great Depression, Canadians have expected the state to adopt policies to reduce these disparities and to attempt to create full employment. Furthermore, since the rise of the welfare state, there has been a strong public bias towards providing uniform services to all Canadians, wherever they live. Yet the Macdonald Royal Commission rejected this tradition and called for a free market approach to the Canadian economy with a minimum of government intervention. Free trade is part of this free market package. Prime Minister Brian Mulroney has regularly claimed that a free trade agreement with the United States will "end regional disparities in Canada" and create hundreds of thousands of new jobs, in spite of the fact that the whole of the Canadian experience points the other way. In view of these contradictions, it is important to know what impact a free trade agreement will really have on regional disparities.

Economic Crisis and Regional Disparities

It is a truism to say that regional disparities can be found in all countries. Yet Canada is an unusual country. It comprises a huge territory, yet most of the population lives in a narrow band along the 8900-kilometre U.S. border. Furthermore, this population is unevenly distributed, with the majority concentrated in what is commonly referred to as "Central Canada," comprising southern Ontario and southern Quebec. Central Canada also contains the most diversified part of the economy, three-quarters of its manufacturing, the major capital markets, and high finance.

In a 1965 comparative study of regional disparity, J.G. Williamson concluded that of six highly developed countries (Canada, United States, United Kingdom, Sweden, New Zealand and Australia) Canada had the highest degree of regional differences. Over the period 1945-60, Canada was the only one of the six which did not achieve a significant reduction in inequality, according to the two most widely used criteria for measuring inequality—per capita income and levels of unemployment. In Canada, the regions measured are the provinces. The figures are presented in Tables 13 and 14. Table 13 covers the differences in per capita income in Canada from 1970 through 1985. The major discrepancies are between the Atlantic provinces and Central Canada. But these disparities in income are nothing new. A study by S.E. Chernick, covering the period from 1926 to 1964, recorded that regional disparities in personal income have been a notable feature of Canada for as far back as we have reliable statistics. Over the years, nothing has really changed.

To a significant degree, regional disparities are self-perpetuating. The concentration of economic activity in Central Canada has led to large urban centres in that region. Large urban centres have more diversified job opportunities, leading to a higher percentage of the population in the labour force. Large urban centres have better educational opportunities and have a better trained labour force. The capitalist class, which directs the economy, is highly concentrated in Toronto and Montreal. Even the new middle class of professionals is proportionally twice as large in Ontario and Quebec as it is in the Atlantic provinces. In contrast, the percentage of the labour force working as wage labourers is highest in Atlantic Canada. The general lack of job opportunities in Atlantic Canada results in a lower labour participation rate by females. The level of discouraged workers is also higher in the low-wage, high-unemployment areas.

Table 14 reveals the changes in unemployment levels in the provinces during the period of the recent recession and the recovery, from 1981 to 1987. The most notable fact in the table is the rise in the level of unemployment in western Canada. The increases were not that dramatic in the Atlantic provinces—the level of unemployment there was already well above the national average. During the period from 1981 to 1984, unemployment across Canada rose by 67%; but it rose by 379% in Alberta, 178% in British Columbia and 94% in Saskatchewan. Graham Riches has shown that between 1981 and 1984, the number of social insurance cases rose by 37% in Canada (excluding native Indians). The percentage increase was 92% in

Table 13

Provincial Per Capita Income as a Percentage
of the National Average

Province	1969	1973	1977	1981	1985
Newfoundland	60.8	64.1	70.0	66.0	66.6
Prince Edward Island	61.7	68.8	69.9	69.9	69.5
Nova Scotia	75.4	77.8	77.9	74.7	80.9
New Brunswick	69.2	72.2	73.8	70.7	75.1
Quebec	89.1	90.7	95.5	94.1	94.4
Ontario	118.5	114.2	109.3	105.9	109.8
Manitoba	92.7	93.3	89.5	91.0	93.7
Saskatchewan	78.9	87.9	87.0	94.9	89.7
Alberta	98.3	98.0	101.4	114.1	106.2
British Columbia	108.8	109.6	110.2	111.8	102.3

SOURCE: Department of Finance. *Quarterly Economic Review*, June 1987.

British Columbia, 41% in Alberta and 39% in Saskatchewan, the only three provinces above the national average.

There are other indicators of regional inequality in Canada. The infant mortality rate per 1000 live births varies from a low of 7.8 in Prince Edward Island to 10.8 in Newfoundland. It is much higher in the Yukon and the Northwest Territories. The number of physicians per capita in Ontario, Quebec and British Columbia is around 60% higher than in New Brunswick and Prince Edward Island, and twice as high as in the Northwest Territories. Per capita health care expenditure varies significantly from region to region, as does expenditure on education. The percentage of full-time college and university students varies substantially; the attendance rate in Ontario is 2.5 times that of Newfoundland.

Government Commitment to Regional Development

The Great Depression of the 1930s dramatized the disparities in the standard of living between Central Canada and the "hinterland"

Table 14

Unemployment by Province, April 1981-87

Province	1981 ('000)	%	1983 ('000)	%	1985 ('000)	%	1987 ('000)	%
Newfoundland	29	14.2	47	21.5	56	25.8	51	23.5
Prince Edward Island	8	15.0	8	14.6	9	15.1	9	16.5
Nova Scotia	36	9.9	53	14.5	61	16.1	63	15.9
New Brunswick	39	13.7	55	18.5	51	17.2	48	15.5
Quebec	290	9.9	440	14.9	392	12.6	360	11.0
Ontario	300	6.8	551	12.2	419	8.8	327	6.7
Manitoba	32	6.6	52	10.4	46	9.0	45	8.4
Saskatchewan	21	4.8	39	8.3	42	8.7	38	7.9
Alberta	45	4.0	136	11.5	143	11.7	139	11.0
British Columbia	87	6.6	190	13.4	218	15.4	192	12.9
Canada	886	7.6	1570	13.2	1437	11.5	1271	9.8

SOURCE: Statistics Canada, *Labour Force,* Catalogue Number 71-001.

provinces. One of the tasks of the Royal Commission on Dominion-Provincial Relations (Rowell-Sirois Commission) was to propose policies to deal with this problem. They advanced the concept of "fiscal equity": the federal government would guarantee similar levels of provincial services across Canada. In addition, the Commission proposed that the federal government bail out the bankrupt provinces and assume responsibility for social welfare. However, at the special federal/provincial conference called in 1940 to deal with this question, the governments of Quebec and Alberta opposed the changes. The demands of World War II led the federal government to undertake a dynamic Keynesian policy and to provide direction to the economy; the depression ended, and full employment was achieved. In the period from the end of World War II down to 1956, the federal government played a strong role in regional development through expenditures on infrastructure, designed primarily to facilitate resource extraction.

The onset of the major recession in 1957 led to the appointment of the Royal Commission on Canada's Economic Prospects, headed by Walter Gordon. This Commission documented the persistence of regional disparities; the hinterland provinces were not closing the inequality gap because they were overly dependent on resource extraction. Beginning with the Diefenbaker government in 1957, the system of federal/provincial tax sharing set equalization as its primary goal. The tradition of the richer provinces compensating the poorer ones became entrenched at this time.

But Diefenbaker's policies went well beyond compensation. Through the Winter Works Program, the *Technical and Vocational Training Assistance Act*, the Atlantic Development Board, Roads to Resources, and the *Agricultural Rural Development Act*, the federal government put emphasis on development as well. The key programs were explicitly directed to assist the less developed regions.

The recession of 1957-61 contributed to the defeat of the Diefenbaker government. The Liberal government of Lester Pearson (1963-68) placed its primary emphasis on national social policy. The key programs introduced were medicare and the Canada Pension Plan. The federal/provincial transfer program was extended. But regional development programs were also continued. The Area Development Agency (ADA) was designed to stimulate industrial development, first through tax-exemption strategies and then through direct cash grants to investors. ADA established designated areas where these incentives policies were to operate.

Under the Trudeau government (1968-84) regional development was centralized in the Department of Regional Economic Expansion (DREE). In addition, the Trudeau government created the Regional Development Industrial Assistance program which designated certain areas for assistance. Eligible projects would receive development grants for new plants or for modernization. Special grants were provided for each job created. In 1977 a new tax policy provided additional incentives to businesses establishing in low-income areas.

However, there was a shift in policy direction under the Trudeau government. By 1974 General Development Agreements were signed with each province, detailing programs and sectors identified for assistance. Under these agreements, the provinces took the lead in regional development policy. While Ottawa assumed the major part of the cost of these programs, the provinces decided which ones they wanted.

The amount of funds actually provided for regional development declined in the latter years of the Trudeau government. With the rise of separatism in Quebec, agreement on federal/provincial programs became more difficult to obtain. A major change in direction came in

1980-1, with a shift in the orientation of development to supporting individual sectors rather than regions. In November 1981 the Liberals released their economic development strategy report, which emphasized resource megaprojects; this plan was doomed by the onset of the great recession. In January 1982, DREE and the Department of Industry, Trade and Commerce were replaced by the new Department of Regional Industrial Expansion (DRIE). DRIE supported the corporate reorganization of the Atlantic fishing companies and helped finance the ill-fated Northeast Coal Project in British Columbia. The very controversial abolition of the Crow Rates for grain shipments was part of a policy goal of improving the profit position of the railroads, the potash and the coal industries.

Thus, by the time the Mulroney government was elected in the fall of 1984, there was a long, well-established tradition of compensation for regional inequalities as well as direct intervention to try to stimulate development. These development programs had inevitably come under attack. Far too often political patronage seemed to be involved. Many projects failed because of poor planning and market projections. There were instances where a company closed a plant in one province to open it in another, with the subsidy and new machinery making it more competitive. There were objections when unpopular capitalists or foreign corporations received the handouts. Companies often did not hire the number of people they had promised to. These kinds of problems inevitably arise when the method of development relies on the use of taxpayers' money to subsidize private capitalists. In Saskatchewan, for example, there is widespread public support for government assistance to the Co-op oil refinery in Regina, but strong opposition to the grants given to right-wing millionaire Peter Pocklington to establish a pork-processing plant in North Battleford. In a planned economy, subsidization and incentive programs would be necessary but would require commitment to full employment and an emphasis on social or co-operative ownership with local democratic controls.

The Change in Direction
Under the Mulroney Government

The neo-conservative agenda dominated the Report of the Macdonald Royal Commission, including its proposals in the area of regional disparities. The Macdonald Commission proclaimed that the National Policy of 1979 was dead; but it also argued that no new national policy should be created to take its place. Following Adam Smith's advice, government direction or intervention to achieve policy goals was rejected as going against "the genius of the market economy." Governments in Canada should intervene only in the case of very serious market failings. The final report urged free trade with the United States, maximum use of the free market internally, and an open door to foreign investment.

As Daniel Drache and Duncan Cameron have pointed out, the Macdonald Royal Commission carefully chose academics who held political views which "largely coincided with those of the business agenda." Indeed, there are few dissenting voices in the 72 volumes of background studies, almost all of which appear to be retreads of old papers; it is even hard to find a Keynesian view. The Commission had determined that the free market must rule before the "studies" were collected.

In the area of regional disparities, the basic position of the Macdonald Commission and its ideological supporters was that we should give up trying to create viable economic communities in the hinterland areas. This is "inefficient." Instead, we should place first priority on shifting the unemployed to where the jobs are created by private capitalist investment. This would promote "the national welfare." The traditional equalization programs "impede national economic growth and regional adjustment," generally "reduce incentives" and "distort the marketplace." So do "excessive minimum wages" and policies like rent controls. The tax transfer system "prevents the types of market adjustments" necessary in the long run; the worst program, in this view, is unemployment insurance. These compensatory programs "inhibit rather than promote regional development." Furthermore, they tax "efficient behaviour" in the richer provices to aid the inefficient in the hinterland provinces. Trade unions come under attack for trying to organize on an industrial basis, across regions, and for demanding wage parity between provinces.

Academic economists have a deep well of hypocrisy to draw upon. For the most part, the right-wing economists who contributed to the Macdonald Commission are based in Ontario, and they are very well paid by the state. Protected by a guild system inherited from the pre-capitalist era, they themselves are completely immune from any free market competition for their jobs. They grant themselves tenure without any judgement by the consumers of education. They have no fear of competition from Asian imports as they are supported by a tight immigration policy. Furthermore, as they operate as a guild they closely control the number of people to whom they grant certification and who may then compete with them for jobs. At best, this is a classic case of "Don't do as I do, do as I say."

The Mulroney government appears to be following the advice of the academic economists. First, actual spending by the Department of Regional Industrial Expansion is not particularly orientated towards the regions with the most depressed economies. Over the five-year period from 1981 to 1986, 23.7% of the budget was allocated to Ontario and another 39.8% to Quebec. In the west, the large allocation to Quebec is commonly attributed to patronage by both Trudeau and Mulroney in their home province. But regional disparities exist in all the provinces. Four of Quebec's ten administrative areas have average unemployment rates that are almost as high as that of Newfoundland. Nevertheless, the four Atlantic provinces, which experience the highest unemployment rates and the lowest average income per capita, received only 19.3% of the budget.

In the past couple of years, Japanese and South Korean automotive companies have received federal government incentives to locate in Ontario and Quebec. Hundreds of millions of dollars were spent on Chrysler, Ford and General Motors in the same two provinces. The aerospace industry is also located in Ontario and Quebec. The federal government gave de Havilland a $78 million write-off and $240 million in new equity before it was sold to Boeing. The government cancelled $1.1 billion in Canadair's debt to help its sale to Bombardier. Bell Helicopter received over $100 million to set up in Quebec. Spar Aerospace received hundreds of millions of dollars to support technological innovations. In actual practice, the Tory government has demonstrated little commitment to a policy of regional development.

In 1985 the Nielsen Task Force on Program Review, established by the Mulroney government, roundly attacked government economic programs and government intervention in the economy in general. The 1985 budget speech by Finance Minister Michael Wilson announced that DRIE and other government programs would place less emphasis on grants and other subsidies and more on background research for private initiative. The important exception, of course, was in the military area. The Mulroney government has put even greater emphasis on tax incentives to private industry; this approach "gets the government off the backs of private entrepreneurs."

The shift in emphasis in programs for regional economic development was indicated by the joint statement by the prime minister and the premiers in June 1985. Aside from the usual governmentese, the key clause in the statement proclaimed that "the governments should explore opportunities for increasing interregional trade and eliminating barriers between provinces." This has been a major demand of the business organizations in both the United States and Canada, and of the U.S. government. It is a pre-condition to the implementation of a comprehensive free trade agreement with the United States.

In the summer of 1987 federal Industry Minister Michel Coté announced changes in regional development policy for Canada. Following the Macdonald Commission, the new buzz word was "adjustment." The government planned to shift from grants and cash incentives to loan guarantees; direct government spending would concentrate on research and development. The new organization to replace DRIE would be "more pro business." Finally, officials in the federal government stressed that the focus would be on the soundness of the project and not its regional orientation.

What are these provincial policies which have to be ditched? All of them were instituted to try to keep jobs in the hinterland provinces, to prevent even further centralization of manufacturing. A few of the most successful are agricultural marketing boards, provincial liquor regulations which require local manufacturing of beer, government procurement incentives given to local employers, some licensing regulations which favour local businesses, preferential hiring on government-sponsored projects, and provincial investment programs. If one looks at the major private corporations in Saskatchewan, for example, all of them have had major government capital and other subsidies: the potash industry, the uranium industry, Interprovincial Steel and Pipe, Canada Packers, Intercontinental Packers, Gainers, and Weyerhauser.

The main message of the Macdonald Royal Commission and the Mulroney government is that people must be moved from the hinterlands to where the jobs are, in Central Canada. We have already seen how that has worked over the past two years. Jobs are being created, primarily in southern Ontario. But vacancies remain high because people cannot find a place to live in the area. How many people can afford to pay $300,000 for a house? Or $800-a-month rent for a one-bedroom apartment? The alternative, which many people are choosing out of desperation, is to live in the suburbs and spend three to four hours a day creeping along the freeways. This is what the free market offers us: a highly irrational and inhumane society.

U.S. Government Policy and Regional Development

So far we have discussed regional development only from a domestic perspective. But Canadian programs have been greatly affected by U.S. government policy. Under the General Agreement on Tariffs and Trade (GATT) and the principles of the Organization of Economic Co-operation and Development (OECD), national governments are given the right to use government subsidies and procurement policies to aid disadvantaged regions. Such policies are widely used in Europe. However, since the passage of the 1979 *Trade and Tariffs Act*, the U.S. government has regularly invoked its own protectionist laws to attack any Canadian programs which aid products which are exported. Actually, the landmark decision was the U.S. government's case against Michelin Tire in Nova Scotia in 1973. The U.S. International Trade Commission (ITC) and the U.S. Treasury Department imposed countervailing duties on Michelin tires because the Granton plant had received capital grants, tax credits, and low-interest loans from three levels of government, including the Department of Regional Economic Expansion.

In response to the Michelin decision, the new Industrial and Regional Development Program (IRDP) modified its policies, taking the view that if regional assistance programs were "generally available" rather than specific to industries or regions, they might be exempt from U.S. trade action. Assistance would be given under a formula based on the level of unemployment, per capita income and the ability of the provincial government to provide assistance. Nevertheless, in the 1985 Atlantic groundfish case, the ITC identified over 50 government programs as offering "unfair subsidies," including assistance received under IRDP. A similar preliminary ruling was made in 1985 in the softwood lumber case. In these two cases, eight regional development programs were identified as "unfair subsidies."

Scott Sinclair has shown that in response to this unilateral U.S. government action, the Mulroney government has been curtailing traditional regional development programs. Regional assistance had been refused to industries considered "sensitive to Canada/U.S. trade relations." Resource industries which are already competitive in the U.S. market are to be excluded. The federal Fishing Vessel Construction Assistance Program is being phased out. The new Atlantic Agency plans to restrict assistance to projects under $10 million, hoping to avoid U.S. trade actions.

But there is another aspect of U.S. influence which Sinclair emphasizes. The Mulroney government, in the free trade agreement, has accepted Washington's position that government subsidies for military expenditures are acceptable. The Reagan administration has indicated that they will not be subject to U.S. trade action. This is just another example of the unequal nature of the free trade agreement: the Canadian approach to regional development has been ruled out, but the U.S. approach has been accepted without modification. As Sinclair points out:

> A substantial portion of U.S. military purchases and contracts are directed to minorities and small business interests through "set-asides" or to designated city cores through urban renewal programs. The goals of these provisions, to create employment for the jobless and to stimulate economic growth in disadvantaged areas, are not dissimilar to those of Canadian regional development programs.

Thus, it is likely under free trade that our regional development program will become more attached to military spending in order to conform to U.S. policy. Recently we have seen how Canada's Litton Industries, a major U.S. military contractor, introduced a bidding war among the Atlantic provinces. It had already been promised a variety of federal government subsidies. The government of Nova Scotia also used a package of subsidies to attract Pratt and Whitney to a new "aerospace technology park." Aside from the fact that such a development ties Canada even more closely to the U.S. military machine, numerous studies show that spending on the military creates significantly fewer jobs than spending in the civilian sectors of the economy.

Regional development programs are of vital interest to the hinterland provinces of Canada. Yet the free trade agreement does not specify which kinds of government subsidies will be permitted. The two governments could not agree on which subsidies were acceptable. As a result, existing American trade laws are to remain in effect for at least seven years. During this period, a working group will be established to try to develop a substitute regime. It seems highly unlikely that lower-level Canadian civil servants will be able to get the U.S. government to change its well-entrenched position on "unfair subsidies." Indeed, the omnibus trade bill, now working its way through the joint committee stage of compromise in the U.S. Congress, promises to exclude even more government support programs.

But the point is that even without the free trade agreement, the sovereignty of our governments in this area is being steadily diminished. It is astonishing that the premiers of the Canadian provinces suffering the worst inequalities are willing to support a free trade agreement that does nothing to protect the historic Canadian approach to regional development.

Will Free Trade End Regional Disparities?

Brian Mulroney repeatedly states that free trade will end regional disparities in Canada. The orthodox economists and other right-wing ideologues argue that if the free market is given its due, wages and other costs of production will even out across Canada. What evidence is there that this may be the case?

We can begin right at home. The *British North America Act* created a free trade area among the British North American colonies. What was the fate of the Maritime provinces under Confederation? In general, de-industrialization and relative decline. Economic geographers, who rely more on actual facts than on abstract theory and mathematical models, have demonstrated that when transportation and communications link less developed areas to more developed centres, the resulting increase in commerce and economic activity tends to benefit the developed centre more than the hinterland. It is not surprising that recognition of metropolitan dominance and regional dependency has a long tradition in Canadian social science—outside the field of modern economics.

More recently, we can see what is happening in countries where the governments have moved toward a free market approach in economic policy. It is well known that in Great Britain, under the neo-conservative policies of Margaret Thatcher, regional disparities have greatly increased. Even the mass media in Canada carries stories on "divided Britain," split not only on class lines, and between finance and industrial capital, but most notably between southern England and the outlying areas where unemployment remains unusually high.

In August 1987 the U.S. Department of Commerce reported that, since 1979, regional disparities have been increasing in the United States, reversing a 50-year trend. Under the free market policies of Ronald Reagan, the coastal states have been booming while the states depending on farming, energy and heavy manufacturing are lagging behind in economic growth. The Great Lakes area, the Plains states, the Rocky Mountains, the Southwest, and the Southeast were all below the national average. In tiny New Zealand, where the three-year-old Labour government has been following free market policies, dramatic increases in regional disparity quickly appeared.

Here in Canada we have seen regional disparities increase in the last couple of years. Statistics Canada reports that in 1986 there were 137,000 new jobs created in Canada. *Only 5000 of this total were created outside of Ontario.* With 36% of the total Canadian population, Ontario has over 40% of all the jobs. As the recovery continued, this disparity eased somewhat. Yet in July 1987 Statistics Canada could report that one-half of all jobs were being created in Ontario and another one-third in Quebec. In August 1987 *The Report on Business Magazine* concluded that "outside of central Canada, the recession is still on." They attributed this to the fact that Canada's hinterland regions were still too heavily dependent on resource extraction, and the prices for these commodities remained low because of the lingering world recession. The recovery in Canada has been mainly in manufacturing and housing, concentrated in Central Canada.

We also have the example of the agricultural machinery industry, in which free trade was established in 1944. Neil B. MacDonald conducted a study of plant location for the Royal Commission on Farm Machinery (1968). First, he found that the plants of the major manufacturers were concentrated in the centre of the market, the U.S. midwest. The other major factor determining the location of plants was access to metalworking technology: casting, forging, machining and stamping. Again, this was concentrated around the industrial heartland in the United States and Canada.

One of the major objectives of the free trade agreement is to provide a stimulus to manufacturers to rationalize their production process. The econometric model created by Richard Harris and David Cox, repeatedly cited by supporters of free trade, concludes that for the more protected Canadian industries, the number of plants operating under free trade will decline by around one-half. It is widely assumed that the larger firms will be the best able to meet the competition from U.S. firms. They are, of course, already concentrated in Central Canada. Not surprisingly, the Harris/Cox model concludes that the gains from free trade will largely accrue to manufacturing in Central Canada. When asked by *The Toronto Star* what he thought of Mulroney's claim that free trade would end regional disparities, Harris replied, "Bunk!"

R. Wiglie's study for the Saskatchewan Department of Economic

Development and Trade (July 1985) concludes that for the manufacturing industries, the expected restructuring resulting from free trade will lead to increased centralization in Ontario and Quebec, at the expense of smaller firms in Atlantic and western Canada.

The most widely cited study of the effect of free trade on the Atlantic provinces is that by Hugh M. Pinchin, an economics professor at Colgate University. Because of the already low levels of tariffs, Pinchin concludes that the net gain from possible reductions in consumer prices would not likely exceed 3%. On the other hand, foreign subsidiaries might well shift location to the larger U.S. market in New England. He concludes that "corporate rationalization of multi-plant firms under free trade might be expected to reduce the attractiveness of Atlantic Provinces locations, except for resource-intensive industries, due to distance, market potential, and the need to acquire economies of scale."

In August 1987 the question of the regional impact of free trade made the headlines. A background study by the Department of Regional Industrial Expansion, "Regional Adjustment to Free Trade," was leaked to the press. First, the report warned of the U.S. demand that any free trade agreement remove all federal and provincial supports to regional development. This would "negatively affect" all provinces, but would have the greatest impact on the Atlantic provinces and the Northwest Territories, where investment was weakest.

Second, the report listed the industries, by province, which would be most likely to benefit or to face "adjustments" due to the impact of the free trade agreement. Outside of Central Canada, there were relatively few "winners" identified. For all of the hinterland provinces, the report projected that there would probably be more jobs lost than gained. That even included Alberta and British Columbia, where the governing parties, the Tories and the Socreds, were strongly supporting a free trade agreement. At the same time that the DRIE report was leaked, a study by the Ontario Ministry of Agriculture was released which projected a significant drop in farm income if supply management marketing boards lost their powers and the seasonal tariffs on horticulture products were removed.

It was in this atmosphere that the premiers met in Saint John, New Brunswick, in late August 1987. They re-emphasized their position that no free trade agreement was acceptable that "dismantles programs aimed at reducing regional disparity." The premiers from the Atlantic provinces insisted that the free trade agreement could not infringe upon any existing regional development programs. David Peterson, premier of Ontario, said the Canada/U.S. Auto Pact could not be touched. The prairie premiers stated that the free trade agreement must not harm agriculture and must include a mechanism for binding arbitration of trade disputes. Premier Joe Ghiz of Prince Edward Island warned that his province would not support any agreement that undermined agricultural marketing boards. The DRIE report had projected that potatoes would be a big loser under free trade, as U.S. potatoes would be expected to grab the southern Ontario market. At the end of the Saint John meeting, Premier John Buchanan of Nova Scotia warned that we cannot have a free trade agreement which "sacrifices the weaker parts of Canada to the stronger parts of Canada."

In no way does the free trade agreement protect traditional government programs for regional development. Furthermore, no one can seriously believe that the U.S. government is going to change its position over the next seven years. Will the free trade agreement help end regional disparities in Canada? Liberal leader John Turner gave an indication during a speech in Halifax in December 1987:

> If access to the U.S. market is going to solve our regional disparity, why hasn't it solved regional disparity in North Dakota or Montana or Idaho or Mississippi or Askansas? They have access to that market and they have had since they joined the union and they still face very dramatic regional disadvantages.

CHAPTER 11

Policy Harmonization and
Canadian Sovereignty

Canadians have expressed concern that our system of income
security and social services could be threatened by a comprehensive
bilateral free trade agreement with the United States. The issue was
dramatically raised in the summer of 1985 when the U.S. government made its preliminary ruling on the import of groundfish from
Atlantic Canada. Following the position of the New England fishing
industry, the U.S. International Trade Commission identified 58
Canadian government programs which it labelled "unfair subsidies"
to the Canadian fishing industry. Included among them was unemployment insurance for fishermen in the off-season.

The response of the Mulroney government was to assure
Canadians that none of our social programs "would be on the
bargaining table" in the free trade talks. Others were quick to point
out that they did not have to be on the table. With continental integration, and the gross imbalance in power between the two countries,
the pressure would be there for general harmonization of policies.
This would inevitably mean Canada's adjusting to American
standards, or creating "a level playing field," to use the popular
American term. The New Right in Canada agrees that this would be
the outcome. The Canadian public is strongly committed to our
system of income security and social services. No Canadian political
party could begin dismantling this system without experiencing the
wrath of the voters. The Mulroney government backed down when it
tried to de-index pensions. But in the long run, Canada's social
programs could be diluted or worse by a bilateral free trade agreement. In Chapter 7, it was stressed that this is the main reason why
the New Right favours a comprehensive bilateral free trade agreement with the United States. Over the long run, the "forced
harmonization" caused by the free market will inevitably lead to an

adjustment of Canadian policies to conform with the playing field for business and investment which presently exists in the United States.

Trends in U.S. Social Policy

Most people are aware that the Reagan administration has been steadily cutting back the American social welfare safety net. Joel Krieger has reminded us that the attack on labour and social rights did not start with the Reagan administration but was initiated much earlier, around the time of the first round of oil price increases and the onset of the major recession, in 1974. This was the beginning of the general retreat from the post-war "social contract" between capital and labour. For the New Right, the key is to change the attitude of the general public: it is necessary to undermine the prevailing attitude that full employment, the protection of labour and collective bargaining rights, and social services are universal citizenship rights. The move to realize two main elements of the New Right agenda, deregulation and privatization, was well underway by the time Ronald Reagan assumed office. Indeed, they had already been accepted by the mainstream of the Democratic Party. The Progressive Alliance of 1979, a coalition of labour and community group leaders to defend the labour/capital accord, had collapsed. It suffered its most telling blow when the United Auto Workers had agreed to bail out the Chrysler Corporation in 1980. Since then, U.S. trade unions have regularly accepted wage freezes, wage cuts and major concessions in the roll-back of fringe benefits.

The U.S. "social safety net" consists of a number of programs which fall under four basic categories. First, there are social insurance programs, financed by payroll taxes, like unemployment insurance and the Social Security system (the American pension). Second, there are means-test programs for the most needy, including Aid to Families with Dependent Children, the federal social welfare program, Medicaid, Supplemental Security Income, food stamps, housing assistance, child nutrition, and the Special Supplemental Program for Women, Infants and Children. Third, there are the federal/state programs introduced during the Johnson administration, such as social insurance, student loans, veterans compensation, etc. Finally, there are direct transfer funds to state and local governments for education, legal aid, social and health services, etc. However, only Social Security is a universal program. All the rest are subject to means tests, and the benefits provided by all of these programs are considerably less than equivalent programs in Canada. Furthermore, serious cutbacks began during the Carter administration.

In his first year in office, Ronald Reagan cut around $44 billion from the federal budget, mainly in the general area of social programs. In 1982 another $35 billion was cut, largely to permit a $37.7 billion reduction in corporate taxes. Major cuts were made in the Aid to Dependent Children, food stamp, housing assistance and Medicaid programs. Not only were budgets cut, the rules of eligibility were changed. None of these programs was ever considered a citizenship right. Thus, it was relatively easy to reduce the expenditures by changing the criteria for eligibility. Finally, there was a major reduction in the number of government positions made available for administering the programs. Without adequate staff, the programs were much less effective. The victims of the budget cuts were not only the recipients of the services but also the job holders, overwhelmingly women and visible minorities.

The shift in government priorities to the neo-conservative business agenda can be seen in the following table:

U.S. Federal Spending as a Percentage of the Total Budget

Budget Category	1980	1987
Military	26%	30%
Social Programs	35%	28%
Social Security & Medicare	26%	28%
Net Interest	9%	14%
Other	5%	1%

SOURCE: *Dollars & Sense,* September 1987.

Thus it was not surprising when a 1986 U.S. Census Bureau report found that the spread in income and assets between blacks and whites was growing; the median net worth of a white household was about twelve times the median for a black one. In July 1986 a study by the Congressional Joint Economic Committee revealed that the rich were getting richer, and the average family was falling behind. The top 10% of all American families accounted for 82% of all wealth. In the winter of 1986-7 the U.S. Conference of Mayors declared that emergency food services and housing the poor were still their major problems. The number of homeless Americans had risen by 50% in one year and was estimated to be close to three million; the Reagan administration had drastically cut back federal aid to low-income housing. In April of 1987 a study sponsored by the U.S. House of Representatives concluded that there were thirteen million children under eighteen living in poverty. All this was occurring in the richest country in the world. But profits were recovering, and stock market speculation was booming.

Thirty-five percent of Americans have no health insurance at all and find it almost impossible to get hospital service. Most people pay large premiums for private health insurance which covers only a fraction of actual costs. Originally, Medicaid covered all costs for Americans over the age of 65; under neo-conservatism, they now must pay large user (or deterrent) fees. Hospitals are being privatized. Yet the cost of the U.S. system of private medical and health care is the highest in the world; in 1986, it was the equivalent of 10.7% of the gross national product. For doctors, malpractice insurance costs on average around $60,000; in Canada, the maximum premium was $8250 in 1987. The Reagan administration cut federal assistance to community health centres. Even the federal contribution to the children's immunization program was slashed! In the United States, accumulated medical bills are the chief cause of personal bankruptcy.

The Reagan administration has also drastically reduced social welfare spending. The Congress has repeatedly blocked the neo-conservative attempt to cut back on the Social Security program, the universal pension system. Nevertheless, the program was cut by $20 billion in 1981. Furthermore, the Social Security disability insurance program has been gutted, with over 400,000 people told they were no longer eligible. The Unemployment Insurance program in the United States is vastly different from that in Canada; during the worst period of the 1981-2 recession, over two-thirds of unemployed Americans were ineligible to receive any benefits!

Two studies by the Brookings Institute, a mainstream "think tank" in Washington, D.C., in the summer of 1987 summarized the impact on the average American. Gary Burtless concluded that in the last fifteen years "real family income has grown little, absolute poverty has risen, and inequality has gotten worse." The poverty rate for children was the highest in an OECD survey. Frank Levy concluded that since 1973 the income of the middle class has declined

Programs of the Canadian Welfare State

Income Security Programs	Social Services
Universal Transfer Payments:	Universal Services:
Family Allowances Old Age Security	Health Care Primary Education Secondary Education
Selective Cash Transfers:	
	Selective Services (Partial List)
Old Age Security-GIS Canada Assistance Plan	Child Welfare Child Day Care
Social Insurance Programs:	Legal Aid Indian and Metis Friendship
Workers' Compensation Unemployment Insurance Canada and Quebec Pension Plans	Centres Services to Victims of Violence Correctional Services Rehabilitation Services
Tax Credits:	Employment-Related Services Services for People with
Refundable Child Tax Credit Other Nonrefundable Tax Credits	Special Needs Home Care Housing
Other:	
Minimum Wage Employment Strategy Job Creation	

SOURCE: A.W. Djao, *Inequality and Social Policy*. Toronto: John Wiley & Sons, 1983, p. 107; Graham Riches, *Food Banks and the Welfare Crisis*. Ottawa: Canadian Council on Social Development, 1986, p. 60.

absolutely and relatively. The "middle-class dream" has been maintained through demographic adjustments: "more two-earner couples, postponed marriages, and low birthrates."

There already is plenty of evidence around to demonstrate that policy harmonization is well underway. On a number of major fronts, the Mulroney government has been following the lead of the United States. Why is this happening? First, the Mulroney government also supports neo-conservative ideology. Second, many of the changes have been advanced because it will be necessary to have standard practices and regulations under a comprehensive bilateral free trade agreement. Third, business interests are already pushing for standardization so that they will be on a "level playing field" with their American competitors. What follows is a brief look at a few cases where harmonization is already underway.

Deregulation, Privatization and Contracting Out

The effects of deregulation, privatization and contracting out can be seen in the example of the transportation industries. The direction of policy was outlined in the deregulation white paper, *Freedom to Move*, published in July 1985. Here, the Mulroney government is clearly following the U.S.precedent:

Airlines. *The U.S. Airline Deregulation Act* was passed in 1978 during the Carter administration with strong support from the Democratic Party. In August 1981 President Reagan smashed the Professional Air Traffic Controllers Organization, firing 11,400 workers and hiring new non-union workers. Between 1981 and 1987, air traffic increased by 25%, but the number of air traffic controllers declined. The number of "near misses" in the air increased from 584 in 1984 to 839 in 1986. The U.S. Air Line Pilots Association reported in 1987 that there had been "a significant drop in safety since 1978."

With deregulation, competition on the more profitable routes increased but decreased on the others. In the rate war that followed, over 60 airlines disappeared. Deregulation, ostensibly intended to enhance competition, enabled the strong carriers to force the weak into bankruptcy, leaving the industry more monopolized after deregulation than before. If the present mergers are approved, six airlines will control 80% of the U.S. market. Deregulation was intended to foster competition from non-union airlines. It had the desired effect of driving down wages and salaries and of leading many airlines to cut back on staff. The age of the average aircraft in use more than doubled. Around 28,000 jobs disappeared. The rates on prime routes used by businessmen dropped, but they rose substantially on other less-travelled routes. Service to smaller centres declined. In 1987 consumers regularly faced long lineups, sloppy service, flight delays, missed connections, unexplained cancellations, and overbooking.

Airline deregulation began in Canada in 1984; anticipating the deregulation legislation and free trade, there has been a rash of mergers as Air Canada and Canadian Airlines International (the latter had been Canadian Pacific Airlines and Pacific Western Airlines) scramble to establish hub systems with feeders. With the Mulroney government budget cuts, in 1987 Canada had 300 fewer air traffic controllers than it had in 1982. The *National Transportation Act*, which came into effect on January 1, 1988, dropped the old test for airline service, "public convenience and necessity," and replaced it with a test of "fit, willing and able." Already, fares are dropping on the main routes used by businessmen and rising in the less-travelled areas. No longer will a regulatory agency review rates. The new act also makes it much easier for the airlines to drop "unprofitable" services. But as the Canadian Air Line Pilots Association points out, "when the squeeze is on, the only discretionary areas are wages and maintenance."

Railways. The U.S. railway industry was deregulated under the *Staggers Rail Act* of 1980. The key provisions of Mulroney's deregulation are the move away from published shipping rates to secret deals, the elimination of public or collective rate-making, and the introduction of procedures which allow the railroads to speed up branch line abandonment. Big business strongly supports these changes and assumes that their economies of scale will permit them to get advantageous rates.

But one of the main reasons for the new legislation was the anticipation of greater U.S. competition, particularly after a free trade agreement. It is expected that trans-border traffic will increase, as we shift to a North/South trading system. In order to meet growing competition from U.S. transportation interests, Canadian railroads are demanding extensive rail line abandonment, the cutting of staff and track and railcar maintenance, and reducing the purchase of new rolling stock. For example, Canadian National insists that it must cut 15,000 employees to keep labour costs in line with major competitors in the United States.

Trucking. The U.S. trucking industry was also deregulated in 1980. The result was fierce competition which led to the destruction of small and medium-sized companies, domination by the very large firms, and a proliferation of independent operators, running longer hours on degenerating, older equipment. Between 1980 and 1987 the number of independent operators doubled to 34,000. Truck safety standards fell and accidents increased.

The *Motor Vehicle Transportation Act* of 1987 opened the Canadian trucking market to anyone. Inter-provincial rates are now on a free market basis. However, the new National Safety Code is not scheduled to come into effect until 1990. Again, the prime motivation was the impending free trade agreement with the United States. Business interests were pushing for lower shipping costs. The fear of the industry is that the U.S. trucking giants like Roadway Services, Consolidated Freightways and Yellow Freight System will end up dominating the Canadian market. Each of the American "big six" trucking companies carries more freight annually than the entire Canadian industry.

However, the provinces administer trucking regulations, and each province will have to pass its own legislation. In December 1987, Ontario introduced implementing legislation. The Ontario Trucking Association predicts that deregulation will lead to the loss of 10,000 jobs in the Ontario industry and that the large U.S. trucking firms will eventually take control of the industry. Under the new legislation, new trucking firms only have to show that they have adequate insurance and conform to the National Safety Code to get a licence. While the Canadian market is now opened up to U.S. trucking firms, there are 43 U.S. states which prohibit Canadian trucking companies from hauling freight between any two points in their states.

Bus Transportation. The deregulation of motor vehicles also extends to the bus system. Permitting courier services to run on bus lines has already hurt the small bus companies in Canada; packages have traditionally provided needed income on lightly travelled routes. The regulated system of bus transportation was designed to ensure adequate traffic to guarantee high safety standards. Bus companies have pointed out that regulations were also installed to enforce the provision of service to less populated areas. Deregulation only serves the more highly populated money-making areas, and bus service to smaller centres is expected to decline.

"Reforming" the Taxation System

The United States first passed an income tax law in 1913; a progressive alliance successfully changed the ideological purposes of the tax system, basing it on the principles of income redistribution and "ability to pay." This was strongly opposed by business interests and the rich. In 1918 the upper-level personal income tax rate was raised to 77%. Furthermore, there was a relatively high tax floor, so the majority of individuals and families did not have to pay any income taxes. In a major retreat from this basic principle, in 1935 the Roosevelt administration introduced the present Social Security program, which is the only one in the industrialized world based solely on a payroll tax. During World War II the income tax system was expanded to include mandatory contributions by the vast majority of income earners. Since the onset of the Cold War, business interests have been successful in getting corporate taxes and those of high-income earners reduced.

In the 1970s there were further increases in indirect taxes. By nature, these are regressive: they apply to all on an equal basis, regardless of ability to pay. The capital gains tax, which affects almost no ordinary wage earners, was greatly reduced. The Reagan tax changes in 1981 dramatically reduced taxes on the wealthy, and they provided corporations with special depreciation allowances. Over the years, U.S. governments had been giving certain business interests special tax breaks. Other business interests, like those in retail and wholesale trade, had to pay higher rates. The tax reforms of 1981 were an attempt to give all business interests equal cuts. The result of this, of course, was a widening in the gap in income between the rich and the poor.

The second Reagan tax reform act passed in 1986. Because of the mounting U.S. budget deficit, some of the special tax concessions to business interests were taken back, and a number of major tax loopholes were shut. But the top corporate tax rate was reduced from 46% to 34%. The graduated income tax principle was dropped, replaced by three tax levels, with all low-income individuals and families now paying a 15% rate. The top individual tax rate was reduced from 50% to 28%. The pressures this put on Canada were obvious: by 1988 the formal tax rate on upper-income Canadians would be 20% higher than that in the United States; the formal tax rate on corporations would be about 12% higher.

In response to the new U.S. tax system, Finance Minister Michael Wilson introduced the white paper on tax reform in June 1987. Following the U.S. pattern, the number of personal income tax brackets would be reduced from ten to three; those in the bottom tax brackets would pay a minimum of 17% and those in the top bracket only 29%. Corporation taxes would be reduced from 36% to 28%. But in contrast to the U.S. legislation, there would be no minimum tax on corporate profits. While taxes would be raised on financial institutions, they would be reduced for oil and gas firms. Many of the tax loopholes for higher-income Canadians would be eliminated or reduced. But to make up for the cuts for corporations and those in the higher income brackets, there would be a new federal consumption tax.

The proposed changes were broadly attacked by trade unions, the

National Action Committee on the Status of Women, the National Anti-Poverty Organization, and other groups representing the poor. Direct tax benefits for the poor will be reduced. Even the conservative Canadian Federation of Labour, representing U.S. construction unions in Canada, described the changes as "a huge tax break for upper-income Canadians." The federal National Council of Welfare concluded, "What is disturbing is how small the gains will be for low- and middle-income Canadians and how well the better-off will fare." Even the Economic Council of Canada concluded that "middle-income Canadians would gain more than low-income individuals." The working poor, those below the poverty line, would still pay taxes, and at a 17% rate.

John Bossons of the University of Toronto pointed out that Canada was forced to follow the United States, which had begun to lower corporate tax rates for manufacturing companies. With the mobility of capital across the border, "the Canadian rate had to come down or production would shift to U.S.-based manufacturing plants of both Canadian and U.S. companies." In addition, "there would be an erosion of the Canadian tax base if Canadian corporate tax rates did not match those in the United States."

Most controversial was the decision by the Mulroney government to introduce a new federal consumption (or sales) tax. For political reasons, the actual introduction of the tax was postponed until after the next federal election. In many countries, taxes on corporations and high-income earners are being replaced by value-added taxes (VAT). Recently, VATs have been widely introduced in Europe, although most countries have provided some form of rebate for low-income earners. However, the Labour government in New Zealand introduced a 10% VAT on all goods and services without any rebates. When the Labour government in Australia attempted to introduce a similar tax, there was widespread vocal opposition, particularly from the trade unions, and it backed down. Needless to say, the VAT has the strong support of neo-conservatives, from the Economic Council of Canada to the Fraser Institute.

In Canada, controversy surrounded the plan by the Mulroney government to include food under VAT. Minister of Finance Michael Wilson promised that there would be a refundable tax credit for lower-income Canadians. But for people living at the lowest level of poverty, who do not earn enough to even file an income tax return, this is a hollow gesture. They will get no rebate. Public opinion polls conducted in July 1987 for the federal government revealed that 68% were opposed to the VAT, and 93% were opposed to putting a tax on

food. In December 1987 Wilson announced that the VAT would not
be applied to food. Instead, a group of Members of Parliament would
be going to New Zealand to see how it works in that country.

Harmonization of Standards

In other areas, deregulation and harmonization are proceeding in
order to facilitate business under free trade with the United States.
One of the most controversial acts by the Mulroney government was
the repeal of the 1969 Canadian drug legislation which replaced
seventeen-year patent rights for brand-name drugs with a royalty of
4% to be paid by generic drug firms manufacturing the drugs. It has
been estimated that generic drugs have saved Canadians over $200
million per year in the 1980s. Generic drugs are produced by
Canadian companies. The large foreign-owned drug corporations
had the support of the U.S. government. As a result, the revision of
the 1969 Act was pledged by the Mulroney government as part of the
free trade deal under the guise of protecting "intellectual property
rights."

On June 30, 1987, the Mulroney goverment's deregulation of the
banking industry took effect. Canadian chartered banks were given
permission to trade in securities. Foreign interests were given
permission to own up to 50% of Canadian investment firms. By June
1988 the ceiling on foreign ownership of Canadian banks was to be
lifted altogether. In this case, action by the Mulroney government
was unilateral, and no reciprocal concessions were obtained from the
United States. For example, U.S. banks can operate anywhere in
Canada, but Canadian banks are limited by U.S. legislation, which
protects the regional nature of their banking system. These
provisions were reinforced in the free trade agreement. In addition,
U.S. banks were exempted from the requirement that foreign banks
loan a proportion of new capital to the middle market (loans between
$5 million and $20 million).

Business interests are pushing the Mulroney government to
deregulate the telecommunications industry. Their particular goal is
the reduction of long-distance rates. The present rate structure keeps
long-distance rates higher in order to subsidize local household
rates. Deregulation in the United States has permitted the telephone
companies to reduce long-distance rates and to charge for local telephone calls. This has raised local rates in many areas to the point
where a sizeable portion of low-income Americans cannot afford to

have a telephone. Bell Telephone and the B.C. Telephone Company both insist that they need long-distance rate reductions to compete with U.S. rates.

In September 1987 the National Energy Board abandoned the 80-year Canadian tradition of tight controls over natural gas exports. The historic Canadian policy has been to ensure that there was a fifteen-year reserve supply for Canadians before exports were permitted. The free market will now determine sales. Ten days before the decision was made, the federal government reported that Manitoba small-volume consumers were paying 18% to 27% more for Alberta natural gas than the export price to the United States. In British Columbia, local consumers were paying more for B.C. natural gas than were U.S. customers.

Consumer and environmental groups in Canada are concerned over the standardization of products that will inevitably result from a comprehensive bilateral free trade agreement. It is known that there are Canada/U.S. working groups trying to harmonize weights, measures, packaging, labelling, sanitation, health standards, etc. These negotiations are well under way in the area of food and agriculture, even before the free trade agreement has been ratified or formally implemented. It is also known that they are trying to achieve common standards for determining the safety requirements for new drugs and pesticides. In May 1987 the U.S. National Academy of Sciences said that the system of poultry inspection in the United States was inadequate and offered little protection against food poisoning. In that same month both the American Federation of Government Employees and the Community Nutrition Institute told the U.S. Congress that over the past ten years the system of meat inspection in the United States had declined, and that consumers were increasingly at risk. In one government survey, salmonella was found in 37% of U.S. broilers, 12% of raw pork and 5% of raw beef. The National Association of Meat Purveyors said that the recommended corrections "would cost too much."

During the negotiations leading up to the signing of the free trade agreement, the U.S. government pressed Canada to eliminate domestic Canadian grades for grains and oilseeds that were different from those in the United States. Canadian export grades for grain were deemed to be "unfair" because they could not be matched by U.S. grades. Canadian grain licensing procedures and standards were seen as "unfair promotion." The free trade agreement protects Canadian grains for the time being. But will they survive the commitment of the agreement to harmonize or "make equivalent" all the standards in the area of food and agriculture?

Under free trade it will also be more difficult to maintain health and safety working standards, which are superior to those in the United States. An example of what may be in store for us took place in May 1987, when Koolatron Corporation of Brantford, Ontario, which manufactured refrigerators, moved across the border to Batavia, New York. Inspectors from the Ontario Ministry of Labour had ordered the corporation to stop work after an investigation revealed that they were not providing workers with adequate protection against dangerous chemicals.

Many environmental groups in Canada are opposed to the bilateral free trade agreement because they fear that Canada will be forced to lower our standards to those in the United States. The U.S. government strongly opposed the 1970 *Arctic Waters Pollution Prevention Act* adopted by the Canadian government. (The U.S. response was due in part to power politics, as Washington refuses to recognize Canadian sovereignty in the Arctic.) The U.S. Environmental Protection Agency was devastated by the Reagan administration's budget cuts and pro-business policies. This is the president, after all, who said that "trees cause pollution." The history of the acid rain dispute between the two countries should be an indication of what is to come in the area of environmental protection under a bilateral free trade agreement. But this poses no great problem for the Mulroney government. The Nielsen Report of July 1986, following the Reagan model, called for the Canadian government to turn over environmental laws and regulations to the provinces and to abandon national standards. Environment Canada's policy under the Tory government has been to be "more conciliatory" to business and the provinces and to cease playing a role of active enforcement and leadership.

Considering that around 75% of our existing trade is with the United States, and that Canada depends heavily on the U.S. capital market, there are already tremendous market pressures to conform to American standards, practices and policies. Federal and provincial governments are being pressured to match U.S. tax and spending policies. Businesses argue that they must reduce costs if they are to compete in the U.S. market. Deregulation, privatization and contracting out are ways of breaking trade unions and reducing labour costs. They are also techniques for reducing other operating costs. The new business agenda and its New Right supporters are demanding that Canadians give up the whole range of programs that have been achieved over the years through labour struggle and political action. Free trade with the United States will inevitably push

Canadians in the direction of harmonization with U.S. standards and practices. It represents a major surrender of Canadian sovereignty. Over the long run it offers the prospect of a reduction in the standard of living and quality of life for nearly all Canadians.

CHAPTER 12

Sectoral Free Trade Agreements

It is very difficult to predict the long-run effect of a comprehensive bilateral free trade agreement with the United States. Many projections are made, yet they are little more than educated guesses. Those done by orthodox economists have a strong bias in favour of free trade, reflecting their fundamental ideological outlook. However, for some years now Canada has had some form of free trade with the United States in three important manufacturing sectors: agricultural machinery, military production and the automotive industry. The history of these industries can give us good insights into what we can expect from a broad free trade agreement.

The Agricultural Machinery Industry

By the mid-19th century there was a proliferation of small companies in Canada producing agricultural machinery. The most important world market, by far, was North America, and in particular, the United States. However, it was not long before monopoly power developed. In 1902 the five biggest U.S. firms merged to form the International Harvester Company; by 1927 they had 75% of the American market. Following an aggressive takeover policy, and through their branch plant, they also came to dominate the Canadian market. By 1918 Deere & Co. emerged as the second-largest manufacturer in the world. They distributed U.S.-produced machinery in Canada through their subsidiary, John Deere Corporation.

But there were also Canadian producers, protected by a 35% tariff. In the 19th century, Massey-Harris was the dominant manufacturer in Canada, with over 50% of the market. They were soon overtaken by the monopoly power of International Harvester, and by the 1930s their share of the Canadian market had fallen to 20%. The Cockshutt Plow Company, Canadian-owned and controlled, manufactured a full line of farm machinery, and in the 1920s and 1930s had around 12% of the Canadian market.

Under the pressure from farmers, tariffs on farm machinery were reduced and then removed. In 1913 the U.S. government unilaterally removed all tariffs on farm machinery. U.S. corporations, by far the largest, most powerful and technologically advanced in the world, had little to fear from foreign competition. Furthermore, the primary world market was still the United States. The Canadian government reduced the tariff to 6% in 1925. In 1944 it was unilaterally removed by the Mackenzie King government. Unfortunately, countries other than the United States maintained fairly high tariffs. While European companies could export to Canada without tariff barriers, Canadian manufacturers could not export to Europe without paying a high duty. Thus there was an incentive to shift to manufacturing in Europe and then to export to North America. Massey-Ferguson and others followed this path.

From the point of view of the agricultural industry in Canada, the removal of the tariff was a disaster. In 1941, imports were the equivalent of 50% of sales in the domestic market. This ratio steadily rose, reaching a high of 114% in 1956, and then levelled off at around 85% in the 1960s. Exports were primarily to the United States; by the 1960s, less than 10% went to other countries. However, exports accounted for only about one-half the value of imports. Canada's share of the world market for farm machinery declined from 12.4% in 1952 to 8.5% in the mid-1960s. The Canadian industry had been a world leader in industrial innovation and design in the 1940s; after free trade, it went into a steady decline.

Under the free trade agreement, U.S. corporations increased their domination of the Canadian market. Cockshutt found that it could not sell Canadian-made tractors or combines in the U.S. market, even when they were manufactured there. They sold out to White Motor Company of Cleveland. Massey-Ferguson also found that it had a difficult time selling in the U.S. market, even when it manufactured all of its tractors there. Because of the nationalism of U.S. farmers, the corporation adopted a different strategy; by the 1960s, 90% of its production and sales were overseas. Even Versatile, doing well at its Winnipeg plant, established a plant across the border in North Dakota. Production of tractors all but disappeared in Canada. Most combines are now manufactured in the

Table 15

Production and Trade in the Agricultural Implement Industry

($ Millions)

	1980	1981	1982	1983	1984
Value of Shipments	1393	1403	1111	960	1036
Value Added in Manufacturing	620	670	534	433	454
Exports	876	885	652	551	762
Imports	2092	2386	1688	1513	1769
Trade Balance	-1216	-1501	-1037	-962	-1007

SOURCE: Statistics Canada, *Summary of External Trade*, Cat. No. 65-001, various issues; Statistics Canada, *Agricultural Implement Industry*, Cat. No. 42-202, various issues.

United States or Europe. Between 1955 and 1967, plant capacity expanded only 7% in Canada but rose by 40% in the United States. The Barber Royal Commission reported that while Canada accounted for 12% of farm machinery sales in North America, only about 7% of manufacturing was done north of the border.

Furthermore, free trade did nothing to undermine the industry cartel. In the early period, International Harvester set the prices and the other companies followed. In 1968 the Royal Commission on Farm Machinery (Barber Commission) concluded that Deere & Co. was the price leader. By setting prices very high, they protected the smaller, less efficient firms. Under this price umbrella, and with lower wages, Versatile was able to break into the market with a small plant specializing in large tractors. The study by Neil B. Macdonald for the Barber Royal Commission also looked at plant location and cost advantages, and found plants tended to locate in the centre of the market, the U.S. midwest. Versatile was able to exist in Manitoba because the lower labour and power costs there offset higher inbound and outbound transportation costs.

Free trade has not benefited the agricultural machinery industry in Canada. As Table 15 demonstrates, production in Canada continues to lag. The farm machinery industry in North America has been on the verge of collapse because of the depression in agriculture and the disappearance of so many farms. The number of workers in Canadian farm machinery plants declined from 17,425 in 1980 to 7735 in 1984. Plants in Canada are operating at about 50% capacity. Since the onset of free trade, Canada has run a substantial trade deficit in this industry. Table 15 shows that this trend has persisted down to the present.

In 1981 Massey-Ferguson (now known as Varity Corporation), one of Canada's largest transnational corporations, was on the verge of bankruptcy. It was saved from collapse by its financial creditors and the governments of the United Kingdom, Canada and Ontario. The firm received around $700 million in new financing; $200 million in new preferred shares were guaranteed by the governments of Canada and Ontario. Since then the corporation has transferred its large tractor assembly plant from Detroit to Canada, shifted its research and development program and a number of divisional head-quarters to Canada and has established a foundry in Canada. One could easily conclude that government intervention was necessary to guarantee the manufacture of farm machinery in Canada.

For the most part, free trade with the United States in agricultural machinery did rationalize plants—in the United States. The shift in production to Europe demonstrates that if Canada (and the United States) wish to maintain production in North America, they may be forced either to raise tariffs or impose import controls. In either case, this means moving to a common market situation, as in Western Europe. Ivan Porter, president of Massey Combines Corporation, argues that free trade left Canada with little in the farm machinery industry because the Canadian companies could not compete against the U.S. manufacturers which had greater economies of scale. Given the experience of their industry, Porter offers the following conclusion about the free trade agreement with the United States: "Personally, I find it very difficult to see how Canada as a country can expect companies to compete with U.S. companies given that we are one-tenth of the size of the U.S. I tend to be skeptical of the whole thing."

Armaments Production

The armaments industry (sometimes called the "defence" industry) has also had a free trade agreement with the United States. Its history goes back to the development of continental integration during World War II. There was standardization of military equipment with that of the United States; this decision represented the Canadian government's formal break with the United Kingdom and the Commonwealth. In the future, our primary foreign and military policy would be linked closely to that of the United States. In return, the Mackenzie King government obtained major U.S. military procurement orders for Canadian-based manufacturers.

This integration did not formally end when the war was over. Indeed, by 1947, when the Cold War was proclaimed, the two governments were working together again to protect the Western Hemisphere from imminent invasion by the Soviet Union. In 1948 they created the Joint Industrial Mobilization Planning Committee, which began negotiations for joint industrial co-operation. The New Hyde Park Agreement of 1950 was spurred on by the Korean War. Under it there was agreement on a common defence, standardized military procurement and economic controls, rationalization of raw materials, and industry on a continental basis. To a large degree this integration was the brainchild of C.D. Howe, Minister of Industry in the Mackenzie King government.

There are two major sectors in the Canadian military hardware industry, shipbuilding and aerospace. Under federal government direction, the shipbuilding industry rapidly expanded during World War II. No country produced warships or merchant ships of a higher quality. We were in the forefront of an advanced technology. The Canadian fleet was one of the largest in the world. Yet at the end of the war the Mackenzie King government sold off the Canadian fleet of merchant ships for a song. Furthermore, it removed the carriage protection from the Canadian fleet, thus allowing shippers access to non-union, unsafe ships registered in Panama and Liberia. As a result, the shipbuilding industry rapidly declined in Canada. We are now almost completely dependent on foreign-flag shipping for our deep sea trade. In contrast, the *Jones Act* in the United States requires 50% of all American trade to be carried in American-built ships. Furthermore, the U.S. government, with the largest fleet of warships in the world, purchases only from American shipbuilders. Thus the Canadian shipbuilding industry has not been able to participate in the Canada-U.S. Defence Production Sharing Agreement.

Today, what remains of the shipbuilding and repair sector is mainly Canadian-owned, and it depends heavily on sales to the Canadian domestic market. In 1983, these amounted to only $585 million. The survival of the industry depends to a large extent on federal contracts for warships. There is no requirement that government services purchase ships in Canada.

The aerospace industry has been quite different from the shipbuilding industry in that it has primarily been a branch plant industry with little Canadian ownership or control. There are, of course, major Canadian companies in the component parts area. Historically, the most important firms have been Canadair (General Dynamics, U.S.), A.V. Roe (Hawker Siddley, UK), Orenda (Hawker Siddley and Douglas Aircraft, U.S.), De Havilland (De Havilland, UK), Canadian Marconi (Marconi, UK), and Litton Systems (Litton, U.S.). More recently, Canadian firms like Spar Aerospace and CAE Electronics have obtained large government contracts.

For the aerospace industry, the key decision on its future was made in 1947, mainly by C.D. Howe. At that time the Canadian Jetliner had been developed, the first medium-range civilian jet passenger aircraft in the world. Canada also had the second-largest market in the world for non-commercial aircraft. However, the Mackenzie King government, following the "American road," chose to ditch the civilian aircraft industry in order to concentrate on the building of military aircraft. Instead of the Jetliner, A.V. Roe built the CF-100 fighter. However, without any sales to the U.S. government, the cost for the military aircraft was inevitably higher. As it turned out, the CF-100 cost almost three times as much as the Sabre Jet, the primary U.S. competitor. This effectively blocked sales to other countries.

The disaster for the industry came when the St. Laurent government decided to proceed with the building of the Avro Arrow—knowing that it was not at all likely that the U.S. government would buy it, no matter how good it was. The U.S. government had never bought a major weapons system from any foreign country. In 1959, when it was learned that the Avro Arrow would cost more than five times that of its U.S. competitor, the Lockheed F-104, there was no alternative but to give up on the production of major military aircraft. The result was the 1959 Defence Production Sharing Agreement. Military integration with the United States, plus inefficient and unco-ordinated branch plants, nearly destroyed the aircraft industry in Canada.

The Defence Production Sharing Agreement intensified integration of the armaments industry in North America. The purposes of the agreement were as follows:

• To provide the U.S. military with a secure source of raw materials;
• To complete the standardization of military equipment;
• To provide Canadian-based firms with "national treatment" in bidding on U.S. military contracts;

• To exempt Canada from the *Buy America Act*, to include Canadian firms under the U.S. military security system, and to allow Canadian-built military goods to enter the United States duty free;
• To make Canadian-based firms eligible for U.S. government research and development grants; and
• To ensure that the Canadian government would buy major military aircraft from U.S. manufacturers.

There were additional losses of Canadian sovereignty. The 1959 agreement requires Canada to obtain approval from the U.S. military for any Canadian offshore sales which involve any American production. As Stephen Clarkson has argued, the integration has left "a truncated Canadian industry incapable of surviving without American research, development, design components and machine tools." Anyone who has followed the development of Canadian defence policy since 1959 is aware of the fact that strategic perspectives are to a very large degree determined by what major weapons Canada can buy from the United States, and what subcontracts are available for Canadian-based arms manufacturers. For the most part, Canadian manufacturers have been limited to supplying component parts and lower-scale military goods.

In the free trade negotiations, a key objective of the Mulroney government was to obtain "national standing" for Canadian firms in the United States. How has this worked under the Defence Production Sharing Agreement? First, it is necessary to remember that an agreement with the United States is not the same thing as a formal treaty, ratified by a two-thirds vote in the U.S. Senate. Treaties supposedly have the same status as a national law. But agreements are different; they can be modified or cancelled by any president, and they can be amended by the U.S. Congress.

As Stephen Clarkson has noted, since 1959 Congress has been chipping away at the "national status" of Canadian-based firms. Numerous amendments to U.S. defence appropriations bills have excluded Canadian firms from the right to bid on U.S. government contracts. There are eleven acts of Congress which restrict Canadian access to the U.S. military market. Canadian firms are also prohibited from bidding in a growing number of areas because of clauses put in the annual Defense Appropriations Bill by Congress protecting local U.S. industries. In his study for the Macdonald Royal Commission, R.B. Byers estimated that today only around 30% of the annual U.S. Department of Defense procurement program is open to Canadian firms. How naive it is for the Mulroney government and free trade supporters to assume that things will be different under a broader free trade agreement!

Another key component of the agreement is a commitment to balance the trade in military hardware between the two countries. From 1959 through 1980 the trade between the two countries was roughly in balance. However, in the 1980s the trade has shifted markedly in favour of the United States. Byers predicts that a major re-equipment program will likely accelerate this disparity.

The Canada/U.S. Auto Pact

The automotive industry provides a classic example of the problems a country has when a very key sector of the economy is under the ownership and control of foreign economic interests. While there were a number of independent Canadian automobile producers in the early period, and many fine Canadian cars manufactured, it was not long before U.S. capital came to dominate. In 1904 Gordon McGregor signed a licensing agreement with Ford in Detroit, and Ford of Canada was created. The U.S. parent received 51% ownership simply for its licences and patent rights. In 1907 R.S. McLaughlin also began a contracting arrangement, first with Buick and then Chevrolet; in 1918 he sold out to General Motors. In 1921 Chrysler organized a plant in Windsor under the name Chrysler Canada. Tariff protection was 35%; it did not stimulate major Canadian manufacturing but created a branch plant industry.

In 1929 Canada was the second largest manufacturer of automobiles and trucks in the world; we exported 102,000 units and imported only 44,000 units. At that time, 31% of production was exported, primarily to the Commonwealth countries, under the preferential tariff system. The industry was hard hit by the depression. In 1936 the Mackenzie King government cut the tariff to 17%, and Studebaker, Hudson and Packard ceased production in Canada, relying instead on imports from their major plants in the United States.

World War II was a boom period for the American Big Three in Canada, even though no private automobiles were manufactured. Thanks to government contracts and generous subsidies, production capacity expanded, and employment in the industry doubled. However, after World War II Canada lost its overseas markets. First, we lost the Commonwealth trade, as local production was introduced. But the main problem was the fact that Canada produced American cars. They were too big and cost too much to buy and service. They were gas guzzlers in a world where most countries had severe oil shortages. We were also stuck with the costly American practice of multiplicity of models and frequency of model changes. The Canadian market was just too small to duplicate the American market. It was a totally irrational industry for a country like Canada, with a limited domestic market and greater dependence on the export market.

In the period after World War II, imports began to take a growing share of the Canadian market. In 1955 they had 13% of the market; by 1959 their share had risen to 51%. European automobiles were smaller, more fuel efficient and were cheaper. The American Big Three did not fill this demand. Thus in 1960 all of the other major automotive-producing countries exported between 30% and 40% of their production, but Canada exported only 6% and the United States only 4%.

In this crisis period, the Diefenbaker government appointed a Royal Commission headed by the noted Canadian economist V.W. Bladen. His final report recommended continental integration of the industry through a system of managed trade. This central recommendation was strongly supported by the Liberal Party, the Conservative Party and even the CCF leadership. The social democratic leadership in the trade union movement also supported the agreement. However, union locals under the influence of the Communist Party pointed out the dangers of the agreement and instead called for the creation of an independent Canadian automotive industry.

While Bladen was compiling data for the Royal Commission report, he visited Sweden and examined their booming independent automotive industry. Significantly, he made no mention of the Swedish experience in his final report. The European/Japanese approach to the industry would have required major restructuring and Canadian ownership, and this was beyond the ideological scope of Bladen and his Conservative mentors.

The 1965 Auto Pact covered only companies manufacturing automobiles and trucks in North America, and they had to have 50% North American content for inclusion under the treaty. Each corporation was required to manufacture in Canada at a level that maintained the ratio of production to imports that existed in 1963, that is, for every car sold in Canada, there had to be one manufactured locally. The value added in manufacturing in Canada was to be at least as great as in 1963, and manufacturers could ship cars across the border without tariffs or quotas. However, should a party not abide by the rules of the pact, a tariff penalty of 9.2% would be applied. In addition, there were two further safeguards set out in "letters of understanding" at the time of ratification, that Canadian value added in manufacturing should be 60% in automobiles and 50% in trucks, and that U.S. companies would invest $260 million in Canada between 1965 and 1968.

The Auto Pact allowed for North American free trade in new cars and trucks, but only for the manufacturers. It was significant in that it provided some guarantee ("safeguards") of protection in Canada and some protections for Canadian jobs. Thus, it could not be called a free trade agreement. However, the safeguards for Canada applied only to vehicle assembly; they did not apply to automotive parts manufacturers. Furthermore, they also did not apply to the area of product development.

The Auto Pact did result in a restructuring of the industry. Large plants were established for production for the North American market. The gap in productivity between Canada and the United States was closed. Factory prices are now actually lower in Canada than in the United States (primarily due to the devaluation of the Canadian dollar), but prices to consumers are higher because of the federal sales tax. As Table 16 shows, Canada has maintained a favourable balance of trade in vehicles but has consistently run a deficit in the automotive parts area. It is estimated that 85% of the deficit in the auto parts trade is accounted for by the "captive parts" industry, intra-company imports from U.S. parents. Increasingly, auto parts are coming from offshore areas, in particular Mexico, Brazil and South Korea; their parts enter Canada and the United States duty free under the Generalized System of Preferences for underdeveloped countries.

However, the Fortress North America approach of the Auto Pact has brought continuing problems to the industry. Offshore trade is almost entirely one way; Canada exports almost no vehicles or parts. Less than 0.5% of the industry's research and development, marketing and promotion is done in Canada. The industry has concentrated the higher-skilled and semi-skilled jobs in the United States; Canada specializes in low-skilled, lower-paid assembly operations. Canada lags behind in the auto parts industry, which has a much higher percentage of semi-skilled workers. Canada lags behind in heavy parts plants like stamping and engines. These differences in *quality of jobs*, attributed to the fact of foreign ownership, were documented in the 1977 Federal Task Force on the Automotive Industry (the Arthur Report).

Table 16

Canada/U.S. Trade in Automotive Products

($ Millions)

	1971-1980	1981	1982	1983	1984	1985
Canadian Exports of						
Motor Vehicles	46,930	8809	11,311	13,786	19,330	21,981
Parts	27,189	4275	4855	7666	10,107	11,203
Canadian Imports of						
Motor Vehicles	31,385	6927	5422	7904	10,496	14,472
Parts	53,118	9092	8768	10,838	15,163	17,143
Balance of Trade						
Motor Vehicles	+15,545	+1882	+5889	+5882	+8834	+7509
Parts	-25,929	-4817	-3913	-3172	-5056	-5940
Total	-10,384	-2935	+1975	+2710	+3778	+1569

SOURCE: Stephen Clarkson, *Canada and the Reagan Challenge*, Table 5-1; Statistics Canada, *Summary of External Trade*, Cat. No. 65-001, various issues.

Today the automotive industry in Canada is facing a very difficult period of adjustment, made more difficult by the fact that it is a branch plant industry, building vehicles which have no market outside North America. The American Big Three are moving to "kit assembly" operations, with parts from offshore producers. They are also forming joint ventures with Asian manufacturers. In 1987, imports had around 36% of the North American market.

By 1990, it is expected that American manufacturers will have only 55% of the North American market. There are ten new Asian plants which will come on stream by that date, with plants in Canada owned by Honda, Toyota, Suzuki and Hyundai. Canada will then have the capacity to produce 450,000 units, whereas the U.S. will have the capacity to produce 1,700,000. Canadian capacity will be much larger than the historic share of the market.

The Canadian government has been using the duty-remission program to stimulate new Asian investment in Canada. The Canadian government designates "qualified manufacturers," those who maintain a prescribed level of Canadian production and Canadian value added. They are allowed to import parts and motor vehicles free of duty and then re-export them to the United States. However, this reduces the market for cars and parts manufactured in North America. The U.S. government, the Big Three manufacturers, the auto parts industry, and the influential Northeast-Midwest Congressional Coalition have opposed this policy. Under the free trade agreement, the duty-remission program for Canadian content would be phased out by 1996. The duty-remission program, which is tied to export performance, is to be cut off immediately.

The Canadian auto parts industry is also facing serious problems due to the competition from Japan and low-wage offshore manufacturers. The industry, which in 1987 employed around 65,000 Canadians, has asked for import quotas, and they want to see the Canadian value-added part of the Auto Pact raised to at least 60%.

While Brian Mulroney insisted all along that the Auto Pact would be excluded from the free trade agreement, very influential interests in Congress insisted that it be included. In 1986, trade under the Auto Pact accounted for more than one-third of the total trade between the two countries. It could not be excluded from any comprehensive bilateral free trade agreement. Right up to the Ontario election on September 10, 1987, the Mulroney government insisted that the Auto Pact was not part of the free trade negotiations. No one really believed this, as leaked U.S. memoranda repeatedly referred to points under dispute in the automotive area in the negotiations. Then, just two days after the Ontario provincial election, the U.S. administration formally announced that they wanted "automotive issues" placed on the negotiating table.

Over the years, the United States has benefited from the Auto Pact trade, as Table 16 demonstrates. Between 1971 and 1980, the United States achieved a $10.4 billion trade surplus in vehicles and parts. However, this situation turned around in 1982, and down through 1986 Canada achieved a surplus which balanced out the past deficit. The main reason for this is *the devaluation of the Canadian dollar.* While productivity and wages are roughly equal between the two countries, the 25% devaluation had made it more profitable for the American Big Three to manufacture in Canada. The Canadian Auto Workers (CAW), representing the 63,000 employees at the American Big Three, have also been adamant that no changes are to be made in the original Auto Pact. In 1987 General Motors announced plans to close eleven parts and assembly plants in the United States, but they maintained production levels in Canada. Since 1979 the United Auto Workers (UAW) in the United States lost around 30% of its members through shutdowns. But employment in the automotive industry in Canada has increased since 1979.

U.S. political interests demanded that the safeguards for Canada in the Auto Pact be removed. In the early 1980s, Chrysler Canada was failing to meet the Canadian content requirements, and it owed $235 million in tariff penalties. The Trudeau government used the penalty provision of the Auto Pact to force Chrysler into additional investment in their Windsor plant, thereby saving Canadian jobs. In July 1987 it was revealed that Chrysler Canada was still in violation of the safeguard provisions of the Auto Pact. However, the Mulroney government had approved a deal with the corporation which excused them from the tariff penalties.

Around 90% of all auto production takes place in southern Ontario, and it was the key issue in the September 1987 provincial election. The Liberal Party, which won a large majority of the seats, promised to block any free trade agreement which included revisions in the Auto Pact. The New Democratic Party took an even stronger stand against the free trade agreement. The Ontario Conservative Party, which supported the free trade agreement, was routed, finishing third behind the New Democratic Party in seats and in popular vote.

The free trade agreement of October 1987 proposes several major changes in the Auto Pact. The 9.2% penalty tariff would be eliminated over ten years, wiping out any enforcement mechanism for the Auto Pact. In addition, the Canadian content rules (60% for cars and 50% for trucks) would be replaced by a 50% *North American content rule*. These two major changes would grant the American Big Three the freedom to invest either in Canada or the United States. Canada would have to maintain the 25% differential under the present foreign-exchange rate to attract their future investment. The American Big Three can easily meet this new 50% content agreement by producing solely in the United States. The Canadian automotive parts manufacturers point out that the 50% rule does not protect key high-value elements of the automobile, such as transaxles, engines and electronics. They see the low 50% content rule as a concession to the American Big Three, allowing them to greatly increase the use of parts made in Mexico and overseas, costing Canada and the United States high quality jobs.

As mentioned above, Canada's duty-remission programs would be eliminated. The agreement also freezes participation in the Auto Pact to the 1989 automobile model year. Thus, only the proposed General Motors-Suzuki plant would qualify, and other Asian producers would be excluded. Bob White, president of the Canadian Auto Workers, points out that this would prevent Canada from developing an independent auto policy with countries other than the United States, and it would represent a major surrender of sovereignty.

We can contrast the existing automotive industry in Canada with that in Sweden. Volvo and Saab, the two Swedish manufacturers, are world-class operations and export over 40% of production. They are in the forefront of research, development and technology. In 1984 they produced one-half as many vehicles as Canada; however, their population and domestic market is less than one-third that of Canada. Their model offers advantages to the Canadian automotive industry which the Bladen Commission and the Diefenbaker and Pearson governments rejected.

The history of the three industries in which there is some form of free trade with the United States certainly doesn't offer much encouragement for a wider free trade agreement. The agricultural machinery industry really moved out of Canada and left a steady trade deficit. Free trade did not bring lower prices for consumers, as it had no effect on the oligopolistic practice of price leadership. Furthermore, Canadian corporations found they had a very difficult time selling in the quite nationalistic U.S. market.

In the armaments industry, the failure of the Canadian government to continue protection of the shipbuilding industry at the end of World War II was disastrous. Again, Canada lost world leadership in a major industry. The aircraft industry failed because it was a weak branch plant industry and because the federal government put emphasis on military rather than civilian production. Continental integration resulted in a major loss of Canadian sovereignty in the defence area. The experience of the Defence Production Sharing Agreement illustrates that Canadian corporations cannot expect to get "national standing" in the United States in the area of government procurement.

The automotive industry provides another example of the problems inherent in foreign ownership and control of a major industry. The entire orientation of the industry has always been directed from Detroit. The U.S. industry simply saw Canada as a region of the American market. Trapped into building American cars, Canada was cut off from the expanding world trade. But at least the Auto Pact demonstrated that if we are going to follow a policy of Fortress North America, as the Mulroney government and big business are demanding, then it is necessary to have safeguards to protect Canadian jobs, even if they are only unskilled assembly jobs.

CHAPTER 13

The Threat to Labour

Most people are aware that the trade union movement in Canada is strongly opposed to a comprehensive bilateral free trade agreement with the United States. There are a number of good reasons why this is the case. It is expected that the impact of continental harmonization of labour relations and standards will be detrimental to Canadians. The trade union movement is much weaker in the United States, where there is no left-wing political party to defend working people, and under the Carter and Reagan administrations there has been a concerted attack on historic trade union rights. There is also a fear that the pressures of harmonization, as discussed previously, will undermine the social policies which labour in Canada has fought for over the years. Moreover, it is widely believed that further trade liberalization will lead to additional job losses, particularly in the manufacturing sector. In North America, the restructuring of manufacturing, the introduction of new technology, and the growing importance of manufactured imports have resulted in major job losses in this sector of the economy. Many workers who have been forced to find other jobs have been unemployed for long periods of time, others have been forced to take jobs at lower levels of income, and some have just been unable to find new work. The plant shutdown phenomenon has also been devastating to local communities.

The U.S. Climate for Labour

Workers in the United States are experiencing many of the same problems as workers in Canada. With the persistence of high levels of unemployment, their bargaining power has diminished. Between 1979 and 1986, average real wages in the United States declined by close to 10%. Workers no longer expect to get wage increases which keep up with increases in inflation. Cost-of-living clauses are rapidly disappearing from contracts. Indeed, payment by cash bonuses is on the rise. For organized workers, emphasis has been placed on the attempt to protect existing jobs—or at least workers—from layoffs.

The trade union movement is on the retreat in the United States; in 1986, only 18% of the labour force was organized. Unions are fighting a losing battle trying to maintain industry-wide bargaining. The steel industry now bargains on a company-by-company basis. The United Auto Workers set a major precedent by signing a separate agreement with General Motors covering the Saturn plant in Tennessee. In 1986, for the first time in 40 years, non-union workers averaged greater average wage increases than unionized workers.

The U.S. federal minimum wage ($3.35 per hour) has not been raised for five years; in real terms, it has fallen by 23% since January 1981, down to the 1955 level. State minimum wages range from $1.40 per hour in Texas to a high of $3.90 per hour in the District of Columbia; Alabama, Mississippi and South Carolina have no minimum wage at all!

In a study for the Joint Economic Committee of the U.S. Congress, Barry Bluestone and Bennett Harrison examined new job creation in the United States between 1979 and 1985, and they found two clear trends, the rising numbers of part-time jobs and rising numbers of low-paying jobs. In 1985, one out of every six Americans was working part time; they are commonly referred to as "contingent workers." Involuntary part-time workers totalled around 5.5 million. Since 1980, the number of part-time jobs has increased twice as fast as full-time jobs. "Flexible employment" is a euphemism coined to describe a growing style of employment; it includes individuals working through regular agencies, short-term employees, workers employed on an "on-call" basis, and those who do contract work. They receive far less pay than full-time workers and few if any fringe benefits. Between 1981 and 1986, new jobs have been created at a rate of 1.56% per year, well under the levels of 3.30% under President Carter and 2.73% under Presidents Kennedy and Johnson. Furthermore, the new jobs created during the Reagan administration pay on average 40% less than the jobs lost.

U.S. economists Barry Bluestone and Bennett Harrison found that 44% of the 9.5 million jobs created between 1979 and 1985 were low-wage positions, paying less than $7400 per year. These are poverty-level jobs. High-wage jobs, paying over $29,600 per year, accounted for only 10% of the new jobs. This is a new development.

In the period between 1963 and 1973, 50% of all new jobs were in the high-wage category; between 1973 and 1979, 17% were in this category. Bluestone and Harrison note the shift is definitely linked to the decline in high-paying unionized jobs in the industrial sector and the growth of low-wage, non-unionized jobs in the service sector. Furthermore, while some economists have claimed that the low-wage jobs are mainly going to women and youth, Bluestone and Harrison found that since 1979 three-quarters of the new jobs for white men have also been in the low-wage category.

The Reagan Onslaught

The Reagan administration led off with an attack on the unemployed. In the 1981 federal budget, 1.2 million Americans who had been unemployed for over 27 weeks were declared ineligible for extended benefits. Eligibility regulations were tightened. In 1986, 5.5 million Americans, or *70% of those unemployed*, received no benefits (in 1976, two-thirds of those who were unemployed were eligible for benefits). At the same time, the federal budget for training the unemployed was cut from a paltry $9.5 million in 1981 to only $5.6 million in 1986.

A war was launched on trade unions. The Department of Labor simply declined to enforce existing labour laws and regulations. The National Labor Relations Board (NLRB), established by the *Wagner Act* in 1936, has been transformed from a mediation institution into an agency for the owners of capital. The Board and the Department of Labor were both stacked with pro-management personnel. The number of union certification votes was cut in half. Under the leadership of Donald Dotson, the NLRB produced a series of decisions cutting back on labour's historic rights. Employers responded by increasing their discriminatory activity in union organizing drives. And the number of "management consultants," who provide union-busting services, has increased dramatically.

With the decimation of the NLRB, organized labour turned more to the courts in the United States. But even here labour faced defeat, as President Reagan has been packing the federal courts with right-wing judges. Federal courts have permitted corporations to use Title 11 of the Federal Bankruptcy Code to unilaterally abrogate union contracts. Reagan's appointments to the Occupational Safety and Health Administration have also consistently undermined enforcement and have refused to improve standards. The number of federal inspectors has been cut by 25%. The federal budget for research on health and safety matters has been steadily reduced. What data is available indicates that injury and illness rates have reached all-time highs during the Reagan administration.

Job Losses Under Free Trade

One of the major concerns that Canadian labour has with a free trade agreement is the potential loss of jobs. Many fear that an agreement will accelerate the trend towards the loss of relatively high-paying union jobs in industry and their replacement by low-paying service jobs. Furthermore, unemployment is at an all-time high for a recovery period. Trade unionists wonder what will happen if a free trade agreement is implemented at just about the same time that the next recession starts. Will unemployment rise even higher than it did in 1982? The econometric models generated by the economists' computers are not very reassuring. Furthermore, Ronald J. Wonnacott, one of the long-time supporters of free trade with the United States, has put it very plainly in his study for the Macdonald Royal Commission: "Trade liberalization is like technological change. The whole point is to increase efficiency and income, not employment."

In January 1985 the Mulroney Government released its discussion paper "How to Secure and Enhance Canadian Access to Export Markets." In it they predicted that around 8% of Canadian workers would experience "adjustments" due to a free trade agreement with the United States. Adjustment is a nice-sounding phrase for losing your job. Under a free trade agreement, most of the adjustments to change would be made in Canada. To tap into the additional Canadian market, the larger U.S. corporations will only have to expand production by employing some of their unused plant capacity. In contrast, most Canadian firms will have to make major changes to meet new U.S. competition.

In terms of scale, Canadian manufacturing plants are generally smaller than those in the United States. The 1983 studies by economists John Baldwin and Paul K. Gorecki, done for the Economic Council of Canada, concluded that the most vulnerable Canadian industries would be furniture, knitting mills, miscellaneous manufacturing, machinery and the food and beverage industry. Roy A. Matthews' 1985 study, also done for the Economic Council of Canada, concluded that the industries most vulnerable to international competition included those listed above, plus clothing, communications equipment, miscellaneous chemical industries, and electric wire and cable. It identified the weakest Canadian manufacturing sectors to be textiles, leather products, knitting mills, electrical equipment, non-metallic minerals and clothing.

One of the most important studies was done by the Ontario Ministry of Industry, Trade and Technology in 1985. It assessed the potential direct effects of a free trade agreement on employment in Ontario manufacturing industries. First, it identified "highly sensitive" industries, those with fairly high levels of tariff protection and relatively low potential for export. These industries are also characterized by a high level of U.S. imports. They employed 281,000 people, 31% of the total in Ontario manufacturing. The industries identified included commercial printing, metal stamping, publishing and printing, household furniture, paper boxes and bags, miscellaneous paper converters, men's clothing and miscellaneous chemicals.

Second, the study identified "sensitive" industries, those showing an excess of imports over exports and a negative trade balance. These industries employed 275,000 people, or 30% of the total in manufacturing. They included miscellaneous manufacturing, office and store machinery, scientific equipment, plastics and resins, electrical equipment, plastic fabricating, and miscellaneous machinery. The study made no assessment of the food and beverage industry, which alone accounts for 12% of employment in manufacturing. However, a 1985 study by Claude Lanoie for Agriculture Canada found, not surprisingly, that U.S. plants were, on average, considerably larger than similar plants in Canada in terms of size and sales. A study by Pamela Cooper for Agriculture Canada in 1981 found that the assets and sales of foreign-owned food and beverage firms in Canada were, on average, five time larger than those of Canadian-controlled firms.

In early 1986 a similar study by the Quebec government was leaked to the press, although it was not acknowledged by the pro-free trade Bourassa regime. It argued that 446,000 workers were employed in industries (including agriculture) which would be "vulnerable" under free trade. The weakest industries were identified as clothing, footwear, furniture, machinery and equipment, metal refining, printing and publishing, and informational hardware, software and data processing. There are over 115,000 jobs in these industries. Other industries were identified as "infant industries" which required continued protection to succeed. They included crafted gold and jewelry, rubber and plastics, electrical products, metal products and machine tools. These industries employed another 75,000 people. Quebec labour is quite concerned about a free trade agreement because 56% of the apparel industry, 49% of shoe manufacturing and 24% of electrical products industries are in that province. The Quebec study projected the loss of 30,000 jobs in the textile and clothing industry alone. It also identified fishing, agriculture and the food and beverage industries as "likely to be adversely affected" by a free trade agreement.

Against these studies the supporters of free trade advance the econometric model created by Richard G. Harris and David Cox. Their computer projection identifies the following "winners" under a comprehensive bilateral free trade agreement: transportation equipment, paper and allied products, textiles, printing and publishing, rubber and plastics, clothing and primary metals. The reader will note that some of these industries have been identified as vulnerable in other studies. Transportation equipment is mainly the automotive industry, and continental rationalization of production has already taken place under the Auto Pact. How could a free trade agreement bring further benefits? But then, what can we really expect from an econometric model that starts with the premise that there is already full employment in Canada?

Nevertheless, Harris and Cox's model projects that under a free trade agreement real income will rise 9%, there will be a 13% increase in total labour income, and employment in manufacturing will increase by 5.5%. However, there are sceptics in the labour movement. The greatest reduction in tariffs occurred in the 1970s and 1980s, following the Kennedy and Tokyo rounds of the GATT. But during this period the world experienced high rates of inflation, a steady decline in the general rate of economic growth, and increasing unemployment. The historical record of free trade and increased competition certainly does not support the predictions of the econometric models.

The Impact of Plant Relocation

One of the primary concerns of Canadian labour is the possibility that American branch plants will gradually cut back their operations in Canada and shift production to their primary manufacturing plants in the United States. There is also the fear that the larger Canadian corporations will decide to locate their new plants in the United

States to be closer to the larger markets. The single factor that is holding back such a trend is the 25% devaluation of the Canadian dollar (in comparison to the U.S. dollar). If the Canadian dollar moves back towards parity with the U.S. dollar, we can surely expect to find more new investment taking place south of the border.

In 1971 Michael Ray surveyed the location of American branch plants in Canada. Around 70% were found in the Toronto-Hamilton area; the second-largest centre was Windsor. Beyond this, only Montreal had any significant number of branch plants. In the manufacturing area, 83% of U.S. branch plant employment was within 400 miles of Toronto. The fastest growing U.S. industries were in the Toronto area; the older, weaker industries were in Montreal.

Why was there such a concentration of American plants in one area? One key factor, of course, was being close to the centre of the Canadian market. But the survey revealed two other factors in U.S. branch plant location, the economic health of the adjacent U.S. region and the closeness of the area to the centre of the U.S. manfacturing belt in the midwest. Thus, for American corporations, choosing the Toronto area as the optimal market location for their Canadian subsidiaries was determined as much by economic conditions in the United States as by those in Canada.

John H. Britton, a geographer at the University of Toronto, was one of the first to point out the dangers to Canada of the shift in manufacturing production in the United States. The key requirement for Canada was to maintain labour costs which were substantially below those in the United States. In the late 1970s, Britton pointed out that similar industries in the neighbouring U.S. states were moving to the American south and southwest, often referred to as "the sunbelt." Aside from the "better" labour climate for business, there was the advantage of new transportation links provided by the interstate highway system and much lower energy costs due to the warmer climate and relatively cheap natural gas. Assembly operations were quick to move. Furthermore, Britton pointed out that the first major industry to move to the U.S. south, the New England textile industry, was even quicker to move overseas to even lower wage areas. The lack of trade unions in the sunbelt made such moves much easier.

In the restructuring of industrial production, corporations are always searching for ways to reduce costs and raise profits. One of the first of the recent trends in the United States has been the shift in production to the sunbelt states. There, labour unions are practically non-existent; most of these states have so-called "right-to-work" laws which virtually outlaw trade unions. Labour costs are much lower and minimum-wage rates are very low or even non-existent. Almost none of these states have any of the traditional legal protections for workers; for example, there is an absence of laws prohibiting sexual harassment, electronic surveillance and discrimination. Workers in sunbelt states do not have access to personnel files, maternity leave, or even time off to vote. Few states have passed laws which provide maximum hours of work, mandatory pay for overtime, timely payment of wages, and equal pay by sex. There are no laws which guarantee workers the right to know about exposure to hazardous materials on the job or even to obtain information about their pension funds. Alabama and Mississippi have none of the above!

The shift in manufacturing to these states has been documented by Bluestone and Harrison in their widely read 1982 book, *The De-Industrialization of America*. Over the period surveyed, 1969-76, there were 25 million jobs created and 22 million jobs permanently lost. Shutdowns occurred on a national basis, and in every region. During this period, the northeast United States was the hardest hit. There were also a lot of jobs lost in the sunbelt, as the textile, apparel and electronics assembly operations moved overseas or to the free trade zones along the Mexican border. As the study demonstrates, the major gainers during this period were the states which have "right-to-work" laws.

The ability of American (and in the future, Canadian) plants to move from their present locations to the low-cost sunbelt states puts tremendous pressures on workers in present operations. One example will illustrate this situation. In 1986 Mack Trucks Inc., the largest employer in Allentown, Pennsylvania, threatened to move to a new plant at Winsboro, South Carolina, unless their workers, represented by the United Auto Workers, agreed to a long list of concessions. The union local refused, and Mack went ahead and built the new plant; 1800 jobs were lost. When the next round of negotiations began, the UAW local agreed to almost all of the original concessions. They agreed to a six-year contract with a wage freeze; because of other contract concessions, each remaining worker lost an average of $41 per week. The remaining 2300 employees had no other real employment opportunities. The Mack contract, of course, broke the industry-wide master agreement for the automotive industry. The UAW, trying to maintain industry-wide standards, was forced to oppose the local agreement. The case illustrates how weak the trade union movement is in the United States. It also demonstrates how corporate blackmail disrupts the lives of ordinary people and destroys local communities.

The Human Costs of "Adjustment"

In the hinterland areas of Canada, we are well aware of what happens when a key industry shuts down in a smaller centre. This is commonplace in a country which heavily depends on resource extraction. Indeed, there is a Canadian Association of One-Industry Towns, and it has 800 members! This organization has come out in opposition to a free trade agreement with the United States.

As I write this, I am reminded of the recent shutdown of Ocean Falls, British Columbia, when the forest products company there was closed. The vast majority of the people had no option but to abandon their homes and businesses and move elsewhere. Bulldozers were used to raze most of the empty houses, as the provincial government decided they didn't want to create havens for squatters living on welfare. And on the prairies, we know all too well what happens to a town when the branch railroad line and grain elevators are removed. Again, houses are abandoned and businesses close. The tragedy is that places like Ocean Falls and Alvena, Saskatchewan, were once very vibrant, pleasant places to live. The logic of the capitalist free market forces the people who once lived in these smaller centres to cram into an already overcrowded city.

The personal losses from plant shutdowns are extensive and well documented. For example, the United Auto Workers conducted a study of their members who had lost jobs between 1957 and 1975. After two years, the average worker was earning 43% less than their wages as auto workers. A similar study of steelworkers in the U.S. found that after two years they were earning on average 47% less than they had in the steel mills.

The Social Welfare Research Institute in Boston looked at the fate of 674,000 New England textile workers who lost their jobs between 1957 and 1975. Fewer than 3% found jobs in the new electronics industry. Another 16% were still in the area, working in the low-wage retail trade and service sector. The rest had been forced to search for employment outside New England.

The Institute also did a study for the U.S. Centre for Work and Mental Health on employees in the aircraft industry. This industry, closely linked to military contracts, suffers more ups and downs than most. Employees constantly have had to adjust to economic insecurity and the loss of income. Around 40% of aircraft industry workers suffer extensive insomnia, headaches, stomach trouble and ulcers. Child and spouse abuse is at a relatively high level.

In Canada, one of the best studies of the effect of mass layoffs was carried out by the Department of Industry, Trade and Commerce in 1979. While most workers found alternative jobs, often in entirely different industries, there was evidence of de-skilling; for example, many electrical and electronics workers were forced to take clerical jobs. Many also were forced to take jobs in the lower-paying industries. This was particularly true for those in the electronics industry.

Three of the most detailed studies were conducted by J. Paul Grayson of the Institute for Social Research at York University. These were in-depth surveys of the effects on workers of the shutdowns of SKF Canada Ltd., Canadian General Electric at Scarborough, and Black and Decker. The plants of both SKF Canada and CGE were making a profit. The corporations decided they could make even higher profits at other plant operations. SKF had opened a new automated plant in Europe. The CGE shutdown also involved shifting production overseas. The Black and Decker shutdown was part of the process of shifting production to low-wage areas in Asia.

Grayson found that for all three plants, the shutdown resulted in increased long-term unemployment. There was also a high level of de-skilling, which increased over time. Furthermore, de-skilling was not limited to older workers; it was experienced by young workers as well, and by both men and women. As a generalization, those who found alternative work accepted employment at lower wage levels. Those who remained unemployed were not refusing work but were very willing to accept new jobs at lower wages. They were also willing to move. Nor were they unwilling to undertake training for a new job, but retraining was generally not available. Women had a more difficult time finding alternative employment.

The research on these three cases also documented the personal trauma experienced by those who permanently lose what they had expected to be a career job. Employees ranked their plant closure as being equivalent to divorce or the death of a spouse. Their psychological well-being deteriorated. There was also a change in political attitudes; there was a growing feeling of powerlessness. There was a low level of class consciousness, and less faith in the ability of trade unions to defend the rights of workers. As Bluestone and Harrison point out, the mobility of capital became a key strategy in the 1970s to discipline labour, individual communities, and governments which wished to improve general working conditions and the environment.

In the face of this human and social depredation, what do we hear from the economists? A lot of talk about "labour-market rigidities." The advantage of the United States over Canada, they say, is "the greater flexibility of labour markets in the United States." This "flexibility" is identified with more advanced levels of deregulation, more extensive privatization, the plundering of the trade union movement, far greater restrictions on the rights of public servants to organize and strike, and the greater willingness of U.S. trade unions to accept major wage and other concessions in their contracts. This reflects the greater political "realism" that prevails in the United States.

The answer to unemployment, we are repeatedly told, is to allow the free market to work in the area of labour and jobs. We are assured that the market "reallocation of jobs," while creating short-term dislocations, is inevitably a move towards greater efficiency in the reallocation of resources to their most valued use. However, according to this analysis, there are impediments in Canada to the natural free market solution to unemployment, referred to as "rigidities." One of the "rigidities" is that, proportionately, there are more than twice as many members of the labour force organized in Canada than in the United States. Another is that we still have a relatively high degree of industry-wide bargaining, whereas the United States is moving much more rapidly to company unions and contracts. Therefore, workers in Canada have been more effective in resisting concession bargaining. Moreover, trade unions in Canada have also been more successful in negotiating contracts which require severance pay, advance notice of changes, and proof of "just cause" for a permanent layoff. All of these "inhibit the adaptiveness of labour markets" and make it "more costly to lay off redundant workers."

But the major focus of attack in comparing the two countries is Canada's much more extensive system of unemployment insurance. Thus, workers in Newfoundland, for example, may consciously choose to live on subsistence for half of the year or more, backed by UI, rather than move to southern Ontario. They may not wish to abandon their homes which may cost only $200 to $300 a month to occupy. If UI benefits were cut, however, as the Forget Commission has recommended, labour mobility would be increased. Refining the argument, University of Toronto economists Morely Gunderson and Noah M. Meltz argue that a "moral-hazard problem" can emerge when governments put unemployment insurance at a high level. They claim that by reducing the cost of being unemployed, "the parties may not take proper precautions against the rise of being unemployed, and workers may enter the state of unemployment more often and remain there longer than they would otherwise." To put this academic debate in context, it should be noted that the average weekly UI benefit in Canada in 1987 was $161!

For the business community in Canada, free trade with the United States offers an opportunity to overcome these "rigidities" in the labour market. Indeed, they are already beginning to gear up for the change. In December 1987 the Institute for International Research began promoting a conference for businessmen who want to close their Canadian operations and move to the United States. The announced agenda for the conference included a comparison of Canadian and U.S. labour laws, the differences in the "environment for business" between the two countries, the decline in the U.S. trade union movement, and methods of repatriating U.S. branch plants.

But in the end, the new business agenda must collapse on one of the fundamental contradictions of capitalism. All individual capitalists strive to reduce costs and maximize their profits. In times of general falling rates of profit, as in the 1970s and 1980s, the capitalist class as a whole utilizes governments to assist them in restraining the wages and salaries of working people. They have been quite successful, through the policies of monetarism, fiscal cutbacks in social programs, deregulation, privatization, attacks on labour's historic rights, forced unemployment, and the blackmail of capital flight. However, as they create unemployment, expand part-time jobs, break unions and generally reduce wages they also reduce the purchasing power of the great majority. Inevitably, this in turn leads to slower economic growth and lower profits. That has certainly been the central lesson of the New Right experiment of the 1970s and 1980s.

CHAPTER 14

Women and the Service Industry

From the beginning, the National Action Committee on the Status of Women (NAC) has been one of the major organizations opposed to a free trade agreement with the United States. NAC is a broadly based coalition of over 500 women's organizations, covering a very wide political spectrum. Why have they taken this position?

It is the central thesis of this book that the policy of free trade with the United States is part of the overall political agenda of the New Right, which includes an attack on the welfare state and trade unions, deregulation, privatization and rejection of democratic concepts of equality. The fact that neo-conservative ideology has moved from the status of a crank philosophy to the dominant ideology of governments and big business is due to the fundamental changes that are occurring in the world capitalist system. It is also quite clear that the New Right agenda represents a major attack on the general rights of women.

Feminism and the Rise of Neo-Conservatism

The major influences on the New Right in Canada have come from the Thatcher government in the United Kingdom and the Reagan administration in the United States. The approaches of the two governments have varied, probably due to the stronger influence of fundamentalist Christianity in the United States. In Canada, R.E.A.L. Women have enjoyed an influence far beyond their membership because their views are shared by a great many Conservative politicians and Members of Parliament.

Margaret Thatcher has not led an all-out attack on women's rights, but she has consistently asserted that the battle for women's rights has been largely won. Nevertheless, her Conservative Party has placed greater emphasis on the family as the central institution in society and on the need for greater parental control of children. While there has been no outright attack on the position of women since she assumed office in 1979, neither has there been an effort to improve the status of women, partly because the Conservatives recognize that the process of the restructuring of capitalism requires greater participation of women in the work force. While the need for women to return to the home has not been emphasized, the Conservatives have justified cutbacks in welfare on the grounds that liberal welfare policies undermine family and individual responsibility.

However, Thatcher's general policies have had a dramatic effect on the status of women. As Elizabeth Wilson has pointed out, the stress on individualism has "widened the gap between better off women and those at the bottom of the employment hierarchy, and this is in large part due to the loss of women's jobs in the manufacturing sector." The all-out attack on trade unions has undermined efforts to improve women's income and working conditions at a time when there has been a relative increase in part-time and temporary jobs for women, at low pay with poor fringe benefits. Privatization has been accompanied by pauperization; women have been highly represented in the higher-paying public sector jobs which are being replaced by very low-paying jobs in the private service sector. There have been cutbacks in maternity leave and other employment rights. It is now widespread practice to require women to prove that they have adequate child care before they can get a regular job. Those who have been most adversely affected have been black and ethnic minority women.

Elizabeth Wilson, who teaches social policy at the North London Polytechnic, points out that Thatcher's policies have resulted in the "ghettoisation" of women in low-paid part-time work. In the end, this has probably created more hardship than the forced return of women to the home:

> Their exploitation in the worst paid and least protected jobs has been intensified, they have been exposed to greater risk of violence both at home and in the streets, their unpaid labour in the home has if anything increased as what little welfare support there was has been eroded, and the Tories have then had the effrontery implicitly to blame women as parents for juvenile delinquency and the decay of morals.

The approach of the New Right is slightly different in the United States, owing to the powerful presence of elements identified with the Moral Majority and Christian fundamentalism. Their goal is to restore patriarchy, particularly at the level of the family, and one of their strategies has been to attack the welfare state as undermining the traditional family. In their view, the movement of women into the labour force has threatened the authority of the man as head of the family, a role for which they claim biblical authority. The ideal of the economically dependent wife advanced by the religious right has little relevance for black and other non-white families where women have traditionally worked. Nor, of course, for a very large percentage of white working women. In these views and many others, the American New Right reveals itself to be both anti-feminist and racist.

The mainstream of the women's movement in the United States has supported the Equal Rights Amendment to the U.S. Constitution, abortion rights and labour market equity. The basic demand has been for equality of opportunity, a demand in keeping with the American tradition of liberal individualism. While this demand is a threat to the patriarchal system espoused by the New Right, neo-conservatism itself is basically a return to the establishment ideals of early 19th century liberalism. Equality in the period of the rise of capitalism meant equality of opportunity. It was not until the boom period after World War II that capitalism was able to accept the welfare state and social rights. At this point, equality took on a different meaning: social security entitlements for all, the right to employment and equality as a human or collective (rather than individual) right. In the reformist wave of the 1960s, legal equality was extended to visible minorities. However, the new perceptions of rights related to equality are currently under severe attack. In particular, the ideology of liberal individualism is so strongly entrenched in the United States that it tends to work against the establishment of collective rights for women. Hence, it is not likely that they will gain status as a sexual group. This inherent conservatism in the American tradition will have long-term implications for Canadian women under a comprehensive free trade agreement.

Under the Reagan administration, affirmative action programs have been undermined. The famous Sears Roebuck case before the Equal Employment Opportunity Commission took the position that discrimination must be on an individual rather than a group or class basis. Neo-conservatism insists that the problem with American society has been the "excess of democracy," the extension beyond equality of opportunity to equality of conditions (or the outcome of a policy). The Equal Rights Amendment did not move into the area of equality of conditions.

In Canada, R.E.A.L. Women is more closely identified with the neo-conservative Moral Majority position. Their primary focus has been the defence of the traditional male-dominated nuclear family. They have mounted campaigns against reproductive rights, easier divorce, universal daycare, and affirmative action. They are adamantly opposed to legislation which extends human rights to homosexuals of either sex. They oppose child abuse legislation on the grounds that it is "detrimental to families."

Neo-conservatism in Canada is also identified with 19th century liberal individualism. This is best illustrated in the publications of the Fraser Institute, the "think tank" for Canadian big business. In *Discrimination, Affirmative Action, and Equal Opportunity* they take the view that legislation to protect women, minority and ethnic groups actually harms them. They oppose equal pay for work of equal value and any form of preferential treatment for minorities. Walter Block, head of their Centre for Study of Economics and Religion, defends employers who make sexual overtures to female employees or who discriminate against women employees in matters of salary. Such treatment is "part of the package deal in which the secretary agrees to all aspects of the job." Women, after all, have the free choice to quit the job. Lower wages for women should be permitted because "the right to discriminate" is a fundamental individual right. Is there any wonder that women are sceptical about the neo-conservative agenda and, what is essentially tied to it, free trade with the United States?

Women's organizations in Canada fear the effects of harmonization which will come after a Canada/U.S. free trade agreement. U.S. minimum wages are lower, and the majority of minimum-wage workers are women. In the last two decades Canada had greatly improved the income situation for women over the age of 65. On average, the Canada Pension Plan, Old Age Security and Guaranteed Income Supplement benefits are 30% higher than U.S. Social Security benefits. Thanks to the efforts of Canada's public service trade unions, there is a much stronger commitment in Canada to pay-equity programs, better programs for paid parental leaves, and other benefits like protection from sexual harassment. We have much better maternity benefits provisions in the Unemployment Insurance Program, allowing women up to four months unpaid maternity leave while retaining the right to a job. There is a stronger commitment to the principle of affordable daycare in Canada than in the United States. In the long run, free trade will threaten Canadian social programs.

Women and the Manufacturing Sector

In Canada in 1986 women represented around 25% of all employees in manufacturing. But the percentage of women workers was much higher in certain industries: clothing (79%), footwear (65%), leather goods (60%), toys and sporting goods (45%), textiles (40%), tobacco (39%), electrical products (38%), plastics (32%) and food (31%). Many of these industries are unable to compete in the international market: they export very little, and they are protected by relatively high tariffs. The Macdonald Royal Commission identified textiles, clothing, footwear, electrical products and consumer goods among the weakest manufacturing industries, those likely to experience the greatest dislocation under any free trade agreement. Thus, many of the manufacturing industries in Canada most vulnerable to detrimental effects from free trade with the United States also have the highest percentage of women workers.

The Macdonald Royal Commission argued that the restructuring of industry, forced by the free trade agreement, will enable workers in these "low-wage" weaker industries to find employment in new, higher-paid industries. It is true that the wages paid in the weaker industries are considerably below the wages paid in other unionized manufacturing industries where the labour force is primarily male. But on the other hand, the wages paid here are considerably higher than the main alternatives for women, the retail trade or hospitality industries. Furthermore, manufacturing provides a greater opportunity for full-time work. There are two studies which analyze the effects of free trade on these industries: the North-South Institute's 1985 *Women in Industry* and Marjorie Cohen's 1987 *Free Trade and the Future of Women's Work*. Their conclusions are summarized below, by industry.

Textile and Clothing Industries. This is the second largest employer in the manufacturing sector, exceeded only by the food and beverage industry. They are not major exporters; in spite of low U.S. tariff barriers, the industry has a large and growing trade deficit, $1.6 billion in 1985. Around 60% of our textile imports are from the United States. The U.S. industry is much larger, stronger, and is located in the sunbelt states, where wages, and construction and energy costs are relatively low. The decline of the clothing industry in Canada due to imports is also adversely affecting the textile industry.

Electrical and Electronic Products. While very important to women workers, this industry cannot compete with the large world-scale industries but must depend on finding small niches. Foreign ownership dominates this industry, and the American firms are strongly for free trade. Women workers are concentrated in low-skilled production work, while men dominate in scientific and technical personnel. The trade unions in this sector fear that American corporations will shift production across the border, and the Canadian firms fear that much of the locally owned industry, which is small scale, will be wiped out.

Footwear. Canadian production supplies only about 50% of the Canadian market. As imports from low-wage countries increased, quotas were put in place in 1977, but they were removed in 1981. As the industry declined, they were reimposed, and then some were lifted in 1984. Employment dropped dramatically over the next eighteen months, yet while imports increased the average price for children's shoes increased 26% and men shoes by 7%. The United States has much lower tariffs than Canada. It is highly unlikely that Canadian manufacturers can increase their share of the U.S. market in the face of competition from larger U.S. firms and low-wage imports from South Korea, Taiwan and Brazil.

Food Industry. The food processing industry has traditionally been unionized in Canada, and wages are higher than in the United States. Other costs are higher due to climatic differences, energy costs, greater distances to smaller markets, and the existence of marketing boards to protect farm income. The industry is directed to the Canadian market, and very little is exported. As Marjorie Cohen notes, those industries with the highest level of female employees have been hardest hit by imports. The horticulture industry, including grapes, is considered the most vulnerable one. Without the 25% devaluation in the dollar, many more firms would have collapsed in the 1980s. The vulnerability of the meat industry is illustrated by the fact that Iowa alone produces more hogs than all of Canada.

We can get some idea of what to expect by looking briefly at the impact of freer trade on the fruit and vegetable industry in the B.C. interior, stretching from Ashcroft/Kamloops down to Oliver/Osoyoos. During World War II this area boomed as imports were drastically curtailed. Thousands of acres were brought into production, the number of farms actually expanded, and thousands of people were employed in the farm, packing and processing industries. Most plant workers were women, and they were unionized. Canadian Canners, later bought by the U.S. giant Del Monte, operated six processing plants in the area, and there were a number of independent plants as well. Beginning in the late 1950s, imports of fresh and processed fruits and vegetables began to flow in from California, Mexico, Australia, South Africa and Asia. By the 1980s, the fresh market was dominated by imports, and the processing industry totally collapsed. The result was a legacy of unemployment, generally around 18%, and the loss of the agricultural base. Consumers got slightly lower prices.

The study by the North-South Institute reveals the prospects for women workers in these industries. The vulnerable industries are concentrated in Ontario and Quebec; in 1982, 65% of all women working in manufacturing in Quebec were in these industries. Furthermore, the women who work here have had a great deal of trouble finding alternative employment when their jobs have disappeared.

For the leather, textile, clothing and knitting industries, almost 30% of the women workers are over 45 years of age. There is a higher percentage of married women working in these plants (approximately 71%) than in the labour force in general (63%). The vulnerable industries also have a much higher percentage of women workers who were born outside Canada and whose mother tongue is neither English nor French. Finally, the level of educational attainment is considerably lower among workers in these industries than in the work force as a whole; 42% have not gone beyond grade nine. These facts indicate that the degree of mobility to other jobs is certainly limited. And as Marjorie Cohen points out, "women account for less than 20 per cent of the participants in the National Training Program. In the Critical Trade Skills Training area their representation, at 4 per cent of all participants, is an appalling indication of failure of initiatives to integrate women into nontraditional job training areas."

Women and the Service Industry

Most people are aware that the fastest growing part of the economy is the service sector; currently, it accounts for about two-thirds of the national income and provides close to 70% of all jobs. Over the past ten years, 80% of the new jobs created in Canada have been provided by this sector. It is also the one area of the international economy where the United States still has a dominant position. The U.S. deficit in trade in manufactured goods is to a large extent offset by a surplus in the service sector, which was around $25 billion in 1986. Not surprisingly, the U.S. government wishes to include services under the GATT so that other countries cannot raise barriers to American penetration.

Just what is the service sector? As Marjorie Cohen points out, economists have historically categorized economic activity into three sectors: (1) the primary sector, agriculture and resource extraction; (2) the secondary sector, manufacturing and construction; (3) the tertiary or service sector, which more or less comprised anything left over. Goods are easy to identify, but services are intangible. In the past, services have been defined as support for production and trade in goods. However, such a definition is not very precise, and seems out of date in a "post-industrial" society where services have become the dynamic force in the economy.

The Economic Council of Canada includes in the service sector health, education, sports, recreation, accounting, consulting, computer services, accommodation, food services, public administration, wholesale and retail trade, banking, investment, insurance, transportation, communications, storage and utilities. Others have included marketing, management services, entertainment, leasing, construction, legal services, travel services, tourism and franchising.

While the service sector is most important to the Canadian domestic economy, its predominance does not carry over to the area of international trade. In contrast to almost all advanced industrial countries, Canada runs a *deficit* in trade in services. Furthermore, this deficit has been growing quite rapidly over the last couple of decades.

One aspect of Canada's deficit in the current account in our balance of payments has already been mentioned in Chapter 9. Canada has a huge outflow of capital in the form of interest and dividends on foreign investment. We also run a large deficit in the travel account, amounting to over $2 billion per year in the 1980s. The deficit in business services, which is well over $2 billion per year, is also primarily linked to foreign ownership of the Canadian economy and reflects additional payments by branch plants to parent firms. Statistics Canada reports that for 1984 the deficits with the United States alone included management and administration services ($748 million), royalties, patents and trade marks ($846 million), equipment rentals ($259 million), and research and development costs

($221 million).

In contrast to merchandise trade in goods, Canada has been losing its export market for services in the United States. In 1973 the U.S. market accounted for around 68% of Canada's service exports; this fell to 52% in 1982. On the other hand, the United States has provided around 64% of our service imports over the same period. The main problem here is that the service industry is quite labour intensive. If we continue to rely on exports from our capital intensive resource area, which employs relatively few Canadians, and allow our service exports to continue to decline relatively, this will intensify the persistent problem of high unemployment.

U.S. Objectives for a Free Trade Agreement

U.S. trade officials recognize the importance to the U.S. economy of expanding the export of services, and they have pushed hard to include this area in the Canada-U.S. bilateral free trade agreement. The major barriers to trade here are not tariffs but national laws and regulations. Thus, from the beginning the U.S. negotiators have stressed the need to obtain the right of American firms to do business in Canada. George Radwanski has summarized the main U.S. objectives as follows:

Right of Establishment. American firms cannot operate in Canada unless they obtain the legal right to do business in this country. In many cases, there are laws, rules and regulations which prohibit this in order to maintain a Canadian national identity or sovereignty. The removal of such barriers has been a key demand of the American negotiators.

National Treatment. The U.S. government wants U.S. firms operating in Canada to have the same status as Canadian firms. This would eliminate various discriminations in favour of Canadian firms. Many governments, for example, give Canadian or local firms special tax advantages over others, or give preference in assigning government contracts. The right of national treatment would end this practice.

Regulatory Harmonization. Differences in government regulations can have the effect of a barrier to trade. The U.S. negotiators have pushed for harmonization of government regulations between the two countries. This would clearly enhance the operation of U.S. firms in Canada.

Mobility of Labour. The U.S. government and industry want to obtain the right of Americans to come and work in Canada without facing existing barriers which give preference to hiring Canadians. Many governments and industries have hiring quotas to protect jobs for Canadians, citizenship restrictions, or licensing or work permits. This practice is widespread in most professional fields like engineering, law, accounting, etc., where governments and professional bodies grant licences to members based on special examinations or the attainment of training or educational requirements. U.S. firms also want the right to offer their services either from within Canada or from across the border.

As we noted in the introductory chapter, the U.S. government got almost everything it wanted in the service sector. There is a code of specific principles for services which grants U.S. corporations the right to national treatment, the right of establishment and the right to cross-border sales. Canada has agreed to adjust rules governing public monopolies (which include all major utilities in Canada) to reflect the private market. There is to be a special code on telecommunications (data processing) which is to provide "predictability in the way Canadians regulate this rapidly growing area of services trade."

What can Canada gain from free trade in services with the United States? As Marjorie Cohen has pointed out, the Macdonald Royal Commission produced 72 volumes of background studies, but none of the papers dealt with the service industry. The only specific study of the impact of free trade with the United States on the service industry was done by George Radwanski for the Ontario Ministry of Treasury and Economics. His overall assessment follows.

First, there are a number of service industries which Radwanski believes would be only marginally affected either because free trade already exists in the industry or because trade plays a minor role. These include accommodation, food and beverage services, retail and wholesale trade, education, health and social service, public administration and defence, real estate, casualty and property insurance firms, and public utilities. This view is not shared by others. Many of the public service trade unions note that privatization is well advanced for many services in the United States, e.g., health care, nursing, hospitalization, education, the penal system, and utilities. Presumably, under the principles of the right of establishment and national treatment, U.S. firms would have the legal right to enter into competition with established Canadian practices.

Radwanski concludes that two industries—trust companies and life insurance firms—could be adversely affected if the free trade agreement removed the existing government restrictions which prevent takeovers by foreign firms. This removal has certainly been a major thrust of the U.S. negotiators and political leaders. Radwanski also looked at the impact on several important service industries in Ontario. First, banking could be adversely affected. There are many Canadian government regulations designed to keep this most important sector of Canadian finance under the control of Canadians. In contrast, there are no special rules protecting the U.S. market from the intrusion of foreign banks. Furthermore, U.S. banks would have access to the entire Canadian market; in contrast, Canadian banks (and all others) would be limited by legislation restricting U.S. banks to regional status. The free trade agreement appears to have given the Americans what they wanted in this area. U.S. banks may now expand in Canada without limitations on their assets.

Culture and broadcasting is another important service sector. Chapter 16 will outline the protections and supports that Canada has used to try to retain a bit of Canadian culture. The U.S. negotiators wanted many of these eliminated. In contrast, the United States has few barriers to entry by foreign firms. Their protection is their strength in the American market and the high level of American nationalism. As Radwanski concludes, it is clear that if government barriers were removed on each side of the border "we would be overwhelmingly the losers."

In telecommunications area, the Canadian system is characterized by regulated monopolies. Ownership is restricted to Canadians. In contrast, deregulation in the United States has led to fierce competition and a wide variation in the availability of services. In long-distance telephone service, the giant corporation AT&T has emerged with 80% of the market. U.S. firms are much larger than their Canadian counterparts. Radwanski comes to the inevitable conclusion: "there does not appear to be any great potential for Canadian firms to penetrate the U.S. market."

Under free trade there is the distinct probability that transportation will shift from an east-west to a north-south axis. Railroads are already seeking labour and other cost reductions in order to compete with their U.S. counterparts. In trucking, deregulation in the United States has permitted the emergence of six huge firms, and it is feared that Canadian firms will not be able to compete with them because of geographic factors and economies of scale. Radwanski predicts that unrestricted U.S. competition would bring serious damage. Free trade would also force deregulation of the Canadian civilian air service, probably with reduced service to smaller centres. The hub system in transportation would likely lead to Canadian spoke service through American hubs. Because of geographic factors, even large Canadian cities could not serve as hubs for competition in the U.S. market.

The only service industry in which Canada could expect to gain from free trade would be business services. These include professional services, such as engineering, law, accounting, management consulting, etc. In contrast, the computer softwear industry believes that free trade would be disastrous for the smaller, emerging Canadian companies. A key factor here would be the reduction of immigration barriers. In his conclusion, Radwanski agrees with the Macdonald Royal Commission:

> The removal of existing Canadian restrictions on the entry of U.S. firms in some (service) fields could result in significant penetration of Canadian markets by U.S.-based competitors without conferring comparable benefits in the other direction. Overall, it is likely that the United States has more to gain from the reciprocal reduction of barriers to trade in services than has Canada.

The service industry is the most important sphere of economic activity in Canada, and it appears to be the most vulnerable to any bilateral free trade agreement with the United States. Around 83% of all working women are employed in the service sector. In addition, women represent the large majority of employees in the service-related jobs in the agricultural, resource extraction and manufacturing sectors; in all, 87% of working women are in service-related occupations. The following are a few examples of the degree to which these industries depend on women workers: clerical and related (80%); medicine and health (79%); teaching and related (61%); social science and related (57%); sales (44%); artistic, literary, recreational and related (42%); and managerial, administrative and related occupations (34%).

Of major concern to women is the trend towards contracting out, privatization and deregulation. Many working women are in the public sector, and their wages, fringe benefits and working conditions are protected by the existence of trade unions. Granting American firms the right of establishment and national treatment is likely to lead to an infusion of American non-union service firms and the replacement of women in union jobs with low-wage part-time workers.

One of the major fears of women is that bilateral free trade in the service areas will lead to further concentration of jobs in this sector south of the border. For example, the Canadian Independent Computer Services Association, representing Canadian-owned firms in the field, has shown that between 1977 and 1984 around 180,000 jobs were lost as a result of the importation of computer services. There is a distinct trend for companies in Canada to have their data processed by firms in the United States. This is particularly true of American branch plants. For example, American Motors Inc. moved almost all of its data processing to the United States and now handles its \$770 million in Canadian sales with only five data-processing employees in this country.

Deregulation of the transportation and communications industries and free trade pose a major threat to working women. Given the hub system of organization, on a continental basis it is likely that many of the positions held by women, such as office personnel, reservation clerks, flight attendants, etc., will be concentrated in the hubs, in the major U.S. transportation and communication centres. These jobs will be lost to Canadian women. If there is deregulation of long-distance telephone services, women can be expected to lose jobs as contracts go to the American carriers.

There has been very little produced by the supporters of bilateral free trade with the United States on the service industry. This is astonishing in view of its importance to the economy. What is available suggests that free trade really offers little opportunity for expansion into the United States. On the other hand, it presents serious dangers to existing Canadian industries. The harmonization that will be required to facilitate trade in the service area will seriously compromise what political and economic sovereignty Canada still has.

For working women, bilateral free trade has little to offer. The most vulnerable manufacturing industries have a high percentage of women employees. They cannot expect much help from the government in retraining and relocation. While free trade might help certain professionals who could work in the United States, this is certainly not true for the vast majority of women who work in the service area. They can only look forward to the erosion of job opportunities and to the conditions associated with the contracting out of jobs: lower wages, fewer fringe benefits, less than full-time work and unemployment.

CHAPTER 15

Agriculture and the Food Industry

Most farm organizations in Canada have been, at best, sceptical about a free trade agreement with the United States. In presentations to the Parliamentary Committee on Canada's International Relations in August 1985, the Canadian Federation of Agriculture, l'Union des producteurs agricoles, the National Farmers Union and the Dairy Farmers of Canada argued that agriculture should be excluded from the negotiations. This position was endorsed by the Ontario Federation of Agriculture at their 1986 annual convention. It was the position taken by the Macdonald Royal Commission. In addition, strong opposition came from the farm organizations representing egg, chicken and turkey producers. The horticulture industry in general also opposed including agriculture in the talks. In 1986 the prairie Wheat Pools requested that grains covered by the Canadian Wheat Board be excluded. Richard R. Barichello of the Department of Agricultural Economics at the University of British Columbia makes it clear why there is resistance to the free trade deal by the agricultural sector:

> . . . some losses [to Canadian farmers] are likely and there do not appear to be sufficient potential gains to the Canadian agricultural sector to offset them. Most of the gains to Canadian agriculture would come from a subsequent movement to multilateral free trade for agriculture, not just a bilateral U.S. agreement.

The two major exceptions to the general position of Canadian farm organizations were the cattle and hog industries, which are looking for additional markets in the United States. In the summer of 1987, nine of the more right-wing farm and agribusiness organizations formed the Canadian Agricultural Policy Alliance to promote a free trade agreement with the United States. In addition to the Canadian Cattlemen's Association, the organization included the Western Canada Wheat Growers' Association, the United Grain Growers, the Manitoba Farm Business Association, the hog marketing boards from the prairie provinces and Ontario, and the Western Barley Growers. This group took the position that protection from import competition and farm subsidies should be phased out, *provided the Americans do the same.*

Canada is one of the top five export markets for U.S. agricultural products. We are their most important market for fruits and vegetables. In 1986 the United States provided 44% of Canada's agricultural imports, but this accounted for only 10% of American exports. In that same year, 35.6% of Canada's agricultural and food exports went to the United States, but this accounted for only 11% of U.S. imports. Traditionally, Canada has had a favourable balance of trade in agricultural products with the world but has run a deficit in trade with the United States. This changed in 1985; for the first time Canada had a favourable balance of trade in agricultural products with the United States. It is widely recognized that this change is almost entirely due to the 25% devaluation of the Canadian dollar.

The U.S. Position in the Trade Negotiations

Over the past few years spokesmen for the U.S. Department of Agriculture and Congressional representatives from farm states have outlined a set of long-term objectives for a bilateral free trade agreement with Canada. A basic objective has been *to include agriculture in a comprehensive bilateral free trade agreement,* to provide a precedent for the next round of negotiations of the General Agreement on Tariffs and Trade, and for other, more practical, reasons. The U.S. government would like to reduce the large merchandise trade deficit with Canada; a free trade agreement which included the food and agricultural sector would help that situation. In addition, U.S. agricultural interests are looking for new markets, and Canada is the closest high-income market. With the advantages of a better climate and lower costs of production, American farmers believe that they can expand sales in Canada.

The most common American demand has been for *an end to interprovincial barriers to trade in Canada.* They are particularly opposed to the supply management marketing boards. Peter Murphy, the chief U.S. negotiator, stated on several occasions that concessions here were "essential" for an agreement. The wine and brewery interests in the United States were also pushing to end provincial discrimination against foreign imports.

The U.S. Department of Agriculture has been pushing for *the removal of import quotas from Canadian management boards* which exist for milk products and the "feather industries." Spokesmen for the U.S. government say the quota system must be removed to provide for equal market access in both countries. They also claim to be aiming for comparable levels of protection and income support in both countries. The U.S. dairy industry felt that it had the most to gain from a comprehensive agreement as their surplus industrial milk products could take much of the Canadian market. The huge vertically integrated poultry and egg producers and processors, paying only minimum wages for labour and based in the warm American south, now easily supply all the northern states and the Alaskan market. If import quotas are removed, they are sure they can take most of the Canadian market.

U.S. negotiators pushed for the removal of the import monopoly of the Canadian Wheat Board. Canadian high standards and Canadian Wheat Board licensing had effectively excluded lower-quality U.S. grain from the Canadian market. While Canadian farmers had access to the U.S. market, grain surpluses there effectively excluded them. In late August 1987, the U.S. Department of Agriculture was still objecting to "state trading" by the Wheat Board and demanding an end to the Canadian two-price system for wheat. They also wanted to see the removal of the freight subsidies for Canadian grain under the *Western Grain Transportation Act* and the *Feed Freight Assistance Act*. U.S. corn producers feel they can replace western feed grains in the eastern Canadian market.

In the same general area, there are at the present time protections for the Canadian canola market. U.S. soybean producers feel they can take much of the Canadian market for cooking oil and margarine if the 10% duty and freight subsidies are removed.

A major demand by U.S. government and farm organizations was for the removal of the seasonal tariffs for fruits and vegetables. They expect to greatly expand exports to Canada in the summer months. They want all duties and other protections removed from potatoes and onions.

U.S. food and agricultural interests also want to see an end to various Canadian subsidies to the food processing industry. In spite of the fact that the United States has a very extensive system of federal and state supports for agriculture, U.S. interests have objected to provincial income support programs for Canadian farmers.

In the United States the National Pork Producers Council has obtained countervailing duties on the import of Canadian hogs. It is not unlikely that in the near future countervailing duties will be extended to Canadian pork products as well. In June 1986, U.S. cattle producers, acting through influential members of Congress, initiated an investigation of the Canadian industry by the International Trade Commission (ITC). The California Cattlemen's Association is strongly opposed to the importation of additional Canadian beef. In this case the ITC concluded that subsidies to beef producers were about the same on both sides of the border. But in view of the decision of the U.S. International Trade Commission in the case of the Atlantic fisheries, it is probable that additional countervailing duties cases will arise when American investigators discover the extensive subsidies that provincial governments have granted to meat packers in western Canada, including Gainers, Fletcher's, Intercontinental Packers, Canada Packers, Springhill Farms, and now Cargill. In many cases the expansion of their output in Canada was to increase sales in the U.S. market.

Many American farm organizations have called for a return to parity in the two currencies. They see the relative decline in sales to Canada to be the direct result of the 25% devaluation of the Canadian dollar, a view which is supported by the U.S. Department of Agriculture. Some U.S. farm organizations argued that negotiations on free trade in agriculture should not have begun until the currencies of the two countries were closer in value. The U.S. National Farmers Union had demanded that the problem of the fluctuating exchange rate be addressed in the negotiations. U.S. agricultural experts have been suggesting the adoption of a currency parity system such as exists in the European Common Market. There, prices are automatically adjusted when a national currency appreciates or is devalued. The result is stable agricultural prices and trade. Because no agreement could be reached on this very political issue, it was put off until the next round of the free trade negotiations.

The currency issue highlights one of the fundamental differences between the positions of the two countries. Fred Mitchell, president of the Canadian Meat Council, pointed out that the Canadian meat industry can benefit from free trade with the United States *provided our dollar stays at a 25 to 30 percent discount.* The key role of the devaluation of the Canadian dollar in the rise of Canadian exports of hogs and cattle to the United States was identified in the studies by Deloitte, Haskins + Sells Associates for the prairie Wheat Pools and by Katie Macmillan for the Canada West Foundation. If the Canadian dollar returns to parity, the likely result will be a return to the trade patterns of the early 1970s when the United States had a large favourable balance of agricultural trade with Canada, and U.S. hogs, in particular, flooded the Canadian market. The Canadian Cattlemen's Association and Canadian hog producers do not seem to understand that if the exchange rate moves back to parity, their exports to the U.S. will greatly diminish.

Government supports for agriculture are extensive on both sides of the border. In 1986 the U.S. government provided over $25 billion in subsidies to American farmers in the form of direct deficiency payments, price supports, quota protections, etc. U.S. support for grain and oilseed farmers was several times higher than Canadian support. In the seventeen western states, the American federal government has provided enormous subsidies for farmers in the form of water and power for irrigation. Farm income support programs are complicated and different in each country. From the beginning, it seemed highly unlikely that all of these issues could be sorted out within the time frame set by the U.S. "fast-track" approach, spelled out in the 1984 U.S. *Trade and Tariffs Act*, only seventeen months. The final negotiations of the Australia/New Zealand free trade agreement took two years of preliminary negotiations and three years of intensive negotiations, primarily because agriculture was included. The recent U.S./Mexico agreement took six years of negotiation. It is not surprising that government spokesmen on both sides of the border saw this agreement as only a first step towards further liberalization of agricultural trade.

Canada's Agricultural Objectives

The Mulroney government listed three main objectives in the area of food and agriculture: to gain more secure access to the U.S. market for Canadian exporters, to liberalize trade rule in order to improve the existing access for both agricultural and food products, and at the same time to preserve Canada's traditional agricultural programs, both federal and provincial. But it was quite obvious that Canada had far less to gain in any agricultural trade agreement with the United States.

The main goal of Canada's negotiations was to gain assured access to the American market for Canada's cattle and hog producers, who have been threatened by non-tariff barriers. This is one of those cases where the more powerful U.S. government is beating Canada over the head, and the official Canadian response appears to be, "What can we give you to induce you to stop?" The Canadian objective in this area of negotiations was the rather minimal one of trying to maintain the access we had prior to the rise of U.S. protectionism in the 1980s.

Canadian negotiators also pressed for the removal of state health restrictions which have effectively blocked Canadian cattle and hogs from some local markets. However, it does not seem legally possible for the U.S. federal government to override local health regulations, and there was nothing specific on this in the text of the final agreement. On the other hand, Canada has required a 30-day quarantine for pseudorabies on all American hogs which enter Canada, and this has effectively excluded all American hogs from the Canadian market. The annex to the final text reveals that the Canadian negotiators yielded on this point.

Canadian negotiators also hoped that a free trade agreement covering agriculture could set a precedent for the next round of the GATT negotiations. Presently, agriculture is not covered under the GATT. There is also a hope that a precedent could be extended to Japan and the European Economic Community. But this seems highly unlikely, as most governments in the world see the protection of domestic agriculture as an issue of national security, and as support for a traditionally conservative voting bloc. Furthermore, there is a division of opinion within the Canadian farming community on this issue. Grain and meat growers are major exporters and want to liberalize trade. But all the other major farm commodities need substantial protection and support if they are to survive with higher costs due to climatic and environmental factors.

As the Mulroney government stressed, the free trade agreement was to "provide a powerful signal against protectionism and for trade liberalization." And it also reflected the commitment of both governments to push for the general liberalization of trade on a global basis through the multinational trade negotiations under the GATT. In view of this general policy orientation, Canadian farmers were very sceptical of the commitment of the Mulroney government to protect Canada's supply management marketing boards and traditional federal and provincial income support systems.

The Reaction to the Free Trade Agreement

The general reaction of the farm community to the free trade agreement announced in October 1987 was a general sigh of relief: much less had been given away than had been feared. The dairy industry had been exempted in this round. However, with all tariffs to be removed over a ten-year period, the Dairy Farmers of Canada asked the federal government to expand the import control list to include dairy products like yogurt, ice cream and liquid milk in consumer-sized packages.

Provincial and federal farm support programs were not specifically excluded, as the Mulroney government was unable to reach an agreement with the U.S. government on what constituted an acceptable government support program. However, U.S. trade laws and their precedents remain in effect. This means that all the Canadian programs for support of agriculture can still be challenged by U.S. producers under U.S. trade legislation.

The horticulture industry was the hardest hit. All agricultural tariffs are to be removed over ten years, and the fruit and vegetable industry lost its seasonal tariffs. A "snapback" clause would permit reimposition of the existing tariffs for the next twenty years. However, these can be reimposed only after five working days and after 48 hours of consultations, and only if prices were below 90% of those in 1987 and there had been no increase in acreage planted. Farm leaders agreed that this emergency protection was totally inadequate, as one or two days of low prices can permanently break a market. Wineries lost all provincial protection. They might be able to survive by importing grapes and lowering costs by breaking their union contracts, but grape growers face ruin.

The Canadian Wheat Board has come under attack. The two-price system for wheat, with higher prices in the domestic market, has been effectively abolished; this will cost grain growers an estimated $200 million. Furthermore, the Board has been stripped of the power to issue import licences for wheat, oats and barley as soon as support levels for these products are equivalent in both countries.

The agreement also removes the subsidies under the *Western Grain Transportation Act* for all agricultural products going to the United States through British Columbia ports. Millfeeds, canola meal and corn-distilled byproducts have had a $30 per tonne subsidized freight rate under this act, which replaced the Crow Rate agreement. While this might not seem that important, the National Farmers Union has pointed out that this is the first time that the

Canadian government has accepted the definition of a transportation subsidy in Canada as an export subsidy. This action opens up the entire transportation support program to U.S. countervailing actions and actions under the GATT. Farmers have never considered the Crow Rate to be an export subsidy. As a result, the agricultural industry has announced that it will have to look at other transportation routes into the United States. The United Grain Growers has suggested trucking to the United States and shipping 50-car lots on U.S. railroads. This actually costs less than shipping on Canadian railroads through British Columbia ports. In addition, the Western Canada Wheat Growers' Association has been pushing for the right to ship grains down the Mississippi River and out through the Gulf ports. This would have a devastating effect on the Canadian transportation system, and in particular on British Columbia.

The import quotas for poultry and eggs were slightly increased, mainly to try to help Canadian food processors who have to face increased competition from U.S. food processors. Nevertheless, the precedent was set for further reductions in the supply management powers of marketing boards in future rounds of negotiations.

The two countries have agreed to "harmonize" and "make equivalent" all standards in the following areas: animal and plant health, the food processing industry, veterinary drugs and feeds, pesticides, food and beverage additives and contaminants, and packaging and labelling. Many Canadians fear that because of the gross imbalance in power between the two countries, the binational working groups will tend to adopt U.S. standards. With the pro-business changes in regulations by the Reagan administration, Canadian standards are now generally higher. Furthermore, once these standards are harmonized, they can only be changed by mutual agreement. If the free trade agreement is implemented, this would represent an enormous surrender of sovereignty by the Mulroney government.

The only real benefit to Canadian farmers appears to be the mutual exemption from restrictions for beef and veal under meat import laws. However, meatpackers will still be subject to countervailing actions if they have received government subsidies. Almost all of the meatpacking plants in western Canada have received substantial capital and other grants to expand capacity, often for the express purpose of expanding exports to the United States. When the next recession hits, and the U.S. market becomes tighter, Canada can expect protectionist actions in this area.

Hogs and pork are not covered in the meat import laws, and they are specifically excluded from the agreement. In 1985 the U.S.

Department of Commerce imposed a duty of US4.4¢ a pound on all imports of live swine from Canada, concluding that hog producers in Canada benefit from government subsidies. The Canadian negotiators were unable to get that decision reversed. Canadian hog producers, who have been tied up for years in cases before the U.S. Tariff Commission, expressed disappointment that the dispute-settling mechanism in the agreement was too weak to prevent further U.S. actions.

The Mulroney government insisted that the free trade agreement would not adversely affect the Canadian tradition of using marketing boards to support farmers. Article 710 in the free trade agreement states that both parties retain their rights and obligations under GATT Article XI, which permits the imposition of import quotas on agricultural products where there are government-supported supply management programs. However, the chapter on agriculture (Article 703) also pledges both governments to "work together to improve access to each other's markets through the elimination or reduction of import barriers." The U.S. government has always insisted that supply management marketing boards are "import barriers." Furthermore, at the GATT round of negotiations in Geneva, the Mulroney government did not ask for the protection of supply management marketing boards. Indeed, the Canadian delegation was openly supporting the position of the Reagan administration that Article XI should be *removed* from the GATT. Clearly, there is a contradiction between what the Mulroney government is saying on the free trade agreement and its negotiating position at the GATT.

Farm leaders at first expressed hope that over the next seven years the two countries could work out a new set of common trade rules through the designated negotiations. However, that depends on good will on both sides of the border. Just two weeks after the free trade agreement was released, it was announced that the United States had offered millions of tonnes of subsidized wheat, oilseeds and milk to the traditional Canadian markets in the Soviet Union, China and India. Yet according to the free trade agreement (Article 701), the two countries pledged to "take into account the export interests of the other Party in the use of any export subsidy on any agricultural good exported to third countries, recognizing that such subsidies may have prejudicial effects on the export interests of the other Party." The National Farmers Union, the New Democratic Party and the Liberal Party denounced this action as a breach of the free trade agreement and an act of bad faith on the part of the Reagan administration.

The Food and Beverage Industry and Free Trade

In Canada the food and beverage industry is the most important manufacturing industry in terms of both employment and value added to manufacturing production. While the bulk of manufacturing is concentrated in Central Canada, the food and beverage industry is more evenly distributed across Canada, roughly following population patterns, and therefore is important to regional development and regional employment. The proposal for free trade with the United States has caused considerable concern within this industry. In 1985 Claude Lenoie of Agriculture Canada compared the industries in Canada and the United States and found that:

• Canada has more manufacturing plants than the United States for the size of the population;
• Average sales per plant in the United States were almost three times as great as in Canada;
• All of the industries in Canada were already more oligopolistic than those in the United States;
• Foreign ownership and control was five times as high in Canada as in the United States;
• On average, labour productivity in Canada was only 69% of that in the United States; and
• U.S. firms in Canada have an advantage over Canadian firms because of overflow advertising.

The most vulnerable Canadian industries have been identified in several studies. Lenoie singled out bakeries, breweries, confectionary manufacturers, poultry processors, soft drink manufacturers, biscuit manufacturers and wineries. James G. Frank's 1977 study for the Conference Board of Canada included dairy products and slaughtering and meat processing plants. John Baldwin and Paul K. Gorecki's studies for the Economic Council of Canada in 1983 added miscellaneous food processors and distilleries. Richard G. Harris and David Cox, in their simulation model prepared for the Ontario Economic Council, concluded that a comprehensive bilateral free trade agreement would improve output and labour productivity for the food and beverage industry but that employment would decline.

The largest and most influential industry organization in this sector is the Grocery Products Manufacturers of Canada. In 1985 and 1986 this organization established a task force to conduct an opinion survey of their members. They covered 150 corporations, representing the vast majority of grocery products manufacturers in Canada. The survey identified three specific impediments to the international competitiveness of their industry: higher costs for farm products; higher labour costs in Canada; and the fear that the Canadian dollar would rise towards parity with the U.S. dollar. The detailed survey revealed that most of the individual companies had common expectations of the effects of free trade with the United States. No industrial sector expected free trade to lead to plant expansion. Almost all reported that they would put future investment "on hold"; there likely would be dis-investment in Canada and future investment in the United States.

There was general agreement that social benefits were higher in Canada, wages were as high as or higher than in the United States, and fringe benefits were consistently higher. Under free trade, most industries expect a net loss of jobs. All industries except coffee and tea wanted the Canadian dollar fixed at between 70 and 75 cents American. Industries which depend on purchasing farm products from marketing boards feared being put at a decided disadvantage in relation to competitors in the United States.

The second most important industrial group is the Canadian Food Processors Association, representing 87 firms which process horticultural crops. In 1986, the sales of these firms, which employed 27,000 Canadian workers, were $4 billion. However, they export only 6% of their total output. In that year they also conducted an extensive survey of their members on trade options and the expected effects of a Canada/U.S. free trade agreement on their operations. Significantly, 55% of the 78 firms which participated in the survey concluded that the net impact would be a loss of jobs; they were the larger firms, representing 70% of the industry's employment. Only 15% supported a free trade agreement with the United States.

Their major conclusions were: the present exchange rate (US$.75) "must be maintained"; under a free trade agreement, U.S. plants would likely pull back south of the border; for Canadians to compete, it would be necessary to have harmonized regulations in all areas; the cost advantages that are associated with the more favourable U.S. climate must be offset in any free trade agreement; and most likely, further industry expansion would "favour U.S. locations." The disadvantages to Canadian growers and processors were identified as the shorter Canadian growing season, lower Canadian population densities, greater distances over which raw materials and finished products must be transported, and higher construction and energy costs.

Finally, in May 1986, *Food in Canada* conducted an extensive study of manufacturers on the impact of a free trade agreement with the United States. Their findings were very similar. Canadian manufacturers would be at a distinct disadvantage if they were forced to continue buying from Canadian marketing boards while their U.S. competitors could buy farm products from wherever they were cheapest. Competition would be difficult because Canadian labour costs were considerably higher than those in the United States. The industries also reported that the tax burden was higher in Canada than in the United States. They all agreed there was a need for harmonization of packaging, product standards, ingredients, labelling, etc. The foreign exchange issue was identified as the key one: the concensus was that the Canadian dollar should be pegged at around US$.71. If there was to be free trade with the United States, existing interprovincial trade barriers had to be dismantled. Finally, the industries surveyed stated that they much preferred individual sectoral negotiations over a comprehensive free trade agreement.

It seems clear, then, that if the comprehensive bilateral free trade agreement with the United States is implemented, a major restructuring would occur in the food and beverage industry. Many smaller regional plants would be closed. In view of the findings of the industry itself, the Economic Council of Canada release of August 1987 supporting a comprehensive free trade agreement appears to be merely a propaganda piece. This is the report regularly cited by Brian Mulroney as predicting an increase of 350,000 jobs as a result of free trade. The ECC's Candide computer simulation model projected these gains only under ideal circumstances. Furthermore, the report also concluded that in the manufacturing industry as a whole, 69.3% of all plants were "suboptimal" and would probably be shut down in the long run; these plants represent 20% of all manufacturing in Canada. The rationalization process brought on by free trade would achieve only a 3.81% increase in efficiency. Furthermore, the free trade scenario would leave Canada with a much more monopolized manufacturing sector and a much higher degree of plant concentration in Central Canada.

The agreement announced in October 1987 projects the removal of all tariffs on food products entering Canada from the United States. Many manufacturers are concerned because their U.S. competitors have access to cheaper farm and food inputs and relatively low cost non-union labour. A brief survey of U.S. branch plants by *The Financial Post* in mid-October reported that most export very little into their parent company's home market. Many are specifically forbidden to do so. They all expressed concern that under the agreement U.S. processed foods could enter Canada duty free, but they would be forced to continue to purchase their farm products from Canadian farmers, where prices were higher. A spokesman for Proctor & Gamble noted that the key to success was changeover time, running your plant more hours per day. "It's harder up here to do that because the plants have been geared to supply the Canadian markets with all product sizes."

In sum, it is not surprising that the proposal for a comprehensive bilateral free trade agreement has been strongly opposed by so many farm organizations. There is very little potential gain for most of them, and there is much they can lose. It is not surprising that the food and beverage industry is concerned about the possible outcome of an agreement. The traditional Canadian policy of provincial protection and support for agriculture and for a local food and beverage industry made good common sense. They were specifically designed to provide local employment. Not everyone can live in the Golden Horseshoe area. Many of us who live in the hinterland areas of Canada don't want to live in already overcrowded Central Canada. Unfortunately for us, free trade and free market ideology now dominate in the corridors of power.

CHAPTER 16

Canadian Culture and
The Mass Media

From the beginning of the public debate over a free trade agreement with the United States, the position of the Mulroney government on culture and the mass media has been contradictory. On the one hand, the prime minister and Minister of External Affairs Joe Clark have stated on numerous occasions that "our national sovereignty, our independence and our cultural integrity are not at issue in these negotiations." These are the "cards that will never be disposed of or touched." They are "the essence of Canada." However, the Mulroney government also announced that the "cultural industries" were to be included in the talks. Indeed, in 1985 they created a Sectoral Advisory Group on International Trade on the arts and entertainment industries, chaired by Marie-Josée Raymond.

Why has there been so much concern over this development? To an astonishing degree, Canada is a culturally occupied country. While everyone acknowledges that Canada is a rich, advanced industrialized country, our cultural industries and our mass communications resemble those of a colony. Yet the culture industries employ over 4% of the labour force, more than all employees of the federal government, including the crown corporations. Their revenues totalled around $13 billion in 1986, around 66% of which goes directly to wages and salaries. Attendance at museums, galleries, libraries, theatres and live performances is growing rapidly. But for most individual artists, life always borders on the poverty line. For example, around three-quarters of the members of the Alliance of Canadian Cinema Television and Radio Artists (ACTRA) earn less than $5000 per year in professional income.

Given the limited control Canada has over culture and mass communications, it is not surprising that those people directly involved in the area are greatly concerned about the impact over the long run of a comprehensive bilateral free trade agreement with the United States. How much more can we lose? The major organizations representing the cultural industries in Canada have come out strongly against any free trade agreement which makes any further concessions to the United States. Many of them have come out squarely against any free trade agreement whatsoever. The most active groups in opposition include the Writers' Union, the Artists' Union, various Arts Councils, ACTRA, and the very broad coalition, the Canadian Conference of the Arts.

As Rick Salutin, Martin Katz and others have pointed out, the American view of culture is a narrow economic concept. Our culture is not confined to institutions and artistic productions; it encompasses the way we live and do things—it is what makes us different from other countries, particularly the United States. It includes co-operatives, a government-funded university system, the CBC, the National Film Board, crown corporations, hockey, medicare, marketing boards, strict controls on firearms, bilingualism, multiculturalism, a federal banking system, the RCMP, the monarchy, parliamentary government, universal social programs, the absence of capital punishment, a low murder rate, safer cities, regional development programs, and unemployment insurance for fishermen—these are among the things that make our culture unique on this continent.

It is the American definition of culture which is embodied in the free trade agreement. That is, culture is an enterprise which is capable of making money, by means of "cultural industries," including publications, films, videos, music recordings, and radio and television broadcasting. Article 2005 [1] says that these industries, with a couple of exceptions, are "exempt from the provisions of this Agreement." However, what immediately follows is a "notwithstanding clause" which says that the United States may impose a retaliatory duty against any subsidy to a cultural industry which prejudices an American industry. As Rick Salutin has pointed out, it is highly unlikely that any U.S. interests will take action when a Canadian government subsidizes the ballet, the opera or the symphony. From an American point of view, they really aren't part of the Canadian culture market. Retaliation will come if Canadian governments infringe on American profit and control in the areas of popular culture, where the money is to be made. And while a working group has the task of defining a "legitimate subsidy" over the next seven years, the free trade agreement has already concluded that a government subsidy to a culture industry which costs U.S. interests some money is an "unjust subsidy."

The Status of the Culture Industries in Canada

The contrast between Canada and the small states in Europe is dramatic. Those states adjacent to larger ones with the same language (e.g., Ireland, Belgium, Luxembourg, Switzerland and Austria) pursue two basic policy approaches: regulation and subsidy. For example, in the publication area, overflow advertising is prohibited. National control of the distribution of periodicals is protected, with priority required for national publications. All states use quotas, duties and other restrictions on foreign imports. Most have rather extensive requirements for local ownership and control. Subsidies include special postal rates, tax concessions, and regulation of advertising. Indirect subsidies include free transporation, telephone and telegraph services. And there are numerous direct public subsidies through a variety of agencies like the Canada Council.

Even the major countries are concerned about maintaining their cultural identity in the face of the onslaught of American cultural imperialism. For example, France limits foreign investment in publishing to 20% of a joint venture, locally controlled. Film distribution is controlled by a licensing system. Television stations may buy products only from French distributors. France has major subsidies for the film industry. France, Britain, West Germany and Italy have quotas limiting foreign exposure. As the Canadian Conference of the Arts points out, "other countries regulate foreign content; Canada regulates domestic content—and not particularly well." The sorry state of the mass media and culture is summarized below.

Daily Newspaper Publishing. There is a high degree of corporate concentration in the newspaper field in Canada, with two chains dominating, Southam and Thomson. Very few cities have more than one local newspaper. Without competition, profits have been very high. Between 1945 and 1975, advertising space went from 50% to 65% of content. In this situation, publishers prefer to buy their editorial content than produce it themselves. They rely heavily on U.S. sources for columns, editorials and "boilerplate" to fill their newspapers.

However, the major problem we face as Canadians is the fact that our daily newspapers rely almost totally on foreign sources for international news. One recent survey concluded that 95% came from international wire services and from the major U.S. newspapers. The Canadian Press distributes Canadian-produced news articles to members, mainly domestic stories. But the CP has traditionally had only five overseas correspondents; their New York office exists mainly to lift copy from the foreign news services.

The Radio Industry. The radio industry in Canada is domestically owned; this is a requirement under the *Broadcasting Act*. Over the years there has been a proliferation of private AM and FM stations, the development of chains, and a decline in the importance of the Canadian Broadcasting Corporation. This has been a deliberate policy of the federal government, effected through its licensing agency, the Canadian Radio-television and Telecommunications Commission (CRTC).

As several Royal Commissions have demonstrated, radio stations are very profitable. The main content is very inexpensive talk, playing the top forty tunes, and reading the news that comes over the wire services. Again, international news comes primarily from U.S. sources. There is very little news reporting or serious programming. Furthermore, in recent years Canadian private radio has been expanding its reliance on special programs imported from the United States.

Television. The central characteristic of the television industry over the past twenty years is the relative decline of public broadcasting, which has been limited to the Canadian Broadcasting Corporation. Aside from the rise of private television, the most significant change has been the introduction of cable television, which exists almost exclusively to show American programming. Satellite broadcasting also has expanded U.S. influence.

In 1958 the Diefenbaker government introduced private television, but the major change came in 1968, when the Pearson government cut back on regulations on Canadian content and forced the CBC to rely on private advertising. Between 1968 and 1983, cable television was expanded to cover 55% of all households. By 1983, 47% of all English-language programs on television were actually provided by American stations.

While news, current affairs and informational programs are primarily Canadian, television relies almost completely on American sources for international news. By 1980, 88% of all entertainment on English-language television was American, and 98% of all drama was foreign, primarily American. We see very few programs from Great Britain or Ireland. We see almost none from New Zealand or Australia. Occasionally we see a program from a third world country, but almost always it is on the American Public Broadcasting Service! Canadian television is American television.

Despite Canadian content rules set forth by the CRTC, the percentage of prime-time television viewing provided by Canadians has been steadily declining. Around one-half of all advertising on Canadian television is by large U.S. corporations. Canadian governments, whether Conservative or Liberal, have done little to support Canadian programming. Whereas the independent European and American production industries are able to recover 75% to 90% of their costs within their own country because of regulations and subsidies, similar Canadian producers can count on getting back only around 30% of their investment from the Canadian market. For example, a single episode of the popular CBC-TV program *Seeing Things* costs around $500,000 to make. In contrast, a single episode of the American program *Remington Steele* costs about $1 million, has a much greater market, and Canadian television can buy it for only $40,000.

Periodical Publishing. There is a marked contrast between the sales of magazines in Canada by subscription and on the newsstand. Canadian magazines have around 80% of the subscription market in Canada. The industry is highly concentrated. Maclean-Hunter Publications have close to 40% of all revenues from general consumer magazines and close to 60% for trade or business publications.

In contrast, U.S. publications have around 75% of all newsstand sales in Canada. The vast majority of all Canadian publishers are denied access to newsstands in Canada. Certainly one of the major reasons for this bizarre situation is the fact that the two largest distributors of magazines in Canada are owned by big American publishers and insist on carrying and displaying their line of publications, no matter how few they sell.

Book Publishing. The overwhelming majority of book publishers in Canada are Canadian—173 out of 202 in 1983. However, only about 25% of the revenues from book sales accrue to titles published in Canada. The remaining 75% is accounted for by imports. Foreign-owned firms specialize in the text book market, which they dominate; in 1985 they had 64% of the elementary and high school market. In 1980, while they had 70% of the English-language book market, they produced only 15% of the titles in Canada, and only 3% of all new books in the area of Canadian literature.

Most bookstores have a "Canadiana" section. This is most useful for readers who would otherwise have a very difficult time finding a Canadian book in the sea of American imports. But it is also an example of the persistence of colonialism in Canada in the area of culture and communications. Would an American bookstore lump its domestic titles together in an "Americana" section?

The Recording Industry. According to Statistics Canada, in 1983 there were 93 sound recording companies in the country. Ten were foreign-owned, yet they accounted for over 80% of sales.

Most tapes and records that are manufactured in Canada originate from imported master tapes. The foreign-owned companies have their own distribution subsidiaries in Canada, and they are quite profitable. On the other hand, the Canadian companies regularly show a loss. The most lucrative sales market is in popular rock music, with over 60% of the total; here the foreign companies clearly dominate.

Canadian companies in this field point out that the government permits "dumping" of the master tapes in Canada. When they come into Canada, they are assigned the cost value of a blank tape, around $25; the value of their performance is not included. Producing a master tape in Canada can cost from $10,000 to $100,000.

The Film and Video Industry. Around 85% of the film and video production and distribution firms in Canada are locally owned. However, they have only 27% of the market; the other 73% is controlled by the twenty foreign-owned firms. The seven largest American film corporations account for around 90% of all the revenues produced by theatre films in Canada. The most powerful firm is Gulf and Western, which controls Paramount, which in turn owns Famous Players theatres. The other major chain of theatres is Cineplex Odeon, now owned by a Canadian consortium headed by Garth Drabinsky of Toronto (52%) and the giant U.S. conglomerate MCA Inc. (48%).

Films are also distributed through the regular television market, pay TV and videos. Statistics Canada reports that in 1982, 42% of new films in Canada were from the United States, 27% from France, with several other European countries and Australia producing more films than Canada. A major concern in Canada is the fact that the foreign-owned distribution firms invest less than 1% of their earnings from Canadian sales in the Canadian film industry. The average American film costs $14 million to make but has a huge potential market. The average Canadian film costs around $4 million but can't even count on having a shot at the Canadian market. Lewis Selznick, pioneer Hollywood producer, put it this way: "If Canadian stories are worth making into films—companies will be sent into Canada to make them."

In response to the strong opposition to a bilateral free trade agreement by most of the Canadian institutions in the cultural area, Brian Mulroney appointed a "blue ribbon" group of 25 people to advise him on this matter. They were primarily businessmen in the area of culture and communications. There were representatives from Baton Broadcasting Corporation, Telemedia Corporation, TVA Television Network Ltd., Maclean Hunter Ltd., Global TV and Fitzhenry and Whiteside. They met with several cabinet ministers in late November 1986. Speaking for the group, *Toronto Life* publisher Peter Herrndorf said: "Our concern is getting access to our own market. Everyone is interested in expanding into the U.S., but only after we've repatriated our own culture."

U.S. Objectives Under Free Trade

As the negotiations under the "fast track" provisions of the 1984 U.S. *Trade and Tariff Act* were reaching a climax in late September 1987, it was revealed that one of the main areas of fundamental disagreement was cultural policy. This came as no surprise. The United States does have a cultural policy and enormously profitable and pervasive cultural industries. There is the U.S. Information Agency and the state-supported radio stations which broadcast the message of the "free world." On another level there are the American corporations in the cultural industries, which try to sell their products on a world-wide basis. American nationalism is a reality, and it leads to the official position that the nationalisms of other countries are simply barriers or hindrances to what Americans perceived to be "international culture," but which is probably best described as The American Way of Life. Therefore, in their view, national protections for cultural industries are unfair trade practices. It is difficult for Americans to understand the need of smaller countries to use state measures to protect their cultural heritages because the United States itself is almost completely immune to the impact of other cultures. For example, only 2% of television programming in the United States is foreign, and almost all of that is on the stations linked to the Public Broadcasting System.

Unfortunately, we border on the United States, and the majority of Canadians share the same language. Canada has traditionally been the first foreign market for expanding U.S. businesses. Their culture and communications industries have concentrated on the small barriers to trade that Canada has thrown up to try to protect what is

left of Canadian culture. They show far less concern about the major
barriers that exist in Europe because language differences make
penetration of these markets more difficult. The preoccupation with
Canada was reflected in the opinions expressed in a 1984 survey by
the Office of the U.S. Trade Representative. They revealed strong
opposition to Canadian government involvement in the film and
television industries.

The U.S. government has from the beginning argued that the culture industries should be included under a free trade agreement. They
are seen as part of the service industries, which the U.S. wants included under the GATT. While the United States presently runs a
$1.5 billion surplus in trade with Canada in this area, their nego-
tiators see expanded U.S. exports as a chance to cut back on the
overall positive trade balance that Canada presently enjoys.

Thus, in February 1986 Deputy Assistant U.S. Trade Representative William Merkin warned that they would "insist on Canadian
cultural industries not being protected from ordinary commerce in a
free-trade environment." The next month, Thomas Brewer of the
U.S. Department of Commerce argued that there was "no relationship between cultural sovereignty and ownership of cultural industries." He argued that Canada's newspapers, television and radio
were Canadian owned, yet more than 70% of their content was non-
Canadian.

A few other quotations will illustrate the difference in attitude
between the two countries:

> Is printing different from other manufacturing? There are a
> number of barriers that have nothing to do with culture but are
> largely economic barriers that have as their bottom line, the
> clear result of protecting specific industries. (Peter Murphy,
> Chief U.S. negotiator, January 14, 1987)

> All issues should be on the negotiating table. I'm prepared to
> have American culture on the table and have it damaged by
> Canadian influence after a free-trade negotiation. I hope
> Canada is prepared to run that risk, too. (Clayton Yeutter, U.S.
> Trade Representative, February 5, 1987)

> Canadians have nothing to fear because there is no link
> between sovereignty and culture. (U.S. Ambassador Thomas
> Niles, February 5, 1987)

I think that the sooner your culture and ours can blend, the better it is going to be for both our countries and both our peoples. The Japanese used to be very protective, but now McDonald's has gone over there. And the Japanese didn't even know what a hamburger was. It's coming, whether you like it or not. (U.S. Senator Spark Matsunaga, April 9, 1987)

In the United States the arts are supported by individual millionaires and their foundations. For example, one American gave the New York City Opera $5 million to ensure production of his favourite opera. Each of the top twenty U.S. foundations gives more to the arts in one year than all of the Canadian foundations combined. The cultural industries in Canada simply can't raise that kind of private corporate support. Following the European precedent, Canada provides assistance to the arts and to our important cultural and communications industries through subsidies and regulations. All of these are under attack from the U.S. government and private interests. Many of our meagre policies in this area have been placed on various American lists as "unfair subsidies" or "unfair trading practices" which ought to be removed in any free trade agreement. The most commonly cited are as follows:

• Higher postal rates for imported magazines;
• Only 5% of advertisements in imported magazines can be specifically for the Canadian market;
• Advertisements are tax deductible in Canada only if they are carried by print and broadcast media with 80% Canadian content;
• Requirements that pay-TV devote 45% of their revenues to Canadian material;
• Requirements that cable TV simultaneously broadcast U.S. programs on Canadian channels;
• Provincial purchasing preferences for educational textbooks;
• Restrictions on foreign ownership of broadcast and cable television;
• The 30% Canadian content requirements on television and radio;
• Direct Canadian subsidy of film production through the National Film Board, Telefilm Canada, the CBC and provincial programs;
• Canadian cable television stations stealing U.S. broadcast signals without paying royalties;
• Personnel restrictions, both by governments and trade unions,

which require the use of Canadian performing artists and technicians when working in Canada.

While Brian Mulroney insisted that Canadian culture was not on the negotiating table, when the summaries of the agreement were released in early October 1987 it became clear that this was just another case of the prime minister's blarney. When the final text was released on December 11, it was found that the Canadian negotiators had eliminated tariffs on all printed material from the United States and guaranteed to provide copyright protection for satellite retransmissions.

But it was the statement of general principles that really upset people who work in the cultural area. As it was stated in the published background briefing paper that U.S. negotiators prepared for high-level government personnel, they wanted "to assure that Canadian cultural policies do not constitute a discriminatory and unnecessary barrier to U.S. trade." The power of the Canadian government to introduce new government-supported policies would seem to be limited. And while the U.S. team did not specifically get all that it wanted (the list above), the negotiators reported that "Canada has agreed that cultural measures it takes will not impair the benefits the United States would otherwise expect from the provisions of the agreement." Finally, the U.S. negotiators noted that "we retained the ability to take trade remedy actions on these issues," the famous "notwithstanding" clause.

Confronting Cultural Imperialism

Several incidents over the past few years revealed the incredible arrogance of the U.S. government and corporations in the area of culture. We have had free trade in the film industry in Canada for 60 years. What has this produced? Canadian films account for less than 3% of theatre time. The major U.S. corporations take $400 million a year from Canadian theatre-goers and spend virtually nothing on the film industry in Canada. Indeed, Canada is formally identified as a region of the United States. As Joyce Nelson points out, this is the kind of "level playing field" U.S. business has in mind.

In 1983 the Parti Quebecois government introduced legislation that would have brought three changes to the film industry: film distribution companies in Quebec would have to be 80% Canadian-owned; non-French language films could show in the province only for 60 days without producing locally dubbed French copies; and film distributors in Quebec would have to devote 10% of revenues for local film production. The Motion Picture Association of America (MPAA) ran to Washington and the pressure began. The State Department and U.S. Ambassador Paul Robinson attacked the legislation. The Canadian branch of the MPAA denounced Quebec for following the "Mozambican model." The bill passed in 1983, but the PQ government delayed its implementation. In the meantime, hearings were held throughout the province, where opinion was unanimous that the bill did not go far enough. Just before the 1985 provincial election, the U.S. State Department told PQ Minister of Culture Gerald Godin that the U.S. film industry was prepared to pull all U.S. films out of Quebec theatres. The Liberals won the election, and after further direct intervention by the State Department and Ronald Reagan, the new government under Robert Bourassa allowed the legislation to die.

A second example arose when Gulf & Western bought the major book publishing firm Prentice-Hall. Their subsidiary, Prentice-Hall Canada Ltd., is the largest single provider of school textbooks in the country. Even though the Mulroney government had scrapped the Foreign Investment Review Act, there were pressures to increase the percentage of Canadian textbooks used in our schools. To the surprise of many, Minister of Communications Marcel Masse announced that the federal government was reviewing the takeover and its implications in Canada. U.S. diplomatic and business pressure quickly mounted. Gulf & Western told the media that if the Mulroney government blocked the takeover, it would carry out a "scorched-earth policy in Canada." In March 1986, just before the prime minister went to Washington to see President Reagan, the Canadian federal government announced that it would not block the takeover. They did not even demand that shares of the Canadian branch plant be open to purchase by Canadians. Nor did they require any performance guarantees. It was another complete surrender.

Most recently there is the case of the film licensing bill, announced in February 1987 by Minister of Communications Flora MacDonald. The proposed legislation was to prevent foreign film corporations in Canada from controlling distribution rights to movies and videos which they had not entirely financed or for which they did not own world rights. This would allow Canadian film distributors the right to buy non-Hollywood produced foreign films for distribution in Canada. In 1986 the revenues in Canada from movies shown in theatres and on television amounted $1.2 billion, 90% of which went to U.S. corporations. The change in policy would permit Canadian film distributors the possibility of gaining up to 20% of these revenues. Many in the Canadian industry complained that the bill did not go far enough. As one spokesman for the Canadian industry pointed out, "we're the only country in the world where distributors have to compete against the United States for their own market."

The American reaction was predictable. Jack Valenti and the MPAA began a high-pressure campaign against the legislation. He even discussed the bill with Ronald Reagan, a past president of the U.S. Screen Actors Guild. Reagan told Brian Mulroney that he did not like the legislation during their Ottawa summit in 1987. In late April a group of U.S. Congressmen sent a letter to the prime minister strongly opposing the film legislation. In May 1987 a group of U.S. Senators, led by California Democrat Alan Cranston, introduced a resolution in the U.S. Senate which condemned the proposed legislation as "discriminatory" and a "disastrous step" and promised to block ratification of the free trade agreement if it were passed. How did the Mulroney government react? The bill was held back for "more detailed consideration and redrafting." In addition, the proposed new *Broadcasting Act*, which would have extended public broadcasting in Canada, was also put on hold. The U.S. briefing paper published on October 9, 1987, stated that the Canadian negotiators "have also promised to solve Jack Valenti's problem on film distribution within the next two weeks."

The American view that culture is just another economic activity has its supporters in Canada. For example, Steven Globerman and Aidan Vining, economists at Simon Fraser University, argue that "cultural industries are generally characterized by the same properties as other industries studied by economists. Namely, under freer trade, skills and talents will likely be redistributed from one activity to another, but the overall sector will, if anything, expand." They believe that "given sufficiently lower prices, *The Globe and Mail* could displace *The New York Times* in certain markets."

Michael Walker, chief economist and propagandist for the Fraser Institute, argues that the Canadian governments should abolish all the subsidies and protections given to the arts. They should pay their own way. "If that means the culture of Rambo and rock music, so be it. That is the consumer's choice." Walter E. Block, also of the Fraser Institute, argues that "apart from a few hundred Canadian writers, painters, and musicians in this country who make it on their own without subsidies from government, there are no artists in this country." The rest, he states, "are only welfare recipients."

This "free market" ideology may be what the Americans want, but it is entirely foreign to the Canadian (or European) experience. As CBC President Pierre Juneau has pointed out, "freedom of choice" in the television area means choice among a narrow range of commercially successful American programs. "Freedom of choice" for most Canadians is not even being able to see Canadian films which win international prizes at the Cannes Film Festival! Mavor Moore, while not an economist, points out that while we are constantly being polled to find out what we want, at the same time advertisers are simultaneously and relentlessly badgering us to change our wants. "All the resources of applied psychology are employed to persuade people to believe they are choosing freely what in fact they can hardly escape." All this feeds the illusion that when we choose American cop shows and mindless situation comedies, this is what we really want. This is free choice—supplied almost entirely by the Americans.

In December 1986 there was a conference in Montreal on the impact of new technology on film and television. John Eger, former vice-president of CBS and adviser to President Nixon, took the position that free market forces will determine the free flow of cultural products. U.S. programs and films dominate because "they are enjoyed." Jack Petrik, vice-president of Turner Broadcasting, argued for "free cultural trade," which meant the expansion of U.S. programming everywhere. Like Eger, he denied that this had any negative impact on other countries. Governments should stay out of this business.

In contrast, Pierre Juneau argued that in reality public support in this area *increases* choice. "Globalization" means the imposition of a "sterile U.S. force which undermines the rich potential of regional cultural forces." In this he was supported by Kim Williams of the Australian Film Commission. "There is no free exchange," he argued. "It is all one way. The term 'international' as used means American." Hans Geert Falkenberg, former head of programming for the West German WDR public TV network, argued that "American television gives foreign countries a totally distorted view of America on one hand, while alienating them from their own cultural sovereignty on the other."

As Rick Salutin points out, Canadian culture is not a matter of particular industries. "All of them exist in a larger cultural context—the atmosphere in which we live, imagine, and express ourselves. The cultural air we breathe is being altered because of this deal." We are being asked to accept the cultural atmosphere of

Ronald Reagan's America—the marketplace of winners and losers. "In this end, free trade is *entirely* a question of culture," says Salutin, "because it is a matter of the kind of society we and our descendants will inhabit as a result of the deal." Margaret Atwood adds, "Do we really want a country? A level playing field, after all, is one from which all distinguishing features have been removed."

Free trade with the United States can only further undermine what little independent Canadian culture remains. But what can we do? Bernard Ostry, Chairman of TVOntario, has argued that Canada must band together with other countries to resist U.S. domination of culture and communications. Instead of merging ourselves even more with the United States, we should negotiate treaties with other countries which are also worried about American domination, such as Great Britain, France, West Germany, Australia, New Zealand and the Scandinavian countries. Only by a direct policy of diversification can we promote Canadian culture and at the same time allow Canadian citizens access to a diversity of other cultures.

PART III

Alternative Strategies
For a Free Canada

CHAPTER 17

Diversifying Trade

When U.S. industries and commodity groups began to increase their protective actions against Canadian imports, Canadian business leaders and politicians panicked. They saw a free trade agreement as the only means of obtaining secured access to their most important export market, the United States. The American market is the easiest market for exporters, and they were quite wiling to surrender considerable Canadian sovereignty to keep it. But to most other Canadians, the trade actions by the U.S. government in 1986 and 1987 merely illustrated the fact that Canada was *already too dependent* on trade with the United States. As we have seen, almost all countries have been diversifying their trade in the post-war period, reducing their dependence on a single or a few markets. Even the "banana republics" of Central America have been able to substantially reduce their trade dependence on the United States. Only Canada, Mexico and Cuba have become more dependent on their major trading partner, and it is widely agreed that this has considerably reduced their sovereignty and freedom of action. The obvious alternative to Fortress North America is a much greater effort by the Canadian government to foster the diversity of trade.

There is also a genuine fear by a great many Canadians that any bilateral free trade agreement with our much larger and more powerful neighbour would be just the first step towards further continental integration. Even Mitchell Sharp, former Liberal cabinet minister and a strong "continentalist," took this position in a widely cited article in *Policy Options* in June 1987. His concern was not the economic consequences of a bilateral free trade agreement with the United States, but the effect on Canadian independence:

It seems to me to be highly likely, if not inevitable, as a result of having decided to move towards integration of our economy with that of the United States, that our course would be set towards further integration, economic and cultural, and I don't see any practical way of reversing the process once started.

Eventually, Canada and the United States would establish a customs union, and since the primary threat to U.S. manufacturing comes from the newly industrialized countries, there would be pressure to set common tariffs and quotas. The threat, according to Sharp, is not to the existence of Canada as a formally independent state, but, he fears, a free trade agreement would "curtail to a substantial degree the freedom of action of the people of Canada, through their governments, to make decisions . . . " He quite rightly points out that once a comprehensive bilateral free trade agreement is approved, the next step must be negotiations on fixing foreign exchange rates.

A similar position is taken by Dr. Stuart L. Smith, chairman of the Science Council of Canada and formerly head of the Liberal Party of Ontario. He argues that under a free trade agreement Canada could well lose its will to be independent. This would be a step-by-step process,

a chain of events wherein we try to compensate for the lack of a globally competitive industrial structure by linking our economy even more closely to a more successful economy south of the border. With about five years between steps, one can easily envisage arguments for free trade, then customs union, fiscal harmonization, monetary union, free movement of labour, and finally, to obtain some voting control over our circumstances, a political union of some type.

Emphasizing the Multilateral Approach to Trade

Mitchell Sharp argues that Canadian trade policy since the end of World War II has stressed two principles. First, under the General Agreement on Tariffs and Trade (GATT) our policy was to oppose the formation of trading blocs like the European Economic Community, the European Free Trade Association, and bilateral agreements like those between Australia and New Zealand and the United States and Israel. These were inevitably discriminatory and preferential. The approach of the Canadian government was for general trade liberalization—not the formation of new trading blocs with their own external tariffs and non-tariff barriers.

Second, there was the commitment by the Canadian government to multilateralism, particularly through the emphasis on the GATT. Even the Commonwealth preference system was largely abandoned. One of the reasons for this policy was the belief that "Canada has little bargaining power in a one-on-one relationship with our superpower neighbour." Because of Canada's much weaker position, "the pressure within a preferential free trade agreement would be to harmonize our laws and regulations to the United States' pattern so as to remove complaints about unfair trading practices . . . " Sharp notes that the resolution of the softwood lumber conflict and the reversal of policy by the Federal Energy Regulatory Board on natural gas exports are examples of the pitfalls of depending on bilateral trade with the United States.

The dangers of one–on-one bargaining were seen during the last week of negotiations leading up to the Canada/U.S. free trade agreement of October 5, 1987. Giles Gerson, Washington reporter for *The Financial Post*, detailed the issues which were holding up final agreement. Canadian negotiators were still demanding a binding trade dispute settlement process to exempt Canada from U.S. trade legislation; given that from the very beginning this was the primary goal of the Mulroney government, they achieved very little. The second goal was exemption from the 1987 omnibus trade bill, which, in different forms, had passed both the U.S. House of Representatives and the Senate and was in the committee stage of reconciliation; this goal was not achieved. In addition, there were six other major issues outstanding: defining legitimate regional development subsidies, mutual tariff removal, foreign investment controls, financial services, cultural issues, Auto Pact duties, and trade in services. The United States negotiators achieved almost all their goals in these areas.

Why should Canada conduct bilateral negotiations to try to escape U.S. protectionist legislation and actions? We are certainly not the only country adversely affected. The proper approach would have been to take these questions to the GATT. If this route proved unsatisfactory, then the Canadian government should have taken the initiative and formed a political alliance with the other U.S. trading partners who are also adversely affected in order to exert joint pressure. This is the approach that Canada has followed in pursuit of more liberalized world trade in agricultural products. We badly need a new "Cairns Group" (fourteen countries which depend on agricultural exports) to deal with U.S. protectionist actions. Canada would be much more likely to gain favourable action in Washington as part of a strong alliance of U.S. trading partners.

The North-South Institute points out that the United States has been primarily interested in gaining trade liberalization through the GATT. In particular, the U.S. government has sought the expansion of the GATT to include trade in services, high technology and agriculture, and they have sought new codes on patent infringement and counterfeit issues. They turned to the bilateral approach only after 1982 when they felt that the GATT was unwilling to take up these issues. However, the new Uruguay round of GATT negotiations began in 1986. The North-South Institute argues that given this new opportunity, "great attention or priority to bilateral negotiations with Canada is unlikely in the U.S. unless the terms are made irresistibly attractive to American interests, thus almost certainly jeopardizing the Canadian position." There is also the fear, expressed by the Macdonald Royal Commission, that a new North American free trade zone might "jeopardize or undermine the stability of the GATT system," and in this case "it would be a steep price for Canadians to pay in order to secure improved access to the U.S. market."

The Science Council of Canada argues that the major threat to Canada and the United States is imports of standardized products from the newly industrialized countries, which combine low labour costs with new technology. Industrialized countries can compete in these areas only by the development of almost totally automated plants. Canada needs to expand and improve its resource sector and move into the areas of production and services in which we can take advantage of our more highly developed research, knowledge and human capital. In contemplating new exports, we cannot ignore the most rapidly expanding world market, the Pacific Rim, a market of three trillion dollars a year. The North-South Institute believes that a multilateral approach to trade offers Canada a much better future than being tied to a relatively declining U.S. economy.

The Council of Canadians (COC) has also urged Canadians to de-emphasize links with the United States and to make a serious effort to diversify trade. In addition to stressing the GATT, multilateral trade and trade diversification, the COC places greater emphasis on a new industrial policy for Canada. They are strongly opposed to the "free market" approach of the Macdonald Royal Commission and the Mulroney government. The American free market approach has never been appropriate to Canada because of our different history, our relatively small population, the enormous size of our country, our regional diversities, the colder climate and the major problems of transportation and communication.

Throughout 1986 and 1987 the federal Liberal Party, under the leadership of John Turner and its trade critic, Lloyd Axworthy, has been stressing the need for a multilateral approach to trade policy. In this they have had the support of Jean Chretien, who in June 1986 strongly opposed the free trade initiative. Chretien argued that the Mulroney government was "starting to link us so closely to the United States that we may lose our privilege of belonging to an independent country." But the task has been a difficult one for the Turner leadership in view of the fact that the Liberal Party has historically been the advocate of closer links to the United States. Turner himself has close ties to big business, the primary force supporting the free trade agreement. Within the party, there are strong supporters of a comprehensive bilateral treaty with the United States, led by former cabinet ministers Donald Macdonald and Donald Johnson.

The difficulties that Turner and Axworthy have had with Liberal Party activists was illustrated at two party conventions in 1986. In March, the Ontario convention was clearly divided on the issue, and only at the last minute, after most delegates had left, was a resolution passed which opposed comprehensive bilateral free trade with the United States, advocated dealing with protectionist questions through the GATT and supported global liberalization of trade. At a conference of western and northern Liberals held in Edmonton in July 1987, delegates endorsed a statement outlining the dangers posed by bilateral free trade to Canada's social programs and cultural and economic sovereignty. But the convention was clearly divided, and the anti-free trade vote came only after a powerful speech by Mel Hurtig, a prominent Liberal and chairman of the Council of Canadians.

The position of the federal caucus of the Liberal Party was established in a policy paper prepared by Lloyd Axworthy and Professor James de Wilde of the University of Western Ontario in November 1986. It recognizes Canada's dependence on trade with the United States and argues for a "surprise-free environment" of trust and resolution of disputes. But at the same time it rejects using a comprehensive bilateral free trade agreement as a vehicle for restructuring the Canadian economy. Furthermore, the Liberals argue that a free trade agreement poses a risk to Canada's political and economic independence. The preoccupation with U.S. trade undermines efforts to gain access to those areas of the world where trade is expanding, particularly around the Pacific Rim. Canada should be actively seeking leverage to counter our trade dependence by expanding trading coalitions with other middle powers and Third World countries to balance off the "goliaths."

In addition, the Liberals argue that Canada should be relying primarily on the GATT in dealing with the problem of non-tariff barriers to trade. In this, we need the support of other middle-sized trading partners. The Liberals say that Canada should take the lead in proposing a new Bretton Woods agreement to stabilize the foreign exchange problem, preferably along the lines proposed by the Commonwealth Study Group. In the special debate in Parliament on June 16, 1987, and then in the response to the agreement revealed in October, Turner has taken a strong position against a comprehensive free trade agreement with the United States and has stressed the need for multilateral trade and a Canadian industrial strategy.

The general opinion of orthodox economists is that Canada is really not in a position to compete internationally. Their strong support for a bilateral free trade agreement with the United States is based on a fundamental belief that we need a drastic restructuring of Canadian industry. Before we can compete internationally, we need to develop larger, more powerful corporations, what they commonly call "world class" enterprises. Under a free trade agreement, the increased competition from the larger U.S. firms and plants will force this adjustment. Indeed, as we have seen, the projection of the Candide econometric model of the Economic Council of Canada, regularly cited by Brian Mulroney and his colleagues as justification for the free trade agreement, concludes that of the 34,578 manufacturing plants in Canada, no fewer than 23,963 are "suboptimal," unable to compete with the larger American firms, and would be eventual casualties in the comprehensive free trade agreement. These are primarily the smaller manufacturing plants located in the hinterland regions. They account for 19.7% of all Canadian manufacturing production.

This prevailing view has been challenged by Andrew Sharpe, an economist with the Canada Department of Finance, in two articles that appeared in the *Canadian Business Review*. Sharpe looked at a number of studies which assessed the international competitiveness of Canadian business. The studies cited were by Statistics Canada, the Organization for Economic Co-operation and Development, the International Monetary Fund, the U.S. Bureau of Labor Statistics and the European Management Forum. Sharpe concluded that in general Canada has done quite well over the period from 1973 to

1984 compared to the other major advanced industrial countries (the Group Seven).

One area of Canadian improvement has been in unit labour costs in manufacturing, which have decreased in relation to costs in other countries. Among the Group Seven countries, over the 1970-84 period, unit labour costs in Canada were second lowest, with only the United States doing better. While Canada had the lowest increase in labour productivity, this was offset by the relative decline in the hourly rate of compensation. Canada has also done well in other costs areas. In relative export prices for manufacturing over the same period, both the IMF and the OECD conclude that of the Group Seven, Canada had the lowest price increases. An assessment of how well Canada has maintained its share of world trade depends on the base years selected. If we begin with the onset of the major economic crisis in 1973, between this date and 1984 Canada's share of world trade rose slightly, from 5% to 5.1%. Furthermore, during that same period of time, the world share of trade for all the other industrialized countries except Japan fell.

In the area of exports of manufactured goods, over the 1982-4 period, Canada's exports increased by 0.6% while U.S. exports dropped 17.1%, France's by 4.9% and the United Kingdom's by 2.2%. West Germany (+1.2%), Italy (+3.1%), and Japan (+6.2%) did better than Canada. Between 1968 and 1985, Canada's trade balance has been positive in all years except 1975. In the five-year period 1980-4, our manufacturing trade deficit actually decreased. Furthermore, our manufacturing industries have strengthened. Our implicit self-sufficiency ratio (Canadian production to consumption) has improved in eleven industries and declined in nine; on average, this ratio improved significantly in the 1982-4 period.

In 1984 the European Management Forum ranked Canada seventh out of 28 countries in terms of competitiveness. This is a business organization with its own set of values. For example, they rated Canada low in the area of state interference in the economy. But it indicates that international business does not view Canada as a weak economy. Sharpe's conclusion is that "over the past several years, Canada's trade performance has improved greatly, and a significant part of the amerlioration can be attributed to increased competitiveness." The gloom and doom picture painted by orthodox economists and others on the political right is less than convincing.

However, it should be noted that there are some serious difficulties with relying on the GATT as the central policy alternative to bilateral free trade with the United States. As Jim Turk reminded us in his contribution at GATT-Fly's Ecumenical Conference on Free Trade, Self-Reliance and Economic Justice in 1987, "multilateral and bilateral free trade are part of the same package. Senior American officials have repeatedly made clear that the United States wants a bilateral agreement with Canada to help bring about multilateral trade through the GATT." The goals of the U.S. government in the GATT talks include elimination of government agricultural subsidies, such as those used in Canada; free trade in all services, and in particular the cultural industries; the elimination of restrictions on foreign investment; and stricter copyright protections. The decision whether to use the bilateral or multilateral approach to freer trade is a tactical question. However, the principal objective of free trade is to open up the world to the free movement of capital and the trans-national corporations.

For Canada, using the GATT may be a better approach than trying to deal with the United States on a bilateral basis. But the principles and rulings of the GATT itself may conflict with historic Canadian development policies. In 1987 there were three cases which clearly illustrated this point. In 1985 the Canadian Cattlemen's Association (recent converts to free trade in cattle) asked the Canadian government for a countervailing duty against the European Economic Community, which was dumping subsidized beef onto the Canadian market. It was granted. However, the EEC appealed the issue to the GATT. A GATT dispute panel in turn ruled against the Canadian cattlemen. When the ruling was announced in October 1987, Gil Barrows of the CCA told the *Western Producer* that "we want the government to reject the GATT ruling. You can't tell cattle producers they have to play by the GATT rules when the GATT rules say there is no protection for them." Unfortunately, for the Mulroney government to reject such a GATT ruling, as many countries do, would be to undermine their position at the current round of GATT negotiations, that the GATT be amended to include new codes which would oppose all agricultural subsidies.

In November 1987 a dispute panel of the GATT ruled that provincial government pricing, listing and distribution policies discriminate against foreign wine, beer and liquor. Again, this action was brought against Canada by the European Economic Community. Without a doubt these policies give preference to Canadian farmers and manufacturers. But again the Canadian government faced the political dilemma: to reject the GATT ruling would undermine their general policy towards the GATT, largely promoted by grain and oilseed producers. The political nature of the GATT is most evident in this case. The European Economic Community maintains very substantial subsidies for these same industries. European wine is relatively cheap in Canada because it is so heavily subsidized.

Finally, on November 16, 1987, a GATT panel ruled that Canada's policy of prohibiting the export of salmon and herring unless they have been processed in Canada constituted an unfair and discriminatory trade barrier. In this case the action was initiated by U.S. fish processors on the west coast and supported by the U.S. government. Fish plant workers in Alaska, Washington and California are non-union, and they work for around $5 per hour. West coast Canadian workers are members of the United Fishermen and Allied Workers Union and earn between $13 and $17 per hour. If implemented, the ruling would threaten about 5000 jobs on the west coast. Spokesmen for the fishermen's union in Atlantic Canada said the ruling also threatened shoreworkers on the east coast. Others feared that the ruling could also be extended to other Canadian policies on natural resources, such as the general prohibition on exporting logs. One of the big surprises in the final text of the free trade agreement is that the Mulroney government abandoned local processing for the west coast fishing industry but tried to retain it for the east coast fishing industry!

A New Industrial Strategy for Canada

The proponents of a multilateral approach to Canada's foreign trade also insist on the need for a commitment to a Canadian industrial strategy. They reject the industrial strategy supported by the Macdonald Royal Commission, the Mulroney government, the right-wing "think tanks" and our orthodox economists: greater reliance on the free market and the use of the bilateral free trade agreement with the United States to forcibly restructure Canadian industry. While the Macdonald Royal Commission stressed that "the National Policy is dead," many others insist that we need a new industrial policy. Unfortunately, since the end of World War II, Canada has not had a development policy, and various governments have responded to worsening economic conditions in a piecemeal manner, mainly in reaction to regional, industrial and private demands.

During the 1970s the Science Council of Canada, under the influence of a group of Canadian economic geographers, consistently advocated a new industrial strategy for Canada, based on co-operation and planning between private business and government. Programs were advocated which included expanded support for research and development, greater emphasis on higher education, the negotiation of trade pacts with countries other than the United States, preferential purchasing policies by government, and public subsidies for major development programs. Following the linkage theory set forth by Canada's most famous political economist, Harold Innis, they advocated support for industries upstream and downstream from Canada's well-developed resource industries. They also recognized the problems caused by foreign ownership and control; they advocated a tougher policy for the Foreign Investment Review Agency and increased support for Canadian small business. Follow-ing the direction of Japan and a number of European countries, the Science Council called for the identification of new industries where Canada had a chance of succeeding in the world market and advo-cated giving them special government support. Because the proposals called for increased government intervention in the economy, they were vigorously attacked by academic economists.

While the Science Council of Canada has changed direction under the leadership of Dr. Stuart L. Smith, it continues to take the position that Canadians have no choice but to use government to try to in-crease production and reduce unemployment. But they now take the position that the government should subsidize only private industry and should not itself own enterprises, in order to promote the development of "world class enterprises." While this position reflects the ideology of the Mulroney government, it ignores the fact that some of the most successful corporations in Canada have been state enterprises and most of the weakest ones have been privately owned.

The general direction of the Science Council of Canada was supported by the Canadian Institute for Economic Policy (CIEP) under the direction of Walter Gordon and Abraham Rotstein. They advocated a renewed policy of government intervention, using fiscal and monetary measures to stimulate economic growth. This would include a reduction of interest rates, price and wage controls, and a stress on import substitution. The problem of capital flight could be dealt with by a tax on capital leaving the country. A unitary tax on transnational corporations would keep them from declaring their profits elsewhere. The industrial strategy advocated by the Council of Canadians in 1987 followed very closely the framework set out by the Science Council of Canada and the CIEP. However, none would go so far as John Maynard Keynes himself and advocate that the government become the central force in the mobilization and direction of investment.

Jim Laxer is closely identified with the New Democratic Party and the Council of Canadians. His position, as outlined in *Leap of Faith* (1986), is very close to that of the Science Council of Canada, the CIEP and the Council of Canadians. He emphasizes the folly of the Fortress North America strategy advocated by the Macdonald Royal Commission, the Mulroney government and big business. Following the lead of other liberal opponents to bilateral free trade, Laxer concludes that Canada needs to rebuild our major industries to make them internationally competitive. This means identifying "winner" industries, which might include high technology manufacturing in microelectronics and communications equipment, mine/machinery, steel, transportation equipment, petrochemicals, petroleum machinery, the aerospace industry, shipbuilding and fish-plant equipment. Emphasis should be on Canadianization.

To support this renewal effort, Laxer advocates a greater role for the federal government in mobilizing capital, through a "national rebuilding fund." There are certainly adequate internal savings to finance this effort. Development would take the form of investment in private companies, joint ventures between government and private industry, and public-sector enterprises.

The most controversial aspect of Laxer's plan concerns the role for labour. In his view, a new industrial strategy requires joint planning by business, labour and government. This "new partnership," similar to the one proposed by *Business Week* in June 1980, requires the full co-operation of labour. Laxer argues that "the labour movement ought to rethink its historical reliance on the adversarial system (bargaining with business, without sharing in industrial management)." As we shall see, this is one of the fundamental differences between the liberal and socialist alternatives to bilateral free trade with the United States.

For opponents of a bilateral free trade agreement with the United States, a central concern is whether a new Canadian government, whether led by the Liberal Party or the New Democratic Party, will have the political courage to pursue a policy of industrial development and trade diversification. The experience of the recent past is not very encouraging. Stephen Clarkson, in *Canada and the Reagan Challenge* (1985), has documented the pressures imposed by the U.S. government on the Trudeau government when it returned to office in February 1980 and contemplated a very moderate national industrial policy. During the election campaign, the Liberals promised a program of energy self-sufficiency, increased Canadian ownership of industry, more government intervention, and higher Canadian participation in resource megaprojects. They also pledged to restore the imbalances in the Auto Pact and to expand the scope of the Foreign Investment Review Agency (FIRA).

The National Energy Policy (NEP), with its target of 50% Canadian ownership, was denounced by American political and business interests as well as by Canadian oil executives. Clarkson recounts the attacks by the new Reagan administration on the NEP and FIRA. Bills were introduced in the U.S. Congress to retaliate against Canada. The wide range of actions contemplated by the U.S. adminstration revealed how the close bilateral economic ties between the two countries made Canada extremely vulnerable. The U.S. threats included withdrawal from the Canada-U.S. Auto Pact, border harassment, further blocking of Canadian bids under the Defence Production Sharing Agreement, countervailing duties on exports which benefited from cheaper Canadian energy, and actions under section 301 of the U.S. *Trade Act* of 1974, which gives the president power to retaliate against "unfair" trade practices. When it became clear that the Reagan adminstration was serious about retaliation, the Trudeau government caved in. The major economic policy paper produced by the government on November 12, 1981, *Economic Development for Canada in the 1980s*, repudiated the NEP as a model for a new industrial strategy and the election pledge to strengthen FIRA.

The Need for a New Third Option

The 1980s is not the first time that Canada has had serious troubles with an American administration. Many will recall the conflicts between the Trudeau government and the Nixon administration in the early 1970s. In 1970 the Trudeau government introduced the Arctic environmental legislation which proclaimed Canadian sovereignty in the area, a position that the U.S. government has never accepted. In retaliation, the Nixon administration cut back oil imports from Canada. In August 1971, President Nixon abandoned the gold standard and moved to flexible exchange rates. He proclaimed the New Economic Policy, which included an import surcharge on Canadian goods, and the Domestic International Sales Corporation (DISC), designed to subsidize exports. The shocked

Trudeau government responded with a Policy Options Paper and a major statement by Secretary of State for External Affairs Mitchell Sharp. The new policy of the Trudeau government was to be the Third Option, which was to diversify trade to Japan and the European Economic Community (EEC).

However, when it actually came to implementing this policy, little concrete was accomplished. In fact, aside from a few ministerial good-will visits, nothing was done until 1976, when agreements were signed with Japan and the EEC which pledged expansion of trade and industrial co-operation. But nothing that was signed was on the order of the special arrangements that individual countries in Europe have had with the EEC. Without greater incentives, it was very unlikely that business interests in Canada would be enticed to divert trade to Europe. While it has been reported that the Canadian government wished to reach a more formal arrangement with the EEC, several European countries feared that such an agreement would end up as a Trojan horse, used by U.S. firms in Canada to increase their exports to Europe.

But times have changed. Today there is a greater commitment by the opposition forces to diversify trade away from the United States. There is a much better chance that the next Canadian government will undertake serious initiatives for change. As an overall goal, Canada should seek to increase trade with medium-sized and small countries which have the same general standard of living and a similar commitment to trade unions, human rights and the welfare state. It should be remembered that Israel signed a free trade agreement with the European Economic Community before it began negotiations on a free trade agreement with the United States. Australia and New Zealand have all but asked Canada to join their free trade association. This would be an easy first step. Canada should also make a serious effort to join the European Free Trade Association. The latter would provide an opening to the European Economic Community. Because of the high degree of American ownership in the Canadian economy, there would have to be specific rules on Canadian content. In addition, Canada could take the lead in forming a new alliance of countries with a major stake in trade with the United States, pushing for joint action against the highly protectionist omnibus trade bill of 1987.

Diversification would have to be political as well as economic. The New Democratic Party has advocated withdrawal from NATO and NORAD, and public opinion polls indicate that most Canadians want our government to stay at an arms length distance from the

United States and to puruse a more independent foreign policy. Canada could join with the other northern countries in proposing de-militarization of the Arctic. Because of our close ties with the United States, in October 1987 the Mulroney government chose not to respond to a proposal from the Soviet Union for de-militarization of the Arctic. Canada could also participate actively in the Group of Nine, a group of smaller European countries which are seeking to promote detente between the United States and the Soviet Union and to promote arms control and reduction. A policy of non-alignment with the United States hardly means withdrawal from international politics or even political alliances. But if Canada is to avoid becoming another Puerto Rico, a serious commitment to change is absolutely necessary.

CHAPTER 18

Managing Capitalism: Canada in World War II

Capitalism is going through a prolonged crisis that began in the early 1970s. There has always been the boom and bust of the business cycle. The chart in any stockbroker's office will show downturns in business activity in 1946, 1949, 1954, 1958, 1961, 1969, 1974, 1979, and 1982. But the recessions of 1973-4 and 1981-2 have certainly been the longest and deepest since the end of World War II. We are now more than five years into a recovery period, and unless there is something like the Vietnam War to prolong business expansion, another recession is due at any time. With unemployment already at all-time highs for a recovery period, and with governments still running budget deficits, many political economists predict that the next recession will be even worse than that of 1981-2. Furthermore, to one degree or another Western governments have bought the New Right agenda and with it the notion that they should not only be cutting back on social services, they should be getting out of the business of trying to manage the economy. For those who are seriously looking for alternatives to the new business agenda, the experience of the Great Depression and World War II offer a clear alternative. These successful policies, based on the model put forth by John Maynard Keynes, rejected the ideology of the free market and free trade.

The Great Depression and Laissez Faire Economics

Most of us identify the Great Depression with the 1930s. Actually, the first major world depression in the modern era lasted from 1873 through 1896, 23 years. The Great Depression of the 1930s might also have lasted that long except for the onset of World War II. But we all know that in the nuclear era, war is no longer a feasible solution to a general economic downturn.

It is common for today's orthodox economists to blame the extent and duration of the Great Depression of the 1930s on the increase in tariffs. But in reality the problem was not high tariffs but the fact that governments in general did very little to stimulate and direct the economy behind those tariff walls. The dominant economic theory of the day called for cutbacks in government spending and balancing the budget. It was argued that if wages were reduced, businesses would employ more people and unemployment would disappear. Individuals were still encouraged to be thrifty and save; in turn, private entrepreneurs and financial institutions would invest these savings, and the economy would get rolling again. Ironically, the right-wing, laissez faire ideology has reappeared and has once again achieved the status of mainstream orthodoxy.

State intervention in the economy to mobilize for war is conventionally considered to be the catalyst that precipitated the end of the Great Depression. Economic recovery from the Great Depression was relatively early in at least one country, Nazi Germany, where the state intervened extensively in the economy, mobilizing capital for investment in the industrial war machine. Other countries mobilized their economies later. When the Roosevelt adminstration took office in 1933, unemployment was 24.9% of the civilian labour force. It dipped to 14.3% by 1937, but then went up to 19% in 1938. Once the war started, it dropped to 1.9% in 1943 and 1.2% in 1944. Government spending averaged around $10 billion between 1929 and 1932; it rose to $12 billion in 1933 but to only $15 billion by 1936. Sweden is often identified as one country where changes in economic policy independent of mobilization for war brought quick results. Sweden experienced a major depression in the 1920s, with unemployment reaching 30%. When the Social Democratic Party was elected in September 1932, they began a policy of government spending for job creation. But the key to Sweden's relative success was the dramatic devaluation of the national currency, caused by a major flight of capital; the result was a steady expansion of exports. Nevertheless, in 1938 unemployment still stood at 11%.

The Influence of Keynes

John Maynard Keynes, the British aristocrat, brought about a major change in economic thinking with the publication of his *General*

Theory of Unemployment, Interest, and Money in 1936. Keynes was certainly not a socialist. He could not support the Labour Party, for he said that it did not represent his class. He hated the Soviet Union. His aim was to save capitalism from collapse. But he supported the right of trade unions to exist and to bargain collectively, and, like Henry Ford, he believed that higher wages promoted economic expansion. Furthermore, he believed that capitalism couldn't survive unless it solved the problem of persistent unemployment. This became his central focus.

Keynes was concerned by the separation of capital from the actual production process, and the willingness of investors to shift their capital around at a whim, abandoning their country when higher profits could be found elsewhere. He denounced "the decadent international but individualistic capitalism" in whose hands economies were juggled. "It is not intelligent, it is not beautiful, it is not just, it is not virtuous—and it doesn't deliver the goods." He believed that capital flight in times of economic crisis is not only irresponsible but intolerable, and was convinced that the increased international interdependence of countries intensified the extent of the Great Depression.

> I sympathize, therefore, with those who would minimize, rather than with those would would maximize, economic entanglements among nations. Ideas, knowledge, science, hospitality, travel—these are the things which should of their nature be international. But let goods be homespun whenever it is reasonably and conveniently possible, and, above all, let finance be primarily national.

Repudiating the dominant theory of international trade, Keynes argued that while ecology and resource distribution led to natural specialization in some commodities, this did not carry over to general production. "Experience accumulates to prove that most modern processes of mass production can be performed in most countries and climates with almost equal efficiency." Keynes believed that greater self-sufficiency was necessary in order to achieve full employment; furthermore, it would also better serve the cause of peace.

In the 1930s, mainstream economists believed that the business cycle was self-correcting. When rates of interest were high, investment would slow. As investment slowed and the economy stagnated, investment rates would drop, and at this point business would again borrow, invest and expand the economy. However, this did not happen in the Great Depression. Keynes was the first major economist to point out what may seem obvious to all today: when there is a depression, savings decline dramatically. People are forced to consume their savings to survive. Thus, there could be no private stimulus for expansion. Human wants were always there, but the fact of the matter was that there was no "effective demand" for goods as people had no money to spend. Keynes concluded that a depression might persist for long periods of time. The answer, as he set it forth in the *General Theory*, was for government to direct and manage investment. This would include the expansion of public works programs, the establishment of government-owned corporations and joint ventures with private business, state mobilization of capital and direction of investment through planning boards, expansion of credit, and carefully directed tax incentives. To Keynes, this was not just minimal "fine tuning" of the economy; in 1943, observing the recovery from the Great Depression brought on by government actions during World War II, he concluded that "something like two-thirds or three-quarters of total investment [should] be under public or semi-public auspices . . . "

The other major policies that he advocated included permanently low interest rates, which, he believed, would prolong the boom period in the business cycle. Finally, general economic demand should be stimulated through measures which would redistribute income and wealth. Included in this was the proposal for incomes and wage controls, needed to stabilize the inflation which would come from a full-employment policy.

In 1934 Keynes went to Washington, D.C., to advise the Roosevelt adminstration. He urged them to go significantly beyond the Works Progress Administration (WPA) approach and to mobilize capital for investment. But the Roosevelt White House rejected his advice, and unemployment remained very high until U.S. government spending rose to over $100 billion per year during World War II.

World War II and Canadian Recovery

The Great Depression had a devastating impact on Canada. Gross national product declined by 12% per annum over the period from 1930 to 1933. Between 1929 and 1936 national income fell by 30%. Unemployment rose steadily to peak at 19.3% in 1933; it was still over 11% in 1939. The consumer price index fell steadily from 1930 through 1933, and the annual rate of inflation averaged increases of only 1.3% from then down to the outbreak of World War II. Government debt rose, as it was necessary to provide emergency relief for the masses of unemployed, and the provinces and municipalities were impoverished. Government revenues fell, for to a large extent they still relied on tariffs on imports.

The Keynesian prescriptions had little impact on the depression governments of R.B. Bennett and Mackenzie King. Listening to the orthodox economists of the day, and the captains of industry, they remained committed to the principle of balancing the budget. They raised the tariff rates, increased the sales tax, personal incomes taxes and corporate taxes. Despite the persistence of the economic crisis, they managed to raise government revenues. Increased government intervention in the economy came only with the rise in political pressure after the formation of the Co-operative Commonwealth Federation (CCF) in 1932, the expansion of the influence of the Communist Party, and the rapid growth of the militant industrial trade unions organized by the Workers' Unity League and the Congress of Industrial Organizations. But in the end, it was only the pressures of World War II that brought Canada and other countries out of the Great Depression.

The way governments mobilized their economies to fight World War II proved that high levels of unemployment were totally unnecessary. The Canadian experience was really rather incredible. It is interesting that this most dynamic period of Canadian economic development is almost completely ignored by our economists. In fact, there has yet to appear a single book documenting Canada's spectacular economic success during World War II. Why is this? The most likely reason is that the policies utilized were in direct contrast to the free market and free trade ideologies that form the heart of traditional economic theory. Mainstream economists have an absolute faith in the free market and free trade; they cannot accept the fact that other systems can work better and with much greater equity without admitting that their own "religion" is basically flawed. However, there are a few Canadian political economists who have studied the Canadian economy during World War II, and of these David Wolfe is the most prominent. What follows is mainly drawn from his research.

The most significant policies of the Canadian government during the war included the mobilization of industrial capacity, the internal direction of the use of goods and serivces, the broad regulatory policies adopted, government finance, and state control over foreign exchange and trade. The success of these policies was due to the fact that *they came as a total package.*

The task of industrial mobilization was largely given to the Department of Munitions and Supply, headed by C.D. Howe. The key problem was directing capital investment into the proper areas. First, the government channelled private capital into specified areas by granting corporations accelerated depreciation allowances, which provided them with major tax savings. However, this tax incentive was limited to industrial capacity deemed to have little post-war value and to direct war contracts. Depreciation rates were directly administered by the War Contracts Depreciation Board. Special depreciation allowances were also granted to corporations which expanded exports to the United States. Finally, the resource extraction industries were stimulated by the introduction of increased depletion allowances, resulting in major tax savings.

But the mobilization of capital for investment was not limited to tax incentives. Following the model of Keynes, the government also intervened more directly in the economy. During the period from 1939 to 1946, the federal government invested $841 million in plants and equipment needed for the war effort. Furthermore, around 75% of this investment was directed to state-owned crown corporations and the other 25% to privately owned corporations. Over $200 million of government funds were spent to purchase British assets in Canada. Another $814 million was provided for working capital for war purposes.

The Mackenzie King government relied heavily on crown companies established by Order-in-Council; these were directly responsible to a cabinet minister. Twenty-eight such companies were established, and they all performed well; they operated 247 crown plants. But the approach of the government was clearly state capitalism. Most of the crown companies only directed private firms under contract. Paul Phillips and Stephen Watson report that 56% of government investment in war production operations went to crown corporations which contracted with private firms. Another 23% went to alter and expand private plants, although the federal government retained ownership rights of all equipment it paid for. The other 21% went to plants directly operated by the Crown. The crown companies themselves were directed by private businessmen. As Phillips and Watson conclude, "The government instituted what we might call socialism, capitalist style; during the war, Canada had a centrally planned economy in which market mechanisms were largely superseded by adminstrative decisions, while ownership of most of the productive capacity was left in private hands."

While most industrial production was operated by private firms on a contract basis, nine of the crown companies were in direct manufacturing. The Polymer Corporation, which produced synthetic rubber, was a world-class operation. So was Eldorado Mining and Refining Ltd., responsible for uranium development. Research Enterprises Ltd. pioneered in the development of radar. Victory Aircraft, a crown company, operated the largest aircraft plant in Canada and built the Lancaster bomber, one of the best in the world. This was not surprising because Canada has a long history of developing very successful crown corporations at both the federal and provincial level.

There was also extensive government intervention in the economy for the purpose of allocating goods and services. This was done by the Wartime Industries Control Board and fifteen individual controllers appointed by the Minister of Munitions and Supply, which allocated resources on a priority basis. They had the power to buy, expropriate, manufacture or ration designated commodities. The Wartime Prices and Trade Board (WPTB) and the director of the National Selective Service worked together to supply a labour force to essential industries.

The Wartime Prices and Trade Board was given the power to "control price, supply and distribution of necessities of life" and to control all exports and imports. As the economy got back on track and moved towards full utilization of capacity, the spectre of World War I inflation arose. With strong support from the Bank of Canada, in 1941 prices were frozen for the duration of the war. When pressure rose on food prices, the Board stabilized costs by subsidizing selective foods. Farmers initially opposed the freeze on farm prices, but they soon came to recognize that the system allowed them to plan, knowing that everything they produced would be bought at a predetermined price. In 1942, the Board introduced rationing on sugar, tea and coffee, and later extended it to butter and gasoline.

A major controversy surrounded the imposition of wage controls. Under the Industrial Disputes Investigation Act, wage rates were established throughout the economy, and bonuses were used to adjust for increases in the cost of living. The National War Labour Board, consisting of four representatives from labour, four from management, and a government-appointed chairman, administered wage controls policy. Labour was dissatisfied with the administration of the policy, and this was reflected in a wave of strikes in 1943.

254 Free Trade and the New Right Agenda

However, between 1943 and the end of the war wages rose 6.1% while inflation was held to 2.9%. The rising militancy of labour forced the Mackenzie King government in 1944 to finally recognize the right of labour to legally form trade unions and to have the right to bargain collectively. As David Wolfe points out, the imposition by the state of a compulsory obligation upon employers and the owners of capital to bargain collectively represented "an important restraint imposed upon the owners of private property in the disposal and use of their property."

In addition, during World War II there was a significant change in social policy. Only two major pieces of legislation were introduced, the *Unemployment Insurance Act* of 1940 and the *Family Allowance Act* of 1944. But there were significant changes in taxation policy; in particular, there was the introduction of the principle of taxation according to ability to pay. Personal income taxes were raised and exemptions were limited. Taxes on corporate profits were raised. Most important was the introduction of "the excess profits tax." Excise taxes were raised on the imports of all luxury items. Succession duties were introduced for the first time, gift taxes were raised, and sales taxes were raised on luxury items.

The government relied almost exclusively on domestic sources for borrowing. Furthermore, the government relied mainly on personal savings rather than borrowing from the banks. The War Savings and Victory Loans campaigns were very successful in raising enough revenues to balance the budgets; at the same time, they helped to keep down inflation as consumers postponed spending on non-essential items. Between 1939 and 1946, the federal government borrowed $14.8 billion, of which $12.5 billion was raised from the general public.

There was an expansion of the money supply during the war; between 1939 and 1946 it rose to around 133% of the 1939 level. However, during the same period of time the Gross Domestic Product rose from $5.1 billion to $10.8 billion, or by 111%, so that production generally kept up with inflation. Thus, in contrast to World War I, the Canadian contribution to the Second World War was financed in a non-inflationary manner.

There were effective controls over trade and the balance of payments. In 1939 the government established the Foreign Exchange Control Board, and it was given the sole authority to control all financial transactions between Canadians and other countries. All foreign currency acquired by Canadians had to be sold to the Board; those who needed to obtain foreign currency had to obtain a permit through the Board. The government also imposed a 10% war exchange tax on all imports that came from countries outside the Commonwealth. Under the *War Exchange Conservation Act* of 1940, certain classes of imports were simply prohibited. These controls were a major contribution to domestic production and full employment.

The results of the restructuring of the economy were impressive. The annual increase in Gross National Product soared, peaking at 18.6% in 1942. By 1944 the real GNP was 80% larger than it had been in 1938. Real investment rose dramatically. Manufacturing went from 22% of GNP in 1939 to 32% in 1944. Unemployment fell from over 11% in 1939 to only 1.4% in 1944. This result was achieved by massive government intervention in the economy: federal government expenditures rose from 9.2% of GNP in 1938 to 44.6% in 1944. Private investment rose by 80% between 1939 and 1942, but government investment rose by 201%. As a result, public-sector investment rose from 28% of total investment in 1939 to 42.5% in 1943. Certainly, the wartime experience had proven Keynes to be right. The great fear among Canadians was that after the war was over the depression would return.

While Keynesian management of the economy worked very well during World War II, there was a major aspect of the wartime policy which greatly undermined Canadian sovereignty. The Mackenzie King government chose to conduct the war effort on a continental basis. The military aspect of Canada's defence was fully integrated into that of the United States. But in addition, war production was also conducted on a continental basis. As noted before, this integration was formalized in the Hyde Park Agreement of 1941. Canada was to be the natural resource preserve of the American war machine, and actual arms production was to be as specialized as possible. Tariffs on war goods were effectively removed. The United States agreed to place war contracts in Canada to ease our balance of payments problem. Canada was granted special status by the U.S. government, treated not as an independent country but as part of the U.S. economy. This policy of "exceptionalism" became entrenched in the post-war period.

The Abandonment of Keynesian Policy

As early as 1943 the Mackenzie King government began planning for the post-war period. Keynesian policies were implemented during the war, but major world wars are very special circumstances. The cabinet ministers, their economic advisers and the leaders of private enterprise did not want to see the system continued. On the other hand, the CCF was growing in popularity and ranked first in the Gallup Poll in 1943, the Communist Party was increasing in influence, militant trade unions were spreading, and the returning soldiers knew it was not necessary to return to another depression. The compromise position emerged in the White Paper on Employment and Income, released on April 12, 1945. The paper stated the government's commitment to using fiscal and monetary policy to promote stable economic growth. But it rejected the successful World War II policy of expanding manufacturing; instead, it fell back on the old policy of emphasizing exports of natural resources. Furthermore, it specifically rejected many of the policies used during the war. It even argued that public works projects might be counterproductive, undermining business and consumer confidence. The new policy was reflected in the strong support for the American imperial program of free trade, reflected in the Bretton Woods agreements and the General Agreement on Tariffs and Trade.

The result was what British economist Joan Robinson called "bastard Keynesianism." Governments were limited to trying to "fine tune" the business cycle through deficit spending and manipulating the interest rates through their central banks. Keynesian policy became militarized; following the example of Nazi Germany, massive government public works spending was limited to armaments. Under the accord with labour that dominated from 1946 through 1971, investment decisions were left entirely to private capitalists. (This is sometimes erroneously referred to as "The Keynesian Accord.") However, "bastard Keynesianism" could not provide full employment.

The political problems of the Keynesian approach to managing capitalism were pointed out in a widely read article by the Polish economist Michael Kalecki, published in 1943. He predicted that capitalists would oppose Keynesian policies in peacetime for three reasons: fear of losing political power, fear of losing profits, and fear of losing control of labour.

Under a regime of laissez faire or the free market, economic success depends on private business investment and confidence. Government policies which cause a loss of business confidence can lead to capital flight and depression. Under these conditions the capitalist class has enormous political power. When governments take control of the direction of the economy, as they did during

World War II, capitalists invariably surrender some of this power.

Capitalists strongly support state spending when it is for infrastructure and general support of private investment. However, given the experience of government activity in World War II, capitalists fear that Keynesian governments would be tempted in time of recession to move into areas of profitable capital accumulation. Thus, an increase in state power offers a potential threat to the right of private capital to have access to the sectors of the economy where capital accumulation is highest.

Furthermore, under conditions of full employment capitalists lose power over the working class. The discipline which results from fear of being fired or laid off virtually disappears. Trade unions become more militant and they make more demands which cut into profits and management rights, and a shift in the distribution of power from capital to labour is effected.

Kalecki then concluded that without the public pressure of war, the capitalist class would not support a Keynesian policy. "Their class instinct tells them that lasting full employment is unsound from their point of view and that unemployment is an integral part of the normal capitalist system." But Kalecki also argued that depressions and unemployment lead to a rise in working-class political activity and pressure on governments to expand economic and social activity.

As Cy Gonick has pointed out, after the war, business leaders in Canada rejected the continuation of Keynesian policies. The redistribution of income and wealth, begun in World War II, was put on hold. There was general public acceptance of the labour/capital accord and reduced government involvement in the economy as long as the system was delivering the goods. But it could work only as long as there was continued high economic growth rates, steady improvement in productivity, and rising real incomes for the vast majority. This system collapsed in the early 1970s, and the model has lost its credibility and legitimacy. The first response has been the New Right business agenda, but that agenda has failed even more miserably. As conditions deteriorate for a growing percentage of the population, political movements will emerge demanding significant changes.

CHAPTER 19

Social Democracy in Sweden and France

In 1986, four years into the economic recovery after the great recession of 1981-2, levels of unemployment in the industrialized capitalist countries were still at very high levels. For the European countries which are members of the Organization of Economic Cooperation and Development, the average was over 11%; this was actually higher than the 10.9% average in 1984. Equally striking was the wide range in levels of unemployment between countries: unemployment levels remained well over 10% in West Germany, France, the United Kingdom, Italy, Belgium, the Netherlands, and Turkey; they were around 20% in Spain and Ireland. But several countries had much lower levels of unemployment: Austria, 3.4%; Japan, 2.8%; Norway, 1.9%; Sweden, 2.2%; and Switzerland, 0.8%. The policies of the governments of these countries illustrate a range of alternatives which are open to Canadian governments.

This phenomena has been examined by Goran Therborn in *Why Some Peoples Are More Unemployed Than Others* (1986). One explanation has concentrated on the degree of corporatism, or cooperation between labour, business and government. In Canada this is most commonly referred to as tripartism; it has been pushed by the more conservative elements in the trade union movement and the New Democratic Party. In Europe corporatism takes the form of centralized bargaining for wages, which then apply to the entire country and are largely enforced by the trade unions. Centralized labour organizations maintain a strong hegemony over their component unions, which in turn control their bargaining units. Austria, Norway and Sweden have strong corporatist institutions and traditions, and they have been quite successful in keeping down the level of unemployment. But the Netherlands also has a well-entrenched corporatist system, and this country has been one of the

258

least successful in dealing with the prolonged economic crisis.

Switzerland, governed by a four-party coalition which includes the Social Democrats, also has a form of corporatism. But it is widely agreed that their unorthodox policies are the main reason for low levels of unemployment. First, the government has forced a massive repatriation of foreign workers. As early as 1964 the governing coalition legally restricted full-employment programs to Swiss citizens. Therborn points out that this alone reduced the unemployment rate by seven percentage points. A second official government policy, supported by the employers' organizations, stressed laying off women workers and discouraging women from entering the work force. In addition, they carried out a range of government policies which included taxation changes, support for the farm community and direct public investment. Therborn estimates that these policies reduced the unemployment rate by another four percentage points. Only the lunatic fringe of the far right would want to see a similar policy package adopted in Canada.

The Norwegian system of tripartism, with a negotiated incomes policy, is very similar to that of Sweden, which will be examined below. During the period of the economic crisis, the social democratic government of Norway has relied on very large subsidies to small locally owned business enterprises, farmers and rural communities. The level of subsidies reached 4.5% of Gross National Product, one of the highest in Europe. Public-sector employment has increased. However, the success of this policy has rested on the development and export of the limited reserves of the North Sea oil. To develop this industry the government borrowed heavily from abroad. Because of the outflow of payments on these loans, the government was forced to impose wage and price controls in 1978. While they have recovered from this particular crisis, the weakness of non-oil exports has left the economy is an uncertain state.

Austria also has a very dominant system of tripartism, with very strong central control by the trade union federation over local unions and bargaining units. This was the result of the historic compromise between the Social Democratic Party (SPO) and the Conservative Party (OVP) at the end of World War II, an attempt to avoid permanent occupation by the Allied forces. As part of this agreement, there were large-scale nationalizations, including the two largest banks, coal and iron mining, mineral oil, steel and non-ferrous metal manufacture. Today, more than 25% of manufacturing is in the state sector, and two-thirds of the 50 largest corporations are state owned. Nevertheless, private capital continues to dominate. The state industries were prohibited from manufacturing finished goods. The success of Austria in dealing with unemployment is largely attributed to the tough incomes policy, enforced by the tripartite agreement. But others point to the fact that Austria has followed an active labour market policy similar to that of Sweden. The government's strategy has included maintaining high levels of employment in the public sector and in state-owned enterprises. For these enterprises, this has created competition problems, and most recently there has been a trend towards privatization. The major popular criticism of the Austrian system is its centralization, hierarchy, bureaucracy and lack of anything like real democracy.

Therborn identifies a number of common characteristics of those countries which have been successful in reducing the level of unemployment. While they are found in both traditional conservative governments and social democratic governments, they are generally absent from Canada:

• Political and cultural independence is important, but this does not extend to include economic protectionism or isolation from the world market.

• All the countries which were more successful had a strong national capitalist class, very low levels of foreign ownership and control, and diversified foreign trade.

• The adoption of varying degrees of Keynesian state intervention has made a major difference. Furthermore, the most effective policies are those that have been directed towards direct investment. General tax reductions have not reduced employment and have tended to stimulate imports.

• Fiscal policies have to be supported by an expansive monetary policy. This requires low interest rates and a policy of cheap currency.

• The five countries that have been the most successful are the least integrated with the other capitalist countries. None are members of the European Economic Community. All have pursued independent currency exchange policies.

• The key factor, however, is the extent of the institutional commitment to full employment, due either to the assertion of strong working-class interests or to the commitment by the local business class to labour stability, deemed necessary to perpetuate the steady accumulation of capital.

Sweden: Social Democratic Planning

Sweden is a relatively small country, with a population of only 8.5 million. But its per capita Gross National Product is the second highest in the world, behind Switzerland. During the economic crisis, unemployment peaked in 1983 at only 3.1%. Youth unemployment in 1985 was 6.8%, the lowest in the West. Sweden has the highest labour participation rate in the capitalist world, around 85%. In 1985, 78% of adult women were in the labour force.

But Sweden is best known for its extensive social welfare and support system. In 1985, government expenditures were the equivalent of 67% of Gross National Product, by far the highest among the advanced capitalist countries. At the same time, 90% of industry is in private hands. There is a very low level of foreign ownership and control. Sweden has a substantial number of large transnational corporations with extensive overseas investment.

Finally, Sweden is notable for mass participation of the working class in trade unions and in the dominant Social Democratic Party. Around 90% of all blue-collar workers are in 24 national trade unions affiliated with the Swedish Trade Union Confederation (LO); 75% of white-collar workers are in the twenty trade unions affiliated with the Central Organization of Salaried Employees (TCO); and most professionals are members of one of the 26 trade unions affiliated with the Swedish Confederation of Professional Associations (SACO). Only the LO is affiliated with a political party. During the long period of government by the Social Democratic Party, around one-half of all cabinet ministers were from the trade union leadership, a stark contrast to the New Democratic Party in Canada and most other social democratic governments. The Social Democratic Party is also noted for mass participation; around 20% of all voters are also party members. In contrast with other social democratic parties, it has a very large youth membership. The party also puts a great deal of emphasis on political education.

When the Social Democratic Party took office in September 1932, they undertook policies which could be called "bastard Keynesianism." They emphasized an active fiscal policy of government expenditures, low interest rates, stabilization of farm prices, devaluation of the currency, and tax and other incentives to modernize private industry. However, they specifically rejected the central Keynesian policy of control and direction over investment. They also chose to follow a policy of export promotion; there has been a minimum of protection in order to promote industries which would be internationally competitive.

The foundation for corporatism was laid in the historic 1938 agreement between the major trade union confederation (LO) and the Swedish Employers' Federation (SAF). This came after a round of general lockouts and strikes where class conflict was pronounced. The two central bodies agreed to self-regulation to reduce industrial conflict. The goal of the employers was really to remove the Social Democratic Party from the capital/labour conflict. Trade unions were recognized, and labour was to be rewarded by more extensive social welfare policies, higher living standards and government policies to facilitate labour mobility and job training. Full employment was established as the prime national goal. Capital was to gain relative labour peace, uniform wages for two-year periods and management control in the workplace. Public sector wages were to follow wage levels in the private sector. The Social Democratic Party agreed to the system, that is, to the maintenance of a capitalist economy with limited government intervention.

In the 1950s the Social Democratic system of managing capitalism was modified by a new plan designed by Rudolph Meidner and Gosta Rehn, economists with the LO. One of the basic principles of their approach was that Sweden is an open economy, and industries must remain competitive internationally. Thus, the centralized system of wage bargaining should apply to all firms, allowing the weaker firms to be driven out by higher labour costs. This would also encourage investment to increase labour productivity. Following the new plan, the labour movement would undertake a "solidarity" policy of demanding the highest wage increases in the lowest-paid jobs. Under centralized bargaining, workers would receive the same pay for doing the same work regardless of the financial status of the employer or the regional location. The plan called for less emphasis on government spending as an attempt to provide full employment. Instead, the government would introduce an active labour market policy to deal with unemployment and industrial restructuring. The plan proposed that profit levels of private industry should be kept low to help counteract inflation, not through taxation policy but through increasing the bargaining power of organized labour to obtain wage increases.

Since the adoption of the Meidner and Rehn plan, the Swedish government has maintained some direction in the investment area. Beginning as early as 1938 there was the creation of Investment Reserve Funds: companies could get tax incentives by placing a percentage of their pre-tax profits in these blocked funds. In time of a

downturn in the economy, the funds were released by the government for investment in approved projects. Since the 1960s they have
also been used to stimulate development in depressed areas.

The government has also established a program of job creation. In
the public sector, all local governments prepare a priority list of local
improvement projects. When unemployment rises to a certain level,
government funds are released. In contrast to Canada, these
programs pay employees regular wages and fringe benefits. In the
private sector, the government has a stockpiling subsidy designed to
keep companies from laying off employees in economic downturns.

The job training program established as part of the plan is famous.
An extensive program was deemed necessary to meet the needs of
workers after the Social Democratic government adopted the industrial adjustment policy. These retraining programs are open to
anyone who is unemployed and to anyone who is in a designated
"sunset" industry. Job training is free. Those in the program receive a
stipend which is equal to two-thirds of the average wage rate. With
the stipend, those who are on unemployment insurance can receive
up to 11/12 of their previous pay. General unemployment insurance
is two-thirds of the average daily pay of industrial workers, and is
good for up to 60 weeks. Those completing the training program are
then placed in suitable jobs.

While the Swedish system of managing capitalism looks very
favourable in comparison to Canada, all is certainly not perfect.
First, ownership of capital is highly concentrated. The famous "five
families" control close to 25% of all productive assets plus many
banks and insurance companies. The ownership of wealth is grossly
unequal, and the inequality is rising. Despite the cradle-to-grave
welfare system, Sweden is very much a class-divided society.

With the fall in the rate of profit in the 1970s, the government
shifted taxation policy dramatically away from capital and onto individuals and families. Because of the general absence of effective
taxes on capital and wealth, Sweden is saddled with the highest rates
of taxes on individuals and families among the advanced capitalist
states. Personal income taxes are quite progressive; those earning
over $46,000 are in the 80% tax bracket. In 1984, the average take
home pay was only 66% of gross earnings. In recent years the Social
Democrats have introduced regressive, indirect taxes: there is a 40%
payroll tax and a 23.5% value added sales tax on around 70% of
goods and services. Furthermore, during the economic crisis period
of 1979-84, the rate of inflation stayed at around 10%, one of the
highest among the industrialized countries.

Given its export orientation, Sweden has not been immune to the changes in the international economic system in the 1970s and 1980s. Sweden has virtually no oil. The price of raw material exports dropped, causing a balance of payments problem. There has been an increasing national budget deficit. Economic growth has been stagnating, compared to the past. There has been a reduction in national savings. In 1974 there was no foreign debt; now it is a major national problem.

As *The Economist* notes, "big business thrives in Sweden." Overseas investment by Swedish transnational corporations has increased. In 1984 it equalled 60% of all investment in Sweden. Of the twenty largest corporations, 70% to 80% of all new investment in the 1980s has been overseas. Of the ten largest Swedish firms, more than half of its employees are overseas. Capital flight is occurring, and in this case with the tacit support of the Social Democratic government. Interest rates are kept high to try to entice capital to invest in Sweden.

When the Social Democrats were returned to office in October 1982, the first thing they did was devalue the currency by 16%. Furthermore, this was a unilateral action taken without consulting their major trading partners in the European Free Trade Association. They did not even consult with the other Scandinavian countries, to which they are closely tied. There was a great deal of resentment over this action.

The centre-right coalition government which governed Sweden from 1976-82 followed a restrictive fiscal policy and a tight money policy to try to deal with the general economic crisis. To a large extent this policy was continued by the Social Democrats after they returned to office in 1982. However, in 1983 and 1984 profits were high and the trade unions demanded wage increases. The employers' federation, the SAF, refused, and the central bargaining system broke down. Bargaining is now sector-by-sector.

Under the legal terms of national bargaining, industrial action by either capital or labour is prohibited while contracts are in operation. Unions and individuals who engage in illegal strikes can be sued for damages and also fined in the Labour Court. During the biggest industrial dispute in Sweden, in 1980, a strike was met by a nationwide lockout by employers which affected 80% of the industrial work force. While the strike/lockout was resolved by mediation, it is widely agreed that this was the beginning of the end of the Swedish model of labour peace. Strikes now occur more regularly; in 1985 there was a combined strike/lockout of 70,000 state employees.

Furthermore, labour unity is disappearing. The TCO and SACO, representing the 40% of the labour force which are now white-collar workers and professionals, have rejected the solidarity wage policy and are demanding higher increases for themselves. In 1985 the public sector trade unions negotiated a separate contract which provided wage increases which were higher than those granted in the private sector. Many believe that the widely acclaimed Swedish "third way" will disappear with the strains that will inevitably occur during the next general recession.

The Collapse of the French Socialist Experiment

In May 1981 François Mitterand, the candidate of the Parti socialiste (PS), was elected president of France. In the national legislative elections which were held the following month, the PS received a mandate unprecedented in France by winning a majority of the seats in the National Assembly. The strength of the socialist mandate was further enhanced by the support from the Parti communiste de France (PCF), which was granted four seats in the Mitterand cabinet. Both parties had campaigned on platforms which called for a repudiation of the right-wing policies of the previous government and international capital, government fiscal policies to move towards full employment and increased socialization of the economy. The French experiment is of primary importance because after a very promising beginning in 1981, the government reverted to the same orthodox policies of tight money and fiscal restraint followed by most of the advanced capitalist states during the economic crisis. Why did this happen?

The political left in France has always been divided. The PCF, with its close links to the largest trade union federation, the Confédération generale du travail (CGT), traditionally has followed the party line from Moscow. Since its opposition to the May-June 1968 popular revolt, which was supported by spontaneous workers' demonstrations, its electoral support has declined. In the early 1970s it broke with tradition and embraced Eurocommunism; in 1972 it signed the Common Program with the PS. However, when it did poorly in the 1974 and 1977 elections, it withdrew from the alliance and went through a period of internal debate and political purges.

The PS was formed in 1971 out of four currents of the non-communist left. The core was the old SFIO, the socialist party from the Fourth Republic, with its close ties to the more militant trade union confederation, the Confédération française démocratique du travail (CGDT). Ideologically, the SFIO was a reformist party supporting moderate Keynesian policies. The SFIO core was joined by the remnants of the Radicals of the Third Republic, basically a republican liberal party. François Mitterand came from this party. The left-socialist movement, the Parti socialiste autonome (PSA), with its strong commitment to workers' control and opposition to state bureaucracy, also joined, and finally, there was the Centre d'études de résearches et d'éducation socialiste (CERES), a movement of left intellectuals from the 1960s, formed as a socialist movement within the SFIO. Like the Waffle in the NDP in Canada in the late 1960s, it was committed to the transformation of the SFIO into a socialist party. Its policies were very close to those of the PCF.

François Mitterand united the non-communist left and chose an electoral strategy which was based on a political alliance with the PCF. The 1972 Common Program included a set of economic policies which were very close to those of the PCF. Even after the break with the PCF in 1977, the PS maintained a platform which was considerably to the left of the mainstream of the party. After a poor showing in the 1978 legislative elections, Mitterand, facing internal opposition, aligned himself with CERES, the most left-wing element in the PS. In return, CERES was given a prominent role in constructing the 1980-1 electoral platform.

The economic program of the socialist government in 1981 had two objectives. First, they would introduce fiscal policies of re-flation in an effort to counteract the effects of the great recession. Second, there would be extensive nationalizations aimed at con-trolling finance capital and establishing defence against the trans-national corporations which were moving industries and jobs out of France.

The expansion of government spending had an immediate positive effect. The minimum wage was raised 10%. Family and housing allocations were raised 25%. The basic allowance for the elderly and handicapped was raised 20%. The work week was reduced to 39 hours. Holiday pay was extended to five weeks for every working person. The retirement age was lowered to 60. In addition, 55,000 new jobs were created in the public sector. Because of the very high level of youth unemployment, a new youth training program was in-troduced. Transfer payments to households increased by 5.8% in 1981 and 7.8% in 1982. Real disposable income rose by 3.2% in 1981 and 3.1% in 1982.

On the whole, public spending rose by 27% in 1981. Economic growth was 1.5% while it was negative in most of the OECD countries. The reflation policies seemed to pay off; unemployment was at 7.5%, below the 8.5% average for the OECD countries.

The nationalization program began in the fall of 1981. Five of the largest complexes of conglomerate industries were nationalized. The government took majority ownership in iron and steel, the armaments industry, computers, chemicals and telecommunications. In total, around 36% of France's industrial capacity came under state ownership. Compensation was by fifteen-year government bonds, at a total cost of around US$5.3 billion. Financial circles described the prices set by the government for the purchased assets as "ludicrously over-generous."

In the spring of 1982, the Mitterand government moved to take control of finance capital. They nationalized 36 commercial banks, the two largest financial holding companies, and the insurance sector. The object was to enable the government to underwrite its new industrial policy by gaining control over credit. They would then be able to direct it to industrial projects which stressed job creation and to the small business sector. Control over finance capital would facilitate broad economic planning as the government moved forward on a policy of full employment.

The third major area of reform came in industrial relations. The trade union movement in France has always been weak, representing less than 18% of the labour force in 1985. There are five trade union confederations, fragmented and split along ideological lines, each attempting to represent workers in all industries and trades, private and public. Trade unions are also weak because of the structure of French industry: in 1985, 46% of the labour force was still employed in firms which hired fewer than 50 workers. Furthermore, the business firms are united in the Conseil national du patronat français (CNPF), which includes three-quarters of all French enterprises. In addition, French laws have been traditionally anti-union. For example, slow-downs or work-to-rule campaigns are illegal, as are political strikes. Closed shops are also illegal.

Because of the weakness of the labour movement, legislation on industrial bargaining has attempted to extend protection to non-organized workers. Collective bargaining has traditionally been industry-wide, and has usually included unions from several confederations. All employees in an enterprise may benefit from a contract, even if they are not unionized. A union contract comes into effect even if only one representative union has signed and ratified it. This system undermines mutual recognition of other unions and encourages employers to oppose unions at the plant level.

The Mitterand government was pledged to major reforms of the industrial relations system. This took the form of the "Auroux laws," named after the Minister of Labour, and were based on the proposals by the socialist trade union confederation, CFDT. In general, the reforms were designed to strengthen the role of trade unions and the rights of workers at the plant level.

Why did the 1981 experiment end so quickly? Economic problems arose because of the incomplete and contradictory nature of the government's applications of the Keynesian program and because of France's close links to the European Economic Community. The Mitterand government also expected to have to pursue a policy of reflation only for a short period; they fully expected the world economy to recover, led by the United States. They had not planned for a long-term economic crisis. In the first year of office the balance of payments problem worsened, with the deficit rising from FFR26 billion to FFR78 billion. The increased spending power of the average person was translated into greater purchases of imported goods. For example, over 1981-2 the sale of new automobiles rose by 12%, but the sale of French units stagnated while imports rose 22%. There were no controls on imports. The government was forced to borrow heavily from abroad, and foreign debt rose. Currencies within the European Monetary System were realigned several times, resulting in a devalulation of the French franc of around 18%.

The rate of inflation was high, reaching 12% in 1981 and 14% in 1982. There were no price controls at this time. The prices of French goods were increasing while other countries were attacking inflation. Because of the nationalization policy, and the election promise of a wealth tax, there was capital flight from the country. During 1981-2 French corporations greatly increased their overseas investment. While government investment increased, private investment in France decreased by 3.5% in 1981. Unemployment continued to increase in the private sector. In order to try to stem the outflow of private capital, interest rates were kept at very high levels. There were no effective foreign exchange controls.

As Goran Therborn and others have pointed out, the key issue for the government was whether or not to support the French franc in the international money markets. A similar dilemma brought down the 1936 Front populaire government headed by Leon Blum. For the Mitterand government, the balance of payments crisis forced currency devaluations in October 1981, June 1982 and March 1983. To save the overall economic program, the Mitterand government would have had to impose strict import controls, tighten foreign exchange controls and break with the European Monetary System, which tied the franc to the West German deutschmark.

Therborn concludes that the failure of the Mitterand program was not a general failure of Keynesian policies but a lack of political will. It was not necessary to abandon the reform program as early as June 1982. The budget deficit, 2.6% of Gross National Product in 1982, was well below the average of 4% for the Group Seven countries. The government debt was much smaller than in the other major OECD countries. In June 1982, Mitterand's government began its big retreat, introducing wage and price controls, increasing unemployment insurance premiums paid by workers, cutting wages, and introducing users' fees for public services like medicare and hospitalization. There were layoffs of government employees. By the fall of 1982, the Mitterand government had completely changed course; the new strategy announced by the president was to control wages and bring labour peace so that French industry could become more profitable and adjust to international competition. But the real income for ordinary people began to fall and unemployment began to rise. De-industrialization continued. Economic growth stagnated.

The political left remained silent during the policy reversal. The major trade union confederations did not criticize "their government"; the only criticism came from the Force ouvrière (FO), the more right-wing of the trade union confederations. More astonishing, the PCF did not withdraw from the coalition until July 1984. By continuing to support a government now implementing the same policies as Margaret Thatcher, the PCF lost the support of the working class. In the 1983 local elections, both the PS and the PCF were routed. In the elections for the European Parliament in 1984, the support for both parties fell dramatically. The Front national, a fascist party, received almost as many votes as the PCF. Finally, of course, the PCF was soundly defeated in the 1986 elections for the National Assembly.

In contrast to the Blum government of 1936, there had been no broad grass-roots support for the Mitterand government. Their initial success was simply an electoral victory by a left-wing social democratic party, supported by a population fed up with the failure of the policies of the right-wing governments. The Mitterand government also alienated many of its supporting groups. It repudiated its electoral platform on nuclear power, alienating the ecology movement. By maintaining support for nuclear arms, a large military budget, and the continuation of nuclear weapons testing, it alienated the peace movement. By taking a strong policy in support of NATO and the Reagan administration's foreign policy, it alienated the political left in general. In fact, the Mitterand government was much more pro-American than the Gaullist Party. In New Caledonia, Africa and islands in the St. Lawrence River, it continued the support for traditional French imperialism. The bombing of Greenpeace's *Rainbow Warrior* in New Zealand symbolized the total political collapse of the Mitterand government.

For the social democratic governments in Sweden and France, the major problem has been a strike by capital and flight from the country. In each case, the government maintained high interest rates in an attempt to bribe the capitalists to stay at home. But high interest rates cause other serious economic problems. John Maynard Keynes called for "the euthanasia of the rentier class" through permanent low-interest rates. He saw the flight of capital as the main barrier to achieving full employment. "We all need to be as free as possible of interference from economic changes elsewhere, in order to make our own favourable experiments towards the ideal social republic of the future."

The social democratic governments in Sweden and France have given us examples of what can be practically done by a progressive government in a liberal democracy. For Canadians, they offer concrete alternatives to the right-wing program of neo-conservatism and integration with the United States. However, they are also good examples of the shortcomings of incomplete programs for national development. The key problem for both has been the power of capital. The Mitterand government quickly surrendered, choosing to avoid a struggle with European capital. In Sweden, the Social Democratic government is floundering as capital moves its investment overseas. The next recession will force a crisis situation. If Sweden wishes to avoid the Mitterand path, it will have to repudiate a 50-year tradition of corporatism and internationalism.

CHAPTER 20

The Option of Greater Self-Reliance

According to the ideology of free trade, as tariff barriers are lowered everyone benefits: production increases, incomes rise, prices on consumer goods fall, and we move towards full employment. In the real world, however, as tariff barriers fell following the Kennedy and Tokyo rounds of GATT negotiations, the Western world in particular experienced slowing rates of growth and a steady increase in unemployment. With inflation at relatively high rates, the real income of the majority of the people actually declined. Furthermore, what became known as "stagflation" persisted almost uninterrupted after the economic downturn became apparent in 1973.

With the reductions in trade barriers, the advanced capitalist countries experienced an influx of manufactured imports from Eastern Europe, southern Europe and the newly industrializing Third World countries. This was primarily the result of national and international capital seeking higher rates of profit. It was quite clear that the advantages these countries offered the owners of capital were lower labour costs and the lack of environmental, health, safety and other regulations. In the Third World countries, there was massive state repression of trade unions and the political opposition. Furthermore, these right-wing pro-Western governments provided major financial subsidies to the transnational corporations.

The initial political response to this crisis was in Western Europe, where economic growth was stagnant and unemployment was at levels seen only during the Great Depression. Alternative economic strategies, and specific rejection of the policy of free trade, developed in Britain around the Cambridge Economic Policy Group and the left wing in the Labour Party, in France around elements in the socialist and communist parties, and in West Germany around a group within the Social Democratic Party. The debate on alternative

271

policies has had a major impact in Canada, on the political left, on the trade union movement, and on the major established churches.

The Cambridge Economic Group

The British economy was hard hit in the 1970s. The Labour government tried an incomes policy, but it proved to be a hardship on ordinary working people. In 1976, the Labour government's response to the sterling crisis resulted in even more restrictive economic policies. Wages began to fall dramatically in comparison with other countries. Unemployment continued to rise. Because British industry is dominated to a relatively high degree by transnational corporations (in 1971, 20% of industrial output was overseas), foreign exchange controls were less effective. New investment continued to be primarily overseas. Manufacturing peaked in 1973 and then steadily declined. The only sector of the economy expanding was finance capital, based in London. When Britain joined the Common Market in 1973, investment fled to the continent. When the Thatcher government dropped foreign exchange controls in 1979, overseas investment soared in one year from £900 million to £4000 million.

In 1975 a group of economists at Cambridge University advanced an alternative strategy for development, a package of economic policies stressing increased barriers to imports. Following John Maynard Keynes, they argued that there could not be a policy of full employment unless there was also a policy of protectionism. The central problem in the economy was the disappearance of the British manufacturing sector, the resulting increase in unemployment, and growing regional disparities. The Cambridge economists argued that an efficient manufacturing sector could both satisfy the demands of domestic consumers and sell enough abroad to pay for the country's import requirements. It was clear to all that Britain's declining share of world manufactured exports and the increase in import penetration were the major causes of rising unemployment.

The Cambridge economists noted that simple policies of reflation (fiscal and monetary policies to stimulate the economy) would immediately cause balance of payments problems, as imports would increase. Eventually, this would bring a return of stagnation. Under these circumstances, the only alternative was to impose import controls. They also called for high and rising tariffs on all finished manufactured products, starting at 30% and rising to 70%, if necessary, to keep imports under control. They predicted that if such changes were not implemented, unemployment might rise to as high as four million by 1985. The strategy of currency devaluation, pursued by social democratic governments, was opposed on the grounds that other trading partners would simply retaliate with their own devaluations. In contrast, a British economy that was once again experiencing sustained economic growth would actually provide a better market for other countries, even with import controls, than would a continuation of economic stagnation.

At first, the attention of the Cambridge Economic Group was focused on competition from the advanced industrialized countries, primarily West Germany and Japan. The main problems for Britain at this time were imports of manufactured goods from the European Common Market and the exodus of British capital to continental Europe. Thus, the group initially called for the withdrawal of Britain from the Common Market. In the 1980s, when almost all of Europe was caught up in the great recession, they shifted to advocating a general policy of Keynesian reflation for all of Europe, on a co-ordinated basis. They argued that the difficulty was "one of shaking the entrenched belief in the virtues of free trade . . . " The key obstacle to this new approach would be convincing the most successful national economies that, for the overall good of Western Europe, they should accept the shift of trade and production against them.

In 1982 the protectionist alternative won the support of Nicholas Kaldor, one of Britain's best-known Keynesian economists. He drew the parallel to Britain in 1932, when government policy shifted from deflationary measures to import controls. As he noted, "manufacturing output expanded by 7.8% a year in the following five years, manufacturing productivity rose by 3.9% each year and manufacturing employment by 4.7% each year." Increased self-sufficiency was the most likely alternative to the destructive policies of the Thatcher government.

The Alternative Economic Strategy

While in opposition between 1970 and 1974, the British Labour Party and the Trades Union Congress (TUC) worked out an alternative economic program, announced in 1975. It called for planning agreements between the largest corporations, the trade unions and government, with government and workers' representatives on boards of directors. A National Enterprise Board would be responsible for extending public ownership to key areas of the economy. A National Planning Commission would be created to co-ordinate development at the level of the individual firm, industry-wide and at the national level. Finally, there would be public ownership of the major institutions in the financial sector in order to permit the government to direct investment where it was needed. This formed the platform on which the Labour government was elected in 1975.

Once in office, however, the Labour Party reverted to its right-wing traditions. The party program was defeated in the parliamentary caucus. The leading left-wing members, Eric Heffer and Tony Benn, were removed from key positions in the cabinet. The Labour government did not consult with the Trades Union Congress. No nationalization took place. The TUC even agreed to tripartism and an incomes policy. It was within this context that the Alternative Economic Strategy was proposed by the Labour left as a transitional program intended to move Britain towards becoming a socialist society. The program advocated a policy of reflation to provide relief from the existing recession. Reflation would include increased public expenditures, the easing of credit, and a reduction in taxes for low income people. General tax cuts were opposed on the grounds that direct public spending provides more jobs, sooner, and avoids stimulating unwanted increases in imports.

The program recommended that tendencies toward inflation be controlled by price controls, rather than tight-money policies or wage controls. The controls would be necessary for a short time to break the inflation cycle. While this would result in a profit squeeze, investment would be encouraged as it was in World War II, through government credit for approved projects and direct investment spending. A number of strategies were put forward to reduce unemployment: the work week would be reduced to 35 hours, jobs and income sharing and employment subsidies would be increased, and job-training programs and the apprentice program would be expanded.

The Alternative Economic Strategy retained the proposals on labour planning agreements and the expansion of public ownership from the original 1975 Labour platform. It was argued that eventually large capital would have to be brought under social ownership and control. Other fiscal policies and programs proposed included the creation of a National Investment Bank to mobilize long-term savings like Pension Funds and Life Insurance programs, and to take control of windfall royalties from projects like North Sea Oil. The four largest banks and the seven largest insurance companies would be nationalized, and an Investment Reserve Fund, similar to that in operation in Sweden, would be created. Pre-tax profits would be directed to specific projects at specific times.

The strategy also proposed to extend democracy into the economic area. Workers' control and decentralization of industry and government was to be promoted, both for its own sake and to counteract general public hostility to bureaucracies. Increased worker and community control would challenge the exclusivity of capital's decision-making rights. One example of spin-off from the Strategy was the Alternative Corporate Plan proposed by shop stewards at the Lucas plant, which called for "socially useful production," no military work, a major say for workers in what is produced, and a greatly reduced role for advertisement. Unfortunately, the Lucas plan remains only a model of what alternatives workers' control might produce.

Under the program, trade would be planned. Import controls were considered necessary to sustain expansion of the domestic economy. Britain's trade problems are largely created by the large transnational corporations. They make the major decisions on imports and exports, and they decide whether to invest their profits at home or abroad. In the early 1970s a 1% increase in domestic demand led to a 4% increase in imports and a balance of payments crisis that required a 15% to 20% devaluation in the national currency. To prevent a repetition, the Alternative Economic Strategy also proposed introducing higher tariffs, as they would permit the flexibility of giving preference to other deficit countries and less-developed countries. However, import controls and higher tariffs would also be used with quotas and rationing of foreign exchange currency, as during World War II. The latter were considered to be even better policies as they represented a move away from delegating decision-making to the market and capital, and would also permit greater flexibility in trade policy. Finally, the authors of the Alternative Economic Strategy argued that protection should not just be a temporary policy, for such a position appears to endorse the notion of capitalism's inherent efficiency and superiority. The Strategy was founded on the position that the ideology of free trade must be combatted. To achieve this, the power that the rich industrial countries have in the GATT and the International Monetary Fund must be undermined, and strong support given to the UN Conference on Trade and Development, a much more representative institution. Protection is a necessary part of managed trade, according to the Strategy, when trade is conducted on the basis of mutual benefit rather than exploitation. Under new principles of international solidarity, trade could be expanded with the state socialist countries and the less-developed world.

In Britain today the Alternative Economic Strategy remains the basis of the platform of the political left both within and outside the Labour Party. It is the only clear alternative to the policies of the Thatcher government, especially so in that it is not intended as a strategy to reform capitalism but as a transitional program leading to an alternative society based on co-operation and popular democracy.

Protectionism and the French Left

The ideology of free trade has never dominated France as it has Great Britain. Thus, when the oil crisis came in 1973, protectionism appeared as an alternative policy and found advocates across the entire political spectrum. However, since the influence of capital is clearly on the political right, it was not long before the debate over increased self-reliance or self-sufficiency became the preserve of the political left. The initial call for a new protectionism came from Jean-Marcel Jeanneney and André Grjebine. From a Keynesian framework, they both argued for increased self-reliance for Europe as a whole and for the Third World. It is to the advantage of industrialized *and* underdeveloped countries to emphasize internal goals and the domestic market over international trade specialization. Both Jeanneney and Grjebine are critical of the free trade argument. Indeed, they cite evidence that the trade liberalization that took place in the late 19th century benefited only Great Britain and not continental Europe, which experienced slower economic growth, lack of innovation, and slower trade expansion.

For France, the most fearful competition comes from the low-wage countries in the Third World. Increased trade with the newly industrializing countries (NICs) will continue to undermine full employment in France. Grjebine argues that Third World countries distort their own economic development by concentrating on expanding manufacturing for the export market. Because this policy is contrary to the needs of the ordinary people in underdeveloped countries, it requires repressive political regimes to maintain it. The obvious alternative is to redirect production to the domestic market. Trade should be regionalized, with emphasis on countries of similar structure and levels of development. Trade between countries of significantly different levels of development should be negotiated behind general protectionism. The main opposition to such a structured trade would come from the transnational corporations and big capital, the primary beneficiaries of free trade.

The debate in France over free trade and protectionism expanded after the Mitterand government changed direction in June 1982. The policy shift meant a rejection of the early goal of reconquering the domestic market. Those who opposed the policy shift have pointed to the failure of the Mitterand government to confront the power of international capital. CERES, the most left-wing element in the Socialist Party (PS), has concluded that the 1981 strategy failed because it was not sufficiently protectionist. Without adequate foreign exchange controls and import controls, the Mitterand government could not deal with the issue of the flight of capital and balance of payments problems.

The protectionist cause has also been advocated by elements in the Communist Party (PCF), where the chief advocate has been Pierre Juquin. He argues that there cannot be full employment unless there is a serious effort to regain the internal market, in all important sectors. But in contrast to the Keynesians, the left-wing advocates of increased protectionism feel that the main threat to the French economy comes from the industrialized countries, particularly West Germany. According to Juquin, "the dogma of free trade" is a major impediment to the creation of a humane and egalitarian society.

Neo-Protectionism in West Germany

In West Germany, the new protectionist movement is associated with a group of intellectuals within the ranks of the Social Democratic Party (SPD), whose most prominent advocate is Wolfgang Hager. The primary concern of these protectionists is the threat to the extensive welfare state in industrialized Europe, what Hager describes as "the most decent society ever created in history." The main threat to this way of life comes from greater exposure to imports from Japan, Eastern Europe and in particular the newly industrializing countries (NICs) in the Third World. The reaction of the right-wing parties and international capital to the expanded welfare state has been to invest abroad, to induce recessions to break trade unions, and to extend free trade.

The strength of the trade union movement in Western Europe has created "unfree labour markets" and a high-cost society, by international standards. There is no question about that. But it has also created a humane society with an extensive social welfare system and relatively low levels of unemployment. According to Hagar, this just society has been threatened by the less-developed countries which "rely on domestic underconsumption for economic growth," a genteel way of describing deliberate deprivation of the populace, enforced by repressive governments. While actual trade between Western Europe and the industrializing Third World countries is not all that significant, because of the turmoil in the international markets and the relatively free mobility of capital, it has had a much greater impact on the manufacturing sectors.

Hager argues that the industrialized countries cannot keep ahead of the expansion of manufacturing in the less-developed countries. There are too few "sunrise" industries, and there is already very keen competition between Japan, the United States and the larger European countries in all the key areas. Even in the sectors where high technology and government support have given the advanced countries a lead, the NICs are close behind. The days of the natural protection provided by technological advance are gone forever. In the end, the NICs and their successors will always have the advantage of lower wages and the ability to acquire high levels of technology.

In this situation, attempts by the industrialized countries to be competitive can only lead to attacks on trade unions and to a political battle to reduce labour and other costs of production. The end result will be a far less decent society. An alternative approach is for the state to subsidize private industry, a practice that is rapidly expanding, but which is far less efficient than protectionism, as it generally rewards the least efficient firms. The only sound alternative is a form of protectionism on a European basis.

Thus, Hager and his supporters in the West German Social Democratic Party urge the creation of a European bloc, including the countries of both the European Economic Community and the European Free Trade Association, with relatively free trade among themselves. These countries all have a similar level of development, industrialization, trade union traditions, and social democratic parties which have implemented the extensive welfare state. Outside of this bloc, there should be a system of managed trade. This new system would have the advantages of free trade competition but "at a pace and under conditions which do not destroy the fabric of economic exchange, and of decades-old distributional bargains in society, beyond tolerable limits." Imports would be permitted, but at specified levels. The level of imports, and their prices, would be adjusted to take into account the "social dumping" of the exporting countries.

Hager argues that for Europe, individual national protectionism would be "messy and financially costly, coupled with a stateward shift of the mixed economy." As a social democrat, he has a strong preference for maintaining the capitalist economy, with a minimum level of state ownership. The only practical alternative is European community preference. However, he is pessimistic about the ability to achieve this political alternative. The likely result will be the steady erosion of the European experiment, which combined trade union rights, the welfare state, private enterprise and relatively free trade with other European countries.

Labour and the American Debate

In the United States the labour movement has become very nationalistic in the last ten years as they see plants shut down and manufacturing shifting overseas. The American Federation of Labor-Congress of Industrial Organizations (AFL-CIO) estimates that between 1979 and 1985 around 2.3 million industrial workers lost their jobs due to the expansion of imports. Between 1978 and 1985, imports of manufactured goods into the United States have increased roughly four times as rapidly as domestic production. In steel and automobiles, imports now have 25% of the U.S. market. Half of all clothing and 75% of all shoes are imported. To a large extent, this is a result of decisions made by U.S. corporations. For example, between 1970 and 1980 General Electric added 30,000 employees to its operations in the newly industrializing countries; at the same time, it eliminated 25,000 jobs in the United States.

Furthermore, American service jobs are beginning to be shifted overseas, particularly to the Caribbean. For example, American Airlines shifted their keypunch operations from Tulsa, Oklahoma, to Barbados. Management claimed that the lower labour costs would save the company $3.5 million in the first year of operation. This trend has been devastating to the trade union movement. The Steelworkers and the International Ladies Garment Workers' Union have each lost more than half their members. The United Auto Workers lost almost 400,000 members between 1978 and 1985. Since its peak in 1975, the AFL-CIO has lost around one million members.

The major problem for workers is the mobility of capital and production that has come with the reduction of tariffs and the move to free trade. Blue-collar workers in the United States are increasingly non-white, from Third World countries, and/or female. Thus, the real question in industries like textiles and clothing is whether the operation will employ a Chinese-American stitcher in New England at $6 per hour or her sister in China at $0.16.

The first reaction of organized labour has been to call for a repudiation of free trade and the adoption of "fair trade," that is, more managed trade and a new industrial strategy under which imports would not be banned but controlled through quotas and higher tariffs. Furthermore, the AFL-CIO has been pressing the Congress to pass legislation with regard to specific imports and particular countries. They argue that imported products should rise only in proportion to the growth of the U.S. market. They have also supported domestic content legislation, which, as originally proposed by the United Auto Workers, would require a percentage of every car sold in the United States to be built locally, a principle which could be extended to other industries.

American labour has also been pushing for fair labour standards. Through the International Labour Rights Working Group, the American labour movement has obtained the support of churches, human rights organizations, and a broad spectrum of community groups. The 1984 *Trade and Tariff Act* limits the granting of trade preference under the Generalized System of Preferences (GSP) for underdeveloped countries, authorized by the GATT, to countries which have accepted international standards for human rights, child labour, fair wages and hours, and occupational safety and health standards. Workers must have the right to organize and bargain collectively. The AFL-CIO argues that limiting imports from a country like South Korea would reduce the incentive for their government to be so repressive, weaken the power of the transnational corporations and strengthen international trade union solidarity. The 1984 legislation was aimed in particular at the repressive right-wing dictatorships in Asia. However, as these governments are close political and military allies of the U.S. government, the Reagan administration has chosen not to implement it.

Unfortunately, the ideology of economic nationalism can sometimes lead to national chauvinism which borders on racism, which can be sensed in some American unionists' attacks on the economic policies and practices of Japan, South Korea and Taiwan. The nationalist strategy also led the union movement to support the 1987 U.S. legislation to increase tariffs in the textile industry, which in turn trapped them in an alliance with the owners of capital, the same capitalists who have been shifting production to low-wage countries abroad. Economic nationalism can also lead to divisions within the trade union movement itself, as many unionists recognize that import controls on automobiles and clothing, for example, can hurt non-unionized workers with low incomes who need to purchase cheaper products.

Finally, it is not at all clear that the main reason for job losses is foreign imports. The reactionary monetary and fiscal policies of the Reagan administration, including high interest rates, have reduced exports and encouraged imports. The high level of the U.S. dollar made imports cheaper. The low level of economic growth greatly restricted job creation. Internal shifts in manufacturing to low-wage areas was a major cause of job loss and the drop in trade union membership. The other major cause has been the introduction of the new technologies based on computers, and in particular robotization.

As an alternative to a corporatist-led nationalism, the left within the U.S. trade union movement has called for a new national industrial strategy, to include the following:

• Economic policies which once again set as the prime goal full employment, through lower interest rates, reducing the value of the U.S. dollar, and fiscal policies which stimulate growth;
• Policies which would restrict plant layoffs and shutdowns;
• A massive retraining program for workers in industries which are dying;
• The introduction of economic democracy through employee ownership and participation;
• Community-based planning for regional development;
• Using federal procurement policies to support publicly owned enterprises serving social needs;
• A national wage policy which builds equality and promotes economic growth;
• Allocation of research and development funds into new enterprise, worker-owned or joint ventures;
• Allocation of resources on the basis of need;
• Reduction of the role of the armaments industry in economic development.

For those facing the loss of a job, the quick appeal of an alliance with the bosses to pressure for tariff and quota protections seems to be the only feasible solution. But this immediate strategy does not deal with the fact that the transnational corporations are central to the issue of job loss and unemployment. In the final analysis, the key problem for workers in both the Third World and in the industrialized world is social control over capital. The only real answer is to extend political democracy and to include democratic control over the economy.

CHAPTER 21

An Alternative Direction for Canada

The accord between labour and capital formed the basis of the division of income, wealth and power in our society for almost 30 years after World War II. Few found fault with the system which was producing high rates of economic growth, rising real incomes for the large majority of Canadians, and a decline in the percentage of the population experiencing absolute poverty. The good times enabled working people to form trade unions and bargain collectively with management. Working conditions and standards were improved. Through democratic political action, people put pressure on governments to greatly expand the welfare state.

However, this system began to break down around 1971, with the collapse of the international monetary system. The general economic crisis which followed has continued now for over fifteen years. The new business agenda, unilaterally declared by capital, has repudiated the accord. All-out war has been declared on trade unions. Social welfare programs are progressively being reduced and eliminated. Big capital has declared that the free market and free trade are to be the guiding principles of the future. It is not surprising that the popular forces in Canada and elsewhere have begun a search for political, economic and social alternatives.

The Canadian Catholic Bishops and the Economic Crisis

The first major call for a debate on the future of Canada came not from the trade union movement or the New Democratic Party but from the Canadian Conference of Catholic Bishops. In 1983 the Episcopal Commission for Social Affairs issued their widely read and controversial statement, "Ethical Reflections on the Economic

Crisis." It was roundly attacked by economists, big business organizations and the business press. The bishops criticized the trend allowing capital to reassert its role as the dominant force in society, denounced the acceptance of Social Darwinian theories of survival of the fittest, and repudiated the reinforcement of the patterns of domination and inequality.

The bishops noted that their analysis rested on two basic principles within the traditional teachings of the church. First, the Christian tradition is associated with "the preferential option for the poor, the afflicted, and the oppressed." Christians must identify with the victims of injustice, the bishops said. Second, there is "the special value and dignity of human work." In the perspective of the Reflections, it is through work that people exercise their creative spirit and realize their human dignity. Work is a social process which enables people to participate in the development of their own communities and gives meaning to their existence as human beings.

The bishops argued that as we search for solutions to the prolonged economic crisis and continued high levels of unemployment, we must adopt economic policies which "realize that the needs of the poor have priority over the wants of the rich; that the rights of workers are more important than the maximization of profits; that the participation of marginalized groups have precedence over the preservation of a system which excludes them." Given these principles, the following guidelines were recommended:

• Unemployment rather than inflation should be seen as the number one problem;
• There is a need for a new industrial strategy to create permanent and meaningful jobs in local communities;
• Reducing inflation requires an approach which recognizes the existing inequalities in income and wealth;
• Social services must be maintained and improved rather than reduced;
• Labour unions should be supported and provided with a more decisive and responsible role in planning;
• Communities should be involved in economic planning.

An alternative community-oriented economic model would include the following:

Socially-useful forms of production; labour-intensive industries; the use of appropriate forms of technology; self-

reliant models of economic development; community ownership and control of industries; new forms of worker
management and ownership; and greater use of the renewable
energy sources in industrial production.

These and related recommendations were presented by the bishops
to the Macdonald Royal Commission on the Canadian economy.
More emphasis was given to the principle of self-reliant development for Canada. The bishops concluded that "an economy that is
largely organized to provide for external interests and [is] dependent
on externally controlled means of production, cannot serve the basic
needs of its own population." A strategy of self-reliance permits a
society to direct its resources to serve basic needs. It also allows local
communities to participate in the structuring of their own development, permits the empowerment of people, and reinforces the ability
of communities to conserve and protect their local resources. Self-
reliance also permits the cultivation of new forms of solidarity with
poor people and, on an international basis, promotes bonds of respect
between independent nations.

The Position of the New Democratic Party

In March 1985 the federal New Democratic Party adopted an important policy statement, "An Alternative Strategy: Fair Trade vs.
Free Trade," in response to James Kelleher's paper of January 29,
which had advocated a comprehensive free trade agreement with the
United States. One of the major problems facing Canada as a trading
nation, the easy mobility of capital, was identified in the NDP paper.
Plants are being shut down as manufacturing is being shifted to offshore low-wage areas. The NDP questioned whether Canadians
were "prepared to allow the rules of international competitiveness to
dictate our economic destiny?" In today's climate, this means a
Canada with lower wages, poorer working conditions and reduced
social services.
   In addition, the paper noted, Canada is one of the most import-
prone countries in the world, particularly in the area of manufactured
products. We rely heavily on the export of resources. For each job in
the resource extraction area, there are four in processing those
resources into end products, and Canada exports those processing
jobs along with the raw resources. Our reliance on imports is
heightened by the fact that Canada has traditionally been a branch

plant economy. In 1985, 48% of our manufacturing industry was foreign owned, by far the highest of any Western country. Yet, with tariffs disappearing, the need for branch plants disappears. A 1982 study by the Foreign Investment Review Agency concluded that "72% of all Canadian imports were accounted for by foreign owned firms." The limited range of manoeuvre allowed us by the branch plant economy is even further restricted due to our heavy dependence on trade with one country, the United States. Around 25% of our trade in manufactured goods is accounted for by the Auto Pact alone. A bilateral free trade agreement, the NDP paper argues, would only link us even closer to the American economy and further reduce policy choices.

The New Democratic Party concluded that there were three possible strategies available to the federal government at this time. One is to emphasize exports for the international market, that is, to export resources, following our tradition as hewers of wood and drawers of water. However, the NDP paper suggests that once we accept that strategy, we must agree to do what is necessary to compete with low-wage countries. We have only to look at the example of the Swedish shipbuilding industry, probably the most advanced in the world in terms of design and technology, but which could not compete with South Korea, where shipbuilders work for one-eighth of the wages. We would also have to specialize production, making the Canadian economy even more vulnerable to international economic upheavals. How can we raise our standard of living by lowering it?

The NDP paper also examines the strategy advanced by big business and the Mulroney government, freer trade with the United States. This is the easiest road, but in fact Canada would be tying its future to the United States at the very time that the American economy is entering a relative decline. The United States is losing the international trade war, and that is the reason for the protectionist movement in that country. Further continental integration would tie Canada even closer to its traditional role as the resource base for American manufacturing. It would make it more difficult for Canada to diversify trade, particularly with the Pacific Rim countries, the most rapidly expanding market in the world.

The NDP recommends an alternative strategy, a more self-reliant approach to development. A new industrial strategy, based on self-reliance, could provide thousands of jobs for Canadians in building our own ships, producing our own mining machinery, producing finished construction materials, to name a few. To protect emerging Canadian industry the NDP strategy would manage trade with countries which have an "international comparative advantage" due to political repression and authoritarian work environments. NDP "fair trade" arrangements would include the following major policies:

Canadian Content Requirements. Following the pattern of the Auto Pact, any company which wishes to sell its products in the Canadian market must also be willing to share investment and jobs. Content requirements are far superior to quotas, as they provide access to other technologies and products.

Import Replacement. Our trade deficit in manufactured goods cost us around 200,000 jobs in 1983. We must give priority to encouraging production in Canada.

Domestic Procurement. Canada needs a "buy Canadian" policy, especially for manufactured products. In 1979, 49 cents of each dollar spent by Canadian governments went out of the country, or around $30 billion of purchasing power.

Industrial Offsets. For large-scale resource projects, in, for example, the offshore oil industry, local purchasing performance requirements for major contracts would increase production and jobs in Canada.

Research and Development. Spending on R&D is very low in Canada compared to our industrial competitors. Around 94% of all our new patents are granted to foreigners. It is essential for Canada to increase public and private spending in this area.

What the New Democratic Party is calling for is a new industrial strategy based on increased self-reliance. However, as a social democratic party, it is not prepared to advance an alternative vision of Canada based on co-operation rather than competition. Nor is it willing to identify private ownership of capital and capital flight as the fundamental problems causing prolonged economic recession, misery for so many people, and an anti-democratic system based on centralization, hierarchy and domination. The NDP program is not a transitional program for moving Canada from corporate capitalism to socialism. But it is a clear alternative to free trade with the United States and unlimited rule by big capital.

The Program of the Canadian Labour Congress

The position on free trade taken by the executives of the Canadian Labour Congress (CLC) and the Ontario Federation of Labour (OFL) in 1985 followed closely that of the NDP. A more comprehensive statement of objectives and strategies was adopted at the CLC convention in 1986, which endorsed two important position papers, "Full Employment and Fairness—the Workers' Agenda for Canada" and "Our Canada or Theirs? Workers Confront the Corporate Blueprint." As an alternative to the new business agenda and a return to the free market, the CLC called for a strategy based on a renewed commitment to full employment and fairness, including creating jobs, promoting socially useful investment, raising real wages and living standards, and supporting public services. In the CLC view the new strategy "must be built on publicly controlled, democratic, economic planning" and on solidarity with others in the community who are also suffering. In this effort to create a new democracy, the CLC argued, "nothing short of a complete restructuring of the Canadian economy will do." Immediate emphasis should be put on fiscal policies of reflation to reduce unemployment, on tax reform, reduced interest rates, "public control and democratization of the investment process," the extension of public ownership at least into the financial and resource sectors, and the expansion of social programs.

The documents recognized the fact that free trade with the United States, cutbacks in social programs, the broad attack on traditional trade union rights, deregulation, privatization and contracting out were all part of a unified strategy by business interests. To combat the unity of big business and the political right, the CLC concluded that it was necessary for trade unions to organize the unorganized, unify the trade union movement, and "work to build links around a common program with other groups in society that are also under attack." But for a secure future, "we must go beyond this, and we must begin to use our resources, as workers, to begin to build the kinds of institutions, the kinds of enterprises that will be the foundation for a new society." Trade union organizations need to get control of pension funds so they can be used for socially useful and job-creating purposes; they need to place emphasis on local community development, on the creation of jobs in Canadian communities and on the development of secondary industries based on our resources; and they need to develop an action plan to create and support unionized workers' co-ops as agents of economic development.

The CLC remains totally opposed to a bilateral free trade agreement with the United States because they believe it guarantees severe economic dislocation, will force Canada to abandon traditional tools of economic management, and will undermine our economic, political and cultural sovereignty. Free trade with the United States, in their view, will also "limit our scope to follow an independent course in the wider field of international affairs."

As an alternative, the CLC argues, we must see trade policy as "an important subordinate part of an economic strategy that is designed to provide full employment, a high and rising standard of living for all Canadians, and a more equal distribution of income and wealth." We have to face the problems inherent in the weakness and lack of diversity of our manufacturing sector. There must be planned trade, beginning with diversification away from the United States. "Both multilateral and bilateral trade negotiations must be approached on a sectoral basis, and job and production guarantees must be accepted as a necessary part of any agreement." Examples of this kind of managed trade, based on mutual benefit rather than the free market, would include the oil agreement between Petro-Canada and Mexico and the grain sales agreements between the Canadian Wheat Board and the USSR and China. Diversification would give Canadians greater freedom to determine their economic future "rather than have it imposed on them as a result of businesses pursuing their self-interest in a continental market."

The position of the Canadian Labour Congress, like that of the New Democratic Party, proposes a reform of capitalism through a limited Keynesian approach. Within the labour movement, the Canadian Union of Public Employees (CUPE) advanced a more radical approach to the economic crisis, based on the Alternative Economic Strategy (AES) put forward by the left wing of the Labour Party in Britain. First published in *CUPE Facts* in February 1983, it later appeared in John Calvert's book, *Government, Limited,* in the same year. Like the AES, it can be seen as the beginning of a transitional program moving towards a democratic socialist society.

While many of CUPE's proposals are familiar, the overall program is much more radical. It recommends stimulating the economy through the usual fiscal policies, but opposes the traditional use of across-the-board tax cuts for business. The union believes interest rates should be lowerd, and that it is absolutely necessary not only to stop the cuts in public services, but to expand services. These are the policies advocated by the social democratic left. But CUPE and Calvert have gone much further. They take the view that it is necessary to establish foreign exchange controls on currency trans-actions immediately to help solve the balance of payments problem and capital flight. They would then nationalize the banks in order to control credit, to help stop the flight of capital, and to be able to direct investment to socially useful projects.

Should inflation increase, CUPE would respond with price controls. They would restructure government finances on the expenditure side in order to direct economic incentives to the most productive sectors of the economy. On the revenue side, they would bring in tax reforms based on the ability to pay as a means of redistributing income and wealth. They would expand public ownership to break the power of the transnational corporations, and to redirect profits to socially necessary projects, such as government financing to expand affordable housing. Capital investment would be diversified, and directed away from the resource area to manufacturing and the service sectors. CUPE believes public ownership of the energy industry is a necessity. However, in their view crown corporations must also be drastically changed through democratization, so that employees, the local community and the public at large may assume control and direction; inherent in this is the revamping of the decision-making process to permit the broadest participation. They do not consider it appropriate for crown corporations to operate according to the same principles as private companies.

However, the fact that most of the far-reaching changes advocated by CUPE and Calvert were not adopted by the Canadian Labour Congress reveals the extent to which the leadership of the CLC is still firmly committed to social democracy and believes that we can save the post-war accord beween capital and labour. But at least they are moving in the right direction and offer a clear alternative to the Mulroney government and big business.

The Canadian Centre for Policy Alternatives

The Canadian Centre for Policy Alternatives is an independent "think tank" on the political left, closely linked to the New Democratic Party and the Canadian Labour Congress. In the 1980s, it has produced a number of books, independent studies, research reports and working papers advocating increased self-reliance for Canada and greater independence from the United States. Their collective effort has been in opposition to a free trade agreement with the United States. On the political level, they have advocated the expansion of coalitions involving organized labour and popular groups. The women's movement, the peace movement and the environmental movement have demonstrated the effectiveness of such coalitions.

At the 1984 national conference of the Centre a special session was held on the question of Canadian economic self-reliance, alternative paths to jobs, development, equality and peace. Sam Gindin, research director for the Canadian Auto Workers, argued that trying to become "internationally competitive" is a dead end street. To be competitive internationally we have to accept wage restraints, we cannot raise minimum wages, we cannot increase social services, we cannot support manufacturing in our hinterland areas, and we cannot increase taxes on corporations, as to do so makes Canadian firms less competitive in the international market. The business agenda for Canada, Gindin warns, means "subordinating social goals and ideals to the priority of strengthening the status quo, to strengthening the power of corporations over our lives. It means undermining our national autonomy in every positive sense of the term."

The alternative he proposes is planned trade and greater self-sufficiency, including bilateral deals and Canadian content proposals. Greater self-sufficiency means strengthening our manufacturing base. An alternative program for Canada begins with "challenging the role of international markets, and therefore corporate power, in determining economic and social outcomes in our society." Specifically, Gindin concludes that we need to nationalize the banks and other financial institutions and introduce foreign exchange controls over currency. We must also limit the ability of corporations to move their capital and profits at will, blackmailing workers and local communities. Aside from strong legislation on plant closures, the government must play a more central role in directing investment. In addition, because Canada has the world's highest per capita deficit in manufactured goods, we need a policy of import replacement. On the export side, we need to promote greater processing of our natural resources in Canada. Finally, we need improvements in the labour market; "we must replace any tendencies toward international competition between workers with international solidarity." This means a joint fight against lowering wages, reducing standards of working conditions, and restricting trade union rights.

Michael Bradfield, an economist at Dalhousie University, questions the traditional dependence of Canada on megaprojects for development, particularly in the resource sector and in the hinterland areas. He believes there is adequate capital being created in Canada's hinterland areas, through personal and business savings. The problem is getting control of this capital and directing investment to local projects, identified by the community. As a beginning, he argues, capital could be mobilized by local financial institutions, credit unions and pension funds. As an example of co-operative, worker-controlled projects, he points to the very successful Mondragon co-operatives in Spain. Until the people of Canada actually get control over their governments and the direction of the economy, says Bradfield, workers and local communities must take the initiative and strike out on their own.

Alexander Lockhart, a development specialist at Trent University, stresses that self-reliance is not just an economic development strategy but also enhances social and political development. He believes that while economic development for "international competition" must inevitably rely on human exploitation, self-reliant development must be a form of human development. For self-reliance to work, he writes, there has to be "orderly growth in a direction that a self-conscious community of interests agrees to be necessary or desirable," a process of building shared commitments to the common well-being, the attainment of health and satisfaction. He would include in "common well-being" cultural diversity, social stability, local economic diversification, and political empower-ment, all of which create a good place to live. Rather than have our lives determined by corporate decision-making, Lockhart argues, planning decisions must be made by those who have to live with the outcomes.

Many large energy projects in Canada provide classic examples of decisions made contrary to community interests by people who do not have to live with the consequences. In the early 1980s I worked on the environmental assessment project for a hydroelectric dam proposed by B.C. Hydro and the Social Credit government for the Peace River in British Columbia, the "Site C Dam" near Fort St. John. The government megaproject, costing $3 billion, would em-ploy a few thousand people (mainly brought into the community) for two to three years during construction, completely disrupt local services and housing, cause all the well-known social problems, and when it was finished, employ only 25 people. The most beautiful part of the Peace River would be flooded, wildlife habitat destroyed, some of the best farmland in B.C. would be gone, and the potential for a viable fruit and vegetable industry, providing long-term jobs, would be undermined. What would be gained? It was hoped that the surplus power could be exported to the United States. The govern-ment-appointed commissioners naturally approved the project. How many times has this been repeated in the history of Canada?

In a major paper for the Centre, Jim Turk, research director of the United Electrical, Radio and Machine Workers of Canada, also takes the position that the only real alternative to free trade with the United

States and the commitment to "international competition" is greater self-reliance. He does not reject trade, he merely recommends that it be made "subsidiary to meeting Canadian needs." He believes that the primary emphasis should be on production for the needs of Canadian society, and that full employment must be a primary goal. Genuine international co-operation requires a rejection of international competition, which, he argues, suits only the interests of the transnational corporations. He believes trade must be based on mutual support, not exploitation.

A common theme in the recent work of the Centre is the need to restrict the mobility of capital and to subordinate it to social goals. Another stresses the concomitant need for state control of our major financial institutions, of foreign exchange, of imports and of prices. Achieving this new agenda for Canada requires a strong and politically active working class and the formation of coalitions with other groups in Canadian society.

The GATT-Fly Proposal for Community Self-Reliance

The most comprehensive proposal for a self-reliant Canada has been advanced by GATT-Fly, a project of the mainstream churches in Canada. Its mandate is to "do research, education and action in solidarity with peoples' organizations struggling for economic justice in Canada and the Third World." Their major study, *Community Self-Reliance: A Canadian Vision of Economic Justice*, was published in June 1987. It is a thorough analysis, well worth careful examination. In it, GATT-Fly identifies three basic characteristics of a self-reliant Canada:

> Canadians produce the essential goods and services we need, in the quantity and quality needed.
>
> Families and individuals who now receive average or below average incomes, and who make up the vast majority of Canadians, have enough income to purchase the goods and services which they collectively produce.
>
> Canada's foreign trade continues, but only as a planned extension of production and trade at home.

The GATT-Fly study expresses self-reliance in terms of community and place, and not solely in terms of individuals. A "community" can be a neighbourhood or humankind in general, but the most common identification is the nation. The GATT-Fly view is that given the political divisions in the world, it is at the national level that most people seek self-reliance. Thus, for the GATT-Fly group, self-reliance also includes the concept of democratic control and popular participation.

The GATT-Fly project encompasses most of the ideas already expressed in this chapter. The model that it advances is quite specific and detailed; perhaps that is its major shortcoming. As Cy Gonick has commented, very few Canadians have seriously considered a political economy that is so different from our entrenched tradition of continental integration. We need more time to develop a popular consciousness about self-reliance. According to GATT-Fly, the basic steps to be taken to establish a self-reliant Canadian economy are:

• reducing Canada's dependence on external trade;
• stimulating modest economic growth to achieve full employment and improve the quality of life for the poor and low-income workers;
• paying off our foreign debt;
• changing minimum wage, taxation and public spending policies to redistribute wealth and expand human services;
• redeploying domestic savings;
• ending foreign ownership and control and substituting various forms of democratic control;
• developing appropriate technology;
• establishing new international relations of solidarity with other peoples seeking self-reliance in their own right.

A political strategy to develop popular support must focus on the expansion of extra-parliamentary coalitions made up of trade unions and community groups. A major task of popular education among all Canadians must be undertaken to enable the existing coalitions to grow in strength and commitment and to unite the people in a popular movement for change.

But there should be no illusion about a strategy of self-reliance for Canada. It will be strongly opposed by big capital and its agents in the "think tanks," the mass media and the universities. It will be strongly opposed by the U.S. government and U.S. capital. As Cy Gonick has pointed out, the GATT-Fly program for self-reliance "is far more radical than anything tried in Allende's Chile, and we know what happened there." Furthermore, anyone who has read Stephen

Clarkson's book, *Canada and the Reagan Challenge*, knows the tremendous pressure American business and the U.S. government put on the Trudeau government to get rid of the National Energy Program, the *Foreign Investment Review Act* and plans for a modest industrial policy. Despite the opposition—or because of it—it is time to seriously advance an alternative development strategy for Canada. When the next recession hits, we may find that a lot of Canadians are eagerly looking for a real alternative to dependence on a failing American giant.

CHAPTER 22

Mobilizing for Popular Democracy

One of the central themes of this book is the major change taking place in the structure of world capitalism. The prolonged economic stagnation of the 1970s and 1980s seems very much like the profound depression which lasted from 1873 to 1896. The Great Depression of the 1930s was ended early by the onset of a war which was truly world-wide. However, in the nuclear era world war offers no solution to the current economic crisis, even for the capitalists. We are witnessing the end of what political economists refer to as "Fordism": the long post-war boom in the advanced capitalist countries where the driving force for the economy was mass production for a mass domestic market. Gone are the high rates of economic growth, high profit levels, rising real incomes, low unemployment and the expansion of social services.

After the Second World War, the owners of capital were willing to accept the class compromise with labour and the extensive welfare state because of the consistently high rate of profit. But conditions changed during the 1970s with the onset of the prolonged general downturn in the world economy, and so did capital's willingness to compromise. In order to restore the high rate of capital accumulation, a new business agenda was created, supported by right-wing political parties and governments.

Joel Krieger has argued that the modern welfare state, and government fiscal and monetary policies having full employment as a goal, were "a transitory motif of class compromise" made possible by political compromises between labour and capital within the context of a period of *exceptional* economic performance. The social policy package of the welfare state was "typical of an unusual period, perhaps never to be repeated." What we are seeing now is a return to the more unstable period of capitalist development which was characteristic of the period prior to World War II.

Alain Lipietz reminds us that the economic recovery after 1983 has been primarily in the United States; hence, everyone has been trying to sell in that market. The newly industrialized Asian countries and Japan have been most dependent on the U.S. market. Because of the reductions in tariffs under the GATT, imports into the United States have risen significantly. But the U.S. recovery has been based on a huge federal deficit and a major balance of payments deficit; these have been maintained by "pumping capital out of the rest of the world" through very high interest rates. The shocks in the stock markets in October 1987 and the subsequent fall in the U.S. dollar demonstrated the fragility and shallowness of the recovery of the 1980s.

The new system of capital accumulation is based on super-exploitation of labour in the Third World and highly capital-intensive production in the industrialized world, symbolized by the expanding use of computers and robots. The gains in productivity are primarily reserved for the owners of capital. Because of the persistence of high levels of unemployment, the decline in real incomes, and the increasing importance of low-paying "flexible" employment, the new system of capital accumulation cannot produce a steady increase in mass consumption. The result is likely to be what Lipietz calls "competitive stagnation." The inevitable next recession will undoubtedly make things worse for most people, but it will also open the possibility for serious political change.

The Opportunity for Political Change

In all modern states, governments rule through some form of hegemony, the consensual basis of the political system which creates passive support from the citizens. The ruled feel an obligation to follow the dictates of the government. In constitutional liberal democracies like Canada, the exercise of political authority by a ruling elite is unimpeded as long as the government of the day assumes office after elections which are considered to be free and fair. Under our system of representative parliamentary government, citizens expect a political party to outline its policies during an election and to follow them generally once in office. When parties drastically depart from their election platforms after they take office and introduce surprise policies, they quickly lose public support. Recently, we have seen this in the case of the Social Credit government in British Columbia (after 1983) and the Conservative government in Saskatchewan (after 1986). Paradoxically, these now very unpopular governments continue to rule with the consent of the citizens, who can see no practical alternative. The habit of consent has thus deteriorated into a form of coercion. In Canada, the traditional response from most of the alienated majority is grumbling and complaining. On occasion, there are political demonstrations, but organized, sustained extra-parliamentary opposition has been rare since the end of World War II.

All capitalist societies are characterized by domination by the business class. Consent in these societies depends on the ability of the dominant group, through the ideological system (e.g., religion, education, mass media, etc.), to convince the majority of the people that the interests of the dominant group are the same as those of the society at large. But consent and liberal rule can be maintained only as long as the dominant group can provide an adequate economic environment. Group and class conflicts are always present in class-divided societies; for a stable social order to prevail, it is necessary for the mass of citizens to habitually conform. In times of prolonged economic crisis, the voluntary consent given to the dominant capitalist class declines and may disappear. We have only to think of the Great Depression of the 1930s; throughout the world, governments moved to dictatorships and state repression to maintain the domination of the capitalist class in the face of rising popular discontent. In the capitalist Third World today, the normal form of government is repressive dictatorship.

When we enter into a period of general breakdown and structural change, as we are now doing, it becomes possible for the popular forces to contest the established order. The capitalist class and its allies are still dominant, but they no longer rule with uncontested consent. Working people, through their organizations, can begin to move in a new political direction. Class alliances are shifting, and coalitions can be formed with other disadvantaged groups. There is virtual war on the ideological front, as popular groups put forth alternative policies and advocate increased democracy. Real political change becomes a possibility.

In the Third World, popular coalitions are the primary form of political activity today. In part this is made necessary by the repressive nature of the authoritarian states and the fact that elections, if and when they are held, are highly manipulated and are generally seen as illegitimate. In these popular coalitions we always find the trade unions, the peasant organizations, students and teachers, slum dwellers, womens' organizations and religious groups. In 1987 we only have to think of the United Democratic Front in South Africa, the Farabundo Marti National Liberation Front in El Salvador, or the Bayan movement in the Philippines. But this political tradition has also been emerging in the industrialized capitalist world in the 1970s and the 1980s.

The Formation of the New Political Coalitions

Most Canadians are aware of the existence of political coalitions and their successes and failures. There have been coalitions around peace issues at least since the Canadian Campaign for Nuclear Disarmament in the early 1960s. Environmental coalitions have also been on the scene for many years. I participated in the formation of two broad environmental coalitions in British Columbia in the 1970s which were quite effective in opposing indiscriminate use of dangerous herbicides and uranium mining. The National Action Committee on the Status of Women (NAC), first formed in 1972, is a coalition of over 500 different womens' organizations from across Canada. Without a doubt, NAC has been the most impressive and successful political coalition in Canadian history.

Many of the coalitions with which we are familiar centre around a single issue. For example, in recent years there has been the Health Care Coalition organized in 1982 to oppose cutbacks in medicare, the broad coalition formed to oppose the de-indexing of family allowances and pensions, and the coalition formed to put pressure on the Mulroney government not to undermine the existing generic drug legislation. There have also been a number of coalitions working at the provincial level, in British Columbia, Alberta, Quebec, Newfoundland and Saskatchewan. They have had a broader agenda: opposing right-wing provincial governments who are cutting back essential social services and attacking historic trade union rights. Coalitions opposing the free trade agreement with the United States now exist in all the provinces.

On the national level there are two working coalitions at this time. First, there is the Working Committee for Social Solidarity, a broadly based coalition of trade unions, NAC, the National Farmers Union, church representatives and other community groups. This coalition, which has been in existence for several years, released a new popular declaration on economic and social policy, *A Time to Stand Together*, the day before the text of the Canada/U.S. free trade agreement was released to the public. The other national coalition is the Pro-Canada network, the alliance of trade unions and major interest groups leading the opposition to the free trade agreement with the United States.

All popular coalitions in Canada face similar problems. What kind of social classes should be involved in the coalition and what kind of class relationships are possible? How do you build alliances and sustain them? What are the key political strategies? What kind of firm commitments are made when joining a coalition? What is the relationship between the coalition and political parties, especially the New Democratic Party? How can these coalitions be transformed from limited alliances into a new political movement?

In the past, coalitions have been largely based around one dominant organization, with the other groups generally playing only a supporting role. John Dillon of GATT-Fly calls these "power alliances." Such alliances characteristically have only a minimum platform, make no real concessions in policy debates, and tend to have their membership chosen by the leading force. A new form of coalition is emerging which strives for equality, full participation in the formation of policy and strategy, and mutual support on key issues. Group membership in these organizations constantly changes as they develop more political cohesion. One of the interesting developments has been the conscious decision of many of the new coalitions to exclude individual businesses and business organizations. In the past, popular coalitions have often had to restrict their policy goals to conform to the "free market" attitudes of most business interests.

The key challenge for coalitions today is to move beyond single issues and to develop the trust which permits the formation of an opposition program and long-term strategies. We can see this taking place in the Working Committee for Social Solidarity, and in the Solidarité populaire Québec, originally begun in 1984 to oppose the Mulroney government's economic policy. Since then the Quebec coalition has been growing and evolving. In 1986 it mounted a major campaign to oppose the provincial government's three major policy reports, all dedicated to expanding neo-conservatism; to date, the Bourassa government has not acted on the reports.

In my opinion, the key to the future success of coalitions rests with the trade unions. The unions must realize that the era of the post-war capital/labour accord is over. They can't bring it back. There is a new business agenda, and it does not recognize the right of trade unions even to exist. As their membership continues to decline, the trade unions will have to recognize the absolute necessity of forming political alliances with other groups. And, as I will argue below, they also have to see the necessity of breaking their formal ties with social democratic parties like the NDP.

The best-known coalition effort in Canada was that which emerged in British Columbia in 1983. A great deal was learned from this experiment. I was deeply involved in it from the beginning to the end. In May 1983 the Social Credit government, under the leadership of Bill Bennett, was re-elected on a moderately conservative platform which called for fiscal restraint and "downsizing" of the civil service. British Columbia was still in the depths of the 1981-2 great recession. Voters expected the Bennett government to continue as in the past. However, for two months after the election the cabinet consulted with advisers from the Fraser Institute. In early July the government brought in a new budget and 26 pieces of legislation. A brand new neo-conservative agenda appeared: taxation shifts, raising grants to corporations, cutting basic services, cutbacks in education, eliminating programs which aided the poor and other disadvantaged groups, and a broad attack on traditional trade union collective bargaining rights. In addition, there was a dramatic shift in power, centralizing decision-making in the hands of the cabinet and the top level of the civil service. Public opinion polls revealed that a large majority of B.C. citizens believed that the Socreds had no mandate to carry out this new program.

The opposition New Democratic Party limited its criticism to debate in the provincial legislature, an inadequate response to the right-wing assault. The failure of parliamentary opposition led to the formation of Operation Solidarity, the political unification of the trade union movement, and the Solidarity Coalition, a very significant province-wide organization of community groups. Mass meetings and marches were organized over the summer and fall, culminating in a demonstration of 50,000 at the Socred convention in Vancouver. At a dramatic provincial meeting in October, delegates to the conference of the Solidarity Coalition gave unanimous and full support to Operation Solidarity to initiate actions "up to and including a general strike." In November, the B.C. Government Employees Union went on strike, with full support from Operation Solidarity and the Solidarity Coalition. During the progressive escalation of the strike, the top leadership of the trade union movement made a settlement with the Bennett government. Since so little was obtained in the effort, and nothing outside of trade union issues, most people concluded that the coalition effort had been sold out by the trade union leadership. Disillusionment and cynicism set in. Operation Solidarity and the Solidarity Coalition faded away and were disbanded in 1985.

There has been a great deal of debate about the experience of the B.C. Solidarity movement. What can we learn from it? A major error was the Solidarity movement's demand for concessions that could not be achieved: the complete withdrawal of the entire right-wing package. Equally serious, there was no decision-making structure in place which permitted the community groups to have any say in the negotiations during the strike. In addition, the trade union movement heavily bankrolled the Solidarity Coalition. The funding resulted in the creation of a small bureaucracy centralized in Vancouver, made the community groups dependent on this outside financing, and gave the trade unions considerable influence over the community groups.

But equally serious was the problem of the close relationship between the leadership of Operation Solidarity and the Solidarity Coalition on the one hand, and the leadership of the New Democratic Party on the other. Most of the NDP caucus opposed the November strike and publicly stated so. Many NDP leaders expressed the fear that the Solidarity movement would become a new left-wing party. They took the position that they did not want to force an election because Dave Barrett had resigned as leader and the party had no campaign funds; they were unwilling to rely on the strong public opinion opposing the Bennett government and a grass-roots campaign. Then the leadership of the trade union movement, closely linked to the NDP, decided to place all its eggs in one basket: they would concentrate on electing "their party" in the next provincial election, the traditional strategy with which they were comfortable. The alternative, popular education and mobilization for extra-parliamentary opposition—was much more difficult. The Solidarity organizations then faded away. However, the electoral strategy failed, as the NDP lost the next provincial election. As a result, when the new Social Credit government, under the leadership of Bill Vander Zalm, brought in the most repressive anti-union legislation in Canada's history in 1987, there was no coalition in existence to give support to the trade union movement. The B.C. experience demonstrates, among other things, the necessity of the new coalitions in Canada remaining clearly independent of the New Democratic Party.

Dealing with Social Democratic Parties and Governments

Anyone who has been a member of the New Democratic Party for any length of time knows that there has always been a struggle between the leadership and the rank and file over policy. The leadership constantly tries to move the party to the right, while the rank and file, represented at conventions, tries to make the party take more principled positions. As the NDP gains in the public opinion polls (often because of disaffection with the governing Liberals or Tories) the party leadership moves to the right. The left within the party is silenced. Those Canadians who have lived under NDP provincial governments know that once in office they are very quick to abandon much of their platform and what socialist ideals they once held. While the party is in office, the left wing is again effectively silenced. The NDP premier and the cabinet determine policy and declare that they must now govern for all the people, not just those who voted NDP. This is not just a Canadian phenomenon but is typical of social democratic parties everywhere. Coalitions working for serious political change must recognize that social democratic parties, pre-occupied with their electoral agenda of gaining and holding office, are not automatically going to be the defenders of the rights of trade unions and the poor.

A couple of examples from 1987 will serve to illustrate the point. During the last half of that year almost all of the public opinion polls reported that more Canadian voters were supportive of the NDP than of either the Liberals or the Tories. Other polls reported that considerably more voters preferred Ed Broadbent for prime minister to either John Turner or Brian Mulroney. Many began to seriously consider the possibility that the NDP might form the government after the next federal election.

Within this context, it is not surprising that the NDP became silent on a number of key issues and took rather opportunistic, unprincipled positions on others. For example, on the Meech Lake Accord for changing the Canadian Constitution, the NDP supported the agreement, apparently trying to protect its political standing in Quebec. As a result, it ended up taking the same position as Brian Mulroney and the Tories and the right-wing premier of Quebec, Robert Bourassa. All the Meech Lake Accord did, on the Quebec issue, was to state that Quebec was "a distinct society," a rather meaningless pronouncement. The NDP still refuses to accept the position that Quebec is a province different from the others, and in a binational state should have the right to have its own version of major Canadian programs. The Canada and Quebec Pension Plan is the notable model, one which is supported by the left in Quebec. But the NDP position on the Meech Lake Accord was wrong on a second count as well. In the past the NDP (and its predecessor, the CCF) took a strong federalist position on Quebec, similar to that taken by Pierre Elliott Trudeau. But in this case they took the right-wing Alberta position of decentralized provincial power. By accepting the Meech Lake Accord, the NDP leadership undermined the possibility of future new federal social programs and weakened the Charter of Rights, and they broke ranks with the womens' movement and Canada's aboriginal peoples.

The leadership of the NDP has always been uneasy about the party's advocating withdrawal from NATO and NORAD. Yet whenever they bring it up at a party convention, the delegates strongly reaffirm the policy. In 1987 the NDP leadership released a new paper on military policy. Once again, it was couched in the old Cold War rhetoric of the 1950s. The NDP Members of Parliament declared that Canada must increase spending to defend against an attack from the Soviet Union. No one really believes the spectre of Soviet invasion anymore. Yet the NDP proposed spending $19.5 billion over the next twenty years on the military. Given federal revenue constraints, if the NDP were to form the next federal government and carry out these pledges for military spending, needed social programs would clearly have to take a back seat. Furthermore, the leadership of the NDP released their new military policy right at the time when the Soviet Union, under its new leadership, was pushing hard for arms control and disarmament. In early December 1987, the North-South Institute released the results of a public opinion poll it contracted. Only 6.2% of Canadians thought that increasing the size of Canada's armed forces would be the best way to increase Canadian influence internationally. Only 18.8% concluded that if there were extra government funds to spend in the international area next year they should be used for defence.

The NDP's proposal to withdraw from NATO and NORAD was attacked by the opposition parties, the business elite and the press for advocating "neutralism" for Canada. How did they respond? They did not launch a counterattack. They did not try to lead public opinion. They remained silent. When French Premier Jacques Chirac came to Canada and attacked the NDP proposal to withdraw from NATO (which, ironically, was the policy of the French government), what did they do? They said nothing. Senator Jack Austin, a key Liberal campaign strategist, correctly noted that the NDP was "mastering the art of silence. When you are ahead, you say as little as possible."

In 1987 three federal by-elections were called, a major test of NDP support. The party dramatically won new seats in the Yukon and in St. John's, Newfoundland. But they almost lost the seat in Hamilton-Mountain, which they had traditionally held, because the federal party leadership parachuted in a candidate from Ottawa, against the wishes of the local party. In 1986, Robert Toupin, Member of Parliament from Terrebonne in Montreal, quit the Tories. Before that he had been a Liberal. He crossed the floor in the House of Commons and was welcomed with open arms by Ed Broadbent and the NDP caucus. Then in October 1987 he quit the NDP, denouncing elements in the party as radicals. This is the kind of political opportunism we have regularly come to expect from the leadership of the NDP all across Canada. It is another good reason why political coalitions need to remain strictly non-partisan.

There is only a slim possibility that the New Democratic Party may form the next federal government in Canada. If they continue to hold to their principled position that they will reject the free trade agreement with the United States, they will warrant electoral support. But what else can we expect once they are in office? Here we might learn something by looking at the experience of the Labour parties in Australia and New Zealand which have been in office during the economic crisis of the 1980s. These countries are very similar to Canada, and their Labour parties are very similar to the New Democratic Party.

In 1979 the Australian Labour Party (ALP) and the Australian Council of Trade Unions (ACTU) began to work out a voluntary prices and incomes policy, commonly known as The Accord. It was patterned after the corporatist examples in Scandinavia, described in Chapter 19. The agreement called for centralized fixed wages, indexed to productivity increases. In return, the ALP promised to increase social programs. The Accord became the major item in the ALP's platform in the March 1983 election, which they won.

The Labour government tried to implement The Accord between 1983 and 1985, but they failed. Australia suffered from a major balance of payments problem and a large federal deficit. The Australian dollar was devalued by 25%, but even this devalutation was not enough to turn the situation around. The government ended up following a policy of tight money and fiscal restraint that was little different from that of neo-conservatism. Wages were frozen, and labour did not get even the productivity increases promised under

The Accord. Between 1983 and 1987, there was an 8% decline in real wages. Unemployment increased. Inflation rose from 5% to 9.4%. Interest rates rose to 16%. Tax policies were revised to aid private enterprise. Universality was ended for pensions and other social programs. The government began to push privatization. Thus, it was not much of a surprise when Australian big business and the highly monopolized press supported the ALP in the July 1987 election. Since that election victory, the Labour government has only offered more of the same.

In New Zealand the Labour Party (NZLP) was elected in July 1984. It was committed from the beginning to a policy of the free market and free trade. Immediately after the election, they introduced a 20% devaluation of the New Zealand dollar, abolished foreign exchange controls, removed import licences, and froze wages. In the first session of Parliament, the Labour Party reduced income taxes on those in the higher income brackets, abolished the capital gains tax, and substituted a 10% value added tax on all goods and services, with no exceptions. They eliminated the principle of universality for almost all social programs. Users' fees were introduced everywhere. Privatization was undertaken. Unemployment started to rise, but it was held down by increased emigration. The inflation rate rose to 18%. Real wages fell. By 1987 there were one million people living below the official poverty line.

One of the hardest hit sectors of the economy was farming. Farm price supports were drastically cut. Export incentives were removed. The Labour government eliminated subsidized loans, subsidized government goods and services, and subsidies to farm inputs. Legislation was introduced to help farmers get out of farming. Existing legislation limiting farm size and preventing foreign ownership of farmland was repealed. Between 1984 and 1986, average farm net income dropped by 50%.

In spite of all this, the NZLP was re-elected in August 1987. Its overall support fell by 2.9%. Support in traditional labour districts fell, as did voter participation, but this was offset by a dramatic rise in support in the new upper-middle-income areas. Almost immediately after the election, the Labour government announced that it was going to review health, education, housing and social welfare policies. The Minister of Finance announced that state bureaucracies were "not giving full value for the money," and that the government was going to contract out much of this work.

Why was it possible for the Labour governments in these two countries to pursue policies that were scarcely different from those of

Margaret Thatcher? In the face of the economic crisis and the balance of payments problems, they followed the easiest route, adopting the policies being implemented by all the other major Western countries. The lack of organized political opposition was due to the quiescence of the trade union movement; they did not openly oppose "their government." Again, the experience of Australia and New Zealand clearly reveals the need for political coalitions to be separate from social democratic parties. The mass of evidence shows that opposition cannot be mobilized from within ruling social democratic parties. And the difficulty is compounded when the trade unions are closely linked to the social democratic parties.

The lesson is clear. Strong coalitions are needed in Canada to maintain pressure on social democratic parties and governments. Otherwise, the result may be the disaster we have witnessed in Australia and New Zealand.

Expanding Political and Economic Democracy

In May and June of 1987 public attention centred on the Meech Lake Accord, the *Constitution Act* of 1987. It was signed on June 3 by Prime Minister Brian Mulroney and the ten provincial premiers after nineteen hours of uninterrupted negotiations. While debate centred on some important aspects of the agreement, others criticized the complete lack of democracy in the process.

The anti-democratic tradition is well entrenched in Canada. There was no popular participation in the formation and approval of our original constitution, the *British North America Act*. The Special Joint Committee of the Senate and the House of Commons on the Constitution, which issued its report in 1972, held all of its hearings in Ottawa. Again, there was no popular participation. The framers did not even recommend a referendum on the new Canadian Constitution. The Pepin-Robarts Committee on the Constitution did hold at least some public hearings across Canada. Their report, issued in 1979, called for a referendum on a new Constitution, but this was ignored. The Chrétien-Romonow Committee hearings on the Constitution, held in July and August of 1981, limited consulations to key political figures. Again, no popular participation. When the Constitution was "repatriated" in 1982, the general public couldn't have cared less; repatriation was a process involving a minimum number of politicians in Ottawa. Given the British system of parliamentary government, provincial ratification itself is a bad joke. In the case of the Meech Lake Accord, the Mulroney government made it plain that no amendments would be accepted, from either the provincial legislatures or the Canadian Senate. In reality, the 1987 *Constitution Act* was created and proclaimed by eleven men.

Canada's method of acquiring its Constitution contrasts with most other liberal democracies, where constitutional amendments must receive some form of approval from the population, usually through a referendum. The Canadian process stands in stark contrast to the process used, for example, in Nicaragua. The Sandinista government created a national Constitutional Commission representing all political parties, used a broad committee system to prepare the first draft, and then held mass meetings throughout the country, at which ordinary people made oral and written submissions. An extensive debate was held in all the media. Then a second draft was prepared, based on the popular input, and finally approved by the National Assembly.

Canadians are faced with a similar situation concerning the free trade agreement with the United States. The Mulroney government has signed the agreement. A committee from Parliament held a few hearings across Canada, before the text of the agreement was signed and released, and a few special interests were invited to give testimony. General public participation in these "hearings" was rejected. The Mulroney government strongly rejects the position that the provinces can block the free trade agreement or change any of the provisions, even those which may infringe on historic provincial rights! Furthermore, the Mulroney government has made it clear that they plan to push the free trade agreement through Parliament before the next federal election. They regularly dismiss popular demands for an election or even a referendum on the agreement before it is ratified.

It is impossible for the Mulroney government to argue that they have any mandate from the Canadian people to sign and implement a free trade agreement with the United States. In 1983, while running for the leadership of the Conservative Party, Brian Mulroney strongly opposed any free trade agreement with the United States. He repeatedly said that it would be a disaster for Canada and lead to the loss of our sovereign independence. During the 1984 federal election the issue was never raised once.

During the period when the free trade agreement was being negotiated, public support for the Conservatives, reflected in numerous public opinion polls, fell to a low of around 23%, well behind the Liberals and the New Democrats. Furthermore, this did not change after the summary of the agreement was published in early October 1987. Polls still showed the Tories with only 24% support from potential Canadian voters. A poll conducted by Angus Reid in the week of October 7-14 found that 59% of Canadians wanted the prime minister to call an election over the free trade issue, and only 37% said no election was needed on the issue.

The fact that the federal Conservative Party can hold office for three years without any significant popular support from Canadians reveals the undemocratic nature of our system of government. That the Tories can move forward with far-reaching and unpopular legislation during that period underscores the problem. The British parliamentary system of government, when combined with an electoral system based on single-member constituencies, usually results in a de facto dictatorship. Once a party has a majority in the House of Commons, it rules as it pleases, regardless of public opinion. The single-member constituency, with the victor being the candidate with the highest number of votes, allows parties with significantly less than majority popular support to gain very large majorities in the number of seats and to hold office for five years, irrespective of their actions. The only restraint on the rulers is their desire to be re-elected, though we have seen, in B.C. for example, how even unpopular governments are returned to office.

In Britain, Margaret Thatcher's Conservatives received a large majority of the seats in the House of Commons in 1979, 1983 and 1987, but never got more than 42% of the popular vote. In the 1983 election the SDP-Liberal Alliance got 26% of the vote and only 3.5% of the seats. In the Ontario provincial election in September 1987, the Liberals got 48% of the vote and 73% of the seats in the legislature. In the New Brunswick provincial election in October 1987, the Liberal Party got 61% of the popular vote and won every single seat in the legislature! Surely, this is an absurd system of government. Who would call this democracy?

The political coalitions that are developing in Canada must adopt an agenda which calls for increasing political and economic democracy. First, there are ways that a national government can be made more responsive to public opinion. Most countries in Europe have some form of proportional representation (PR), where the number of seats in the legislature is in proportion to the popular vote that a party receives in an election. Historically, PR was brought in primarily to protect the non-socialist diversity of opposition parties when the franchise was extended to men without private property. For some, PR was a way to try to avoid polarization in the legislature along class lines, labour versus capital. In most countries, PR has worked well; while the cabinets may change more often, there is a continuity in personnel. But these governments are much more subject to popular pressure. In the late 1860s, a committee of the U.S. Senate concluded that the U.S. Civil War probably could have been prevented if there had been a system of PR, for the large unionist minority in the South would have been represented in the Congress and in state legislatures. In Canada, the historic political polarization and hostility between Liberal Quebec and Tory Ontario would have been greatly moderated under a system of PR.

More direct popular participation in government would be encouraged in Canada by a system of popular initiatives for new legislation, referendums on issues and acts of government, and recall of elected members. Such a system exists in Switzerland. There, the popular initiative was used to introduce PR and to finally grant the right to vote to women. Most attractive is the Swiss provision for a referendum of confidence in an existing government. A sitting government which fails to get a majority in such a referendum must resign and call a new election. With a similar system in this country, Canadians would no longer be forced to put up with grossly unpopular regimes which have lost the confidence of the electorate.

It is rather amazing that those who rule Canada have convinced us that democracy consists of casting a ballot for a single candidate once every four or five years. The ritual does no more than indicate our meek approval of a system of parliamentary sovereignty by which a handful of men are given the right to govern us. But the concept of democracy, which goes back at least to the New England town councils, the Swiss cantons and Athens, includes direct, equal participation of the citizen in the governmental process. Furthermore, this is a social and not an individual activity.

Why is our form of government characterized by rule by the elite few, by hierarchy, bureaucracy and centralization? The structures of government mirror those of our economic institutions. In our educational institutions and in the workplace, where we spend most of our productive lives, we function in a grossly undemocratic atmosphere. If we had democracy in the political sphere, it would seem only natural to have democracy in our places of learning and work. The notion of democracy in the workplace is heretical, running totally contrary to the basis of economic life under capitalism, where the rule is one dollar, one vote. There is certainly nothing democratic about the way corporations are run. Those with the "votes," the blocks of shares of stocks, are in control. The decision-making process is always from the top down. Expanding the degree of citizen participation as part of a move towards political democracy would at the same time bring forward demands for economic democracy.

One of the central themes in this book is that working people everywhere are at the mercy of the power of the large transnational corporations and big capital. We cannot really have democracy and create a humane society as long as we can be blackmailed by those who move capital abroad, shut down plants at will, and destroy our communities. In my mind, this is the great political challenge of the next decade: Can we bring capital under democratic control? If Canada is tied even closer to the United States through the free trade agreement, that option will certainly be closed.

CONCLUSION

Defeating the Mulroney Free Trade Deal

In early October 1987 Canadians finally learned the substance of the deal between the Reagan administration and the Mulroney government. It was not a traditional free trade agreement covering only goods. As well, there was the continental energy agreement, which surprised even most of the provincial premiers. And it included provisions covering government procurement. It was the first agreement ever signed between two countries which included a comprehensive treatment of the service industry, including finance. A special class of persons, those serving business interests, were to be given the right to employment on both sides of the border. Most of all, it was an agreement which centred on the issue of investment. As the Mulroney government proclaimed, the deal would "chart a new course for the largest and most important trading relationship in the world." Furthermore, it was just a first step to "lay the foundation for further bilateral and multilateral co-operation to expand and enhance the benefits of the agreement."

The Reagan administration was very pleased with the outcome. As the U.S. negotiators reported, "we got everything that we wanted." President Reagan proclaimed that the deal represented "a new economic constitution for North America." It was part of "the American dream," the uniting of the hemisphere from the Arctic Circle to the Tiera del Fuego. Clearly, the Reagan-Mulroney deal, if ratified, would represent a major step towards a North American common market.

Throughout the negotiations the Canadian people were left in the dark. But they are beginning to learn that the Mulroney government did not obtain its objectives in the negotiations. They did not get secure access to the U.S. market. There has been no agreement on what is an "unfair subsidy," and U.S. interests retain the right to use

Conclusion 313

U.S. trade laws to attack Canadian industries. The binational dispute panels have not replaced the long, expensive U.S. system for dealing with trade disputes. The dispute panel is tacked on at the end of the process, and it has no real binding powers. In a great many ways, the proposed system is much worse than the dispute settlement system under the General Agreement on Tariffs and Trade (GATT). The Mulroney government did not succeed in getting exemption from the omnibus trade bill being considered by the U.S. Congress. If it is passed, this bill will further broaden the U.S. definition of an "unfair subsidy." The remaining U.S. tariffs will be removed over a ten-year period, but the Mulroney government paid a very high price for this objective. The same end could have been achieved at the present round of the GATT negotiations simply by offering equivalent tariff reductions.

The Mulroney government has repeatedly claimed that the deal would increase the net balance of trade with the United States, in both goods and services. But the reality of the American political and economic situation is such that this simply cannot be the case. Currently, the United States has a major balance of payments deficit which it is trying to reduce. Canada already has a relatively large favourable balance in merchandise trade with the United States. If the results of the Reagan-Mulroney deal were to increase this net balance, the U.S. government and Congress would undoubtedly take other actions to reduce it.

There is also the claim that the deal will result in a large net increase in jobs in Canada. The figure usually cited by Brian Mulroney is 350,000. It is impossible to predict with any confidence the impact of the free trade agreement on jobs. Some manufacturing industries protected by high tariffs will clearly lose, as everyone admits. But no one knows where the new investment will take place. The mainstream economists predict that there would be a major rationalization of industry as smaller plants are replaced by larger plants. But this process has always resulted in the replacement of labour by capital. Furthermore, the service industry in Canada would be opened to competition from much larger U.S. firms. Many believe that it is in the service area that Canada would experience the greatest loss of jobs. The impact would be felt most heavily by women workers.

Finally, the Mulroney government repeatedly assured Canadians that the Auto Pact, social programs, culture, and regional development were not going to be on the bargaining table. But they are. And while social programs are not specifically covered in the deal, they can still be classified as an "unfair subsidy" under U.S. trade law.

But even more significant is the impact of further integration of the two economies on social programs. The power of capital to move freely back and forth across the border would make it even more likely that the process of harmonization would intensify. As the text of the deal states, "harmonization means making identical." Who would be harmonized? We really know the answer to that.

The major business organizations in Canada and the United States are strongly supporting the Reagan-Mulroney deal. They got what they really wanted, investment rights, including the service sector. This would include the right to establishment and the right to national treatment in either country. Both governments agreed to limit performance requirements on new investment projects, a practice widely used in Canada where there is government participation. U.S. capital would also have the right to provincial treatment; it is uncertain whether under the U.S. system an agreement (in contrast to a treaty) would be binding on the states. There are strict limitations on the nationalization of any industry, which really applies only to Canada, and there is a provision which would prohibit restrictions on the repatriation of profits. Finally, the Canadian practice of reviewing the takeover of Canadian firms by foreign firms would be limited to takeovers involving firms with gross assets of over $150 million, far higher than figures used in the past.

Business interests also support the Reagan-Mulroney deal because it is part of the New Right agenda. They firmly believe that the influence of trade unions needs to be greatly reduced and government-sponsored social programs need to be cut back. A method of achieving these goals is to move towards the free market economy through a tight money policy, fiscal restraint, taxation policy, deregulation, privatization and trade liberalization. However, the New Right agenda has never been very popular in Canada. It does not begin to have the political support that it has in Britain or the United States. Closer economic integration with the United States is seen as the means of moving the Canadian people in the direction of the New Right agenda, a process described as "forced harmonization" through the power of the market and capital.

If the Reagan-Mulroney deal is ratified and implemented it will result in a major shift of power in Canada to the large corporations and finance capital. However, there is a very good chance that the deal can be defeated in Canada. Support for the New Right agenda is on the decline. Public opinion polls continue to show that Brian Mulroney and the Conservative Party have the backing of less than one-third of the Canadian electorate. To date the major problem has been the pro-free trade propaganda campaign by the Mulroney government, some of the provincial governments and the mass media. But I am confident that once Canadians find out what is actually in the deal, they will reject it. It is now up to the Liberal Party, the New Democratic Party and the member-groups of the anti-free trade coalitions to educate the public. Once the deal is defeated, then we can turn our attention to a better alternative.

SELECTED REFERENCES

Ambler, John S., ed. *The French Socialist Experiment*. Philadelphia: Institute for the Study of Human Issues, 1985.

Anthony, Brian. "Negotiating Canadian Culture: What's at Stake?" *Canadian Business Review, 13*, No. 2, Summer 1986.

Audley, Paul. *Canada's Cultural Industries*. Toronto: James Lorimer & Co. for the Canadian Institute for Economic Policy, 1983.

An Automotive Strategy for Canada. Report of the Federal Task Force on the Canadian Motor Vehicle and Automotive Parts Industries. Ottawa: Department of Industry, Trade and Commerce, May 1983.

Axworthy, Thomas S. "Power and Plenty: The Politics of Free Trade." *Canada Not For Sale: The Case Against Free Trade*. Toronto: General Publishers, 1987.

Bamber, Greg J., and Russell D. Lansbury, eds. *International and Comparative Industrial Relations*. London: Allen & Unwin, 1987.

Banting, Keith, ed. *The State and Economic Interests*. Toronto: University of Toronto Press for the Macdonald Royal Commission, 1985.

Barichello, Richard R. "Canada-U.S. Free Trade Negotiations: Anticipating the Effects on Canadian Agriculture." Unpublished paper, University of British Columbia, January 27, 1986.

Baranson, Jack. "Assessment of Likely Impact of a U.S.-Canadian Free Trade Agreement upon the Behaviour of U.S. Industrial Subsidiaries in Canada." Toronto: Government of Ontario, November 1985.

Barber, Clarence, and John C.P. McCallum. *Unemployment and Inflation: The Canadian Experience*. Toronto: James Lorimer & Co. for the Canadian Institute for Economic Policy, 1980.

Bercuson, David J., ed. *Canada and the Burden of Unity*. Toronto: Macmillan, 1977.

"Beyond Free Trade." *Dollars & Sense*, No. 115, April 1986.

Bluestone, Barry. "Abandoning Jobs and Industries in North America." *Policy Alternatives*, Canadian Centre for Policy Alternatives, Winter 1984.

Bluestone, Barry, and Bennett Harrison. *The Deindustrialization of*

America. New York: Basic Books, 1982.

Boltho, Andrea, ed. *The European Economy: Growth and Crisis.* London: Oxford University Press, 1982.

Bowles, Samuel, David M. Gordon, and Thomas E. Weisskopf. *Beyond the Wasteland: A Democratic Alternative to Economic Decline.* Garden City, N.Y.: Anchor Press/Doubleday, 1984.

Britton, John N.H. "Location Perspectives on Free Trade for Canada." *Canadian Public Policy, 4,* No. 1, Winter, 1978.

Britton, John N.H., and James M. Gilmour. *The Weakest Link: A Technological Perspective on Canadian Industrial Development.* Ottawa: The Science Council of Canada, October 1978.

"Building Self-Reliance in Canada." *GATT-Fly Report, 7,* No. 1, February 1987.

Burtless, Gary. "Inequality in America: Where Do We Stand?" *The Brookings Review,* Summer 1987.

Byers, Roderick, B. "Canadian Defence and Defence Procurement: Implications for Economic Policy." In G.R. Winham, ed. *Selected Problems in Formulating Foreign Economic Policy.* Toronto: University of Toronto Press for the Macdonald Royal Commission, 1985.

Calvert, John. *Government Limited: The Corporate Takeover of the Public Sector in Canada.* Ottawa: Canadian Centre for Policy Alternatives, 1984.

Cameron, Duncan, ed. *The Free Trade Papers.* Toronto: James Lorimer & Co., 1986.

Canadian Conference of Catholic Bishops. *Ethical Choices and Political Challenges: Ethical Reflections on the Future of Canada's Socio-Economic Order.* Ottawa: CCCB, December 1983.

Canadian Conference of Catholic Bishops. *Ethical Choices and Political Challenges: Free Trade at What Cost?* Ottawa: Concacan Inc., 1987.

Canadian Conference of Catholic Bishops. *Ethical Relfections on the Economic Crisis.* Ottawa: Concacan Inc., 1983.

Canadian Labour Congress. "Full Employment and Fairness—the Workers' Agenda for Canada." Document No. 18. 16th Constitutional Convention, 1986.

Canadian Labour Congress. "Our Canada or Theirs? Workers Confront the Corporate Blueprint." Document No. 19. 16th Constitutional Convention, 1986.

Canadian Labour Congress. *Position Paper on Canada-United States Free Trade.* July 1985.

Canadian Labour Congress. *The Transportation Acts of 1986.* Ottawa, March 26, 1987.

Clark-Jones, Melissa. *A Staple State: Canadian Industrial Resources in the Cold War.* Toronto: University of Toronto Press, 1987.

Clarkson, Stephen. *Canada and the Reagan Challenge.* Toronto: James Lorimer & Co., 1985.

La coalition Québecois d'opposition au libre-échange. *La politique sociale Canadienne et le libre-échange.* Montreal: CSN, CFL, CTC, UPA, 1986.

Cohen, Marjorie. *Free Trade and the Future of Women's Work.* Toronto: Garamond Press and the Canadian Centre for Policy Alternatives, 1987.

Confederation of Canadian Unions. *Too High a Price: A Policy Paper on "Free" Trade.* Vancouver: CCU, 1987.

Conference of Socialist Economists. *The Alternative Economic Strategy: A Labour Movement Response to the Economic Crisis.* London: CSE Books, 1980.

Crotty, James R. "On Keynes and Capital Flight." *Journal of Economic Literature, 21,* March 1983.

Crozier, Michael, Samuel P. Huntington, and J. Watanuki. *The Crisis of Democracy: Report on the Governability of Democracies to the Trilateral Commission.* New York: New York University Press, 1975.

Dahrendorf, Ralf, ed. *Europe's Economy in Crisis.* New York: Holmes & Meier Publishers Inc., 1982.

Deyo, Frederic, C., ed. *The Political Economy of the New Asian Industrialism.* Ithaca: Cornell University Press, 1987.

Djao, A.W. *Inequality and Social Policy.* Toronto: John Wiley & Sons, 1983.

Drache, Daniel, and Duncan Cameron, eds. *The Other Macdonald Report.* Toronto: James Lorimer & Co., 1985.

"The Economic Crisis." Special Issue of *Studies in Political Economy*, No. 11, Summer 1983.

Eisenstein, Zillah. "Liberalism, Feminism and the Reagan State." In Ralph Miliband et al., eds. *Socialist Register 1987: Conservatism in Britain and America.* London: Merlin Press, 1987.

Flaherty, D.H., and W.R. McKercher, eds. *Southern Exposure: Canadian Perspectives on the United States.* Toronto: McGraw-Hill Ryerson, 1986.

Fowke, Vernon C. *The National Policy and the Wheat Economy.* Toronto: University of Toronto Press, 1957.

GATT-Fly. *Free Trade or Self-Reliance.* Toronto: GATT-Fly, 1987.

Ghosh, Jayati, "Developing Countries and World Economy." *Economic and Political Weekly, 21,* No. 41, October 11, 1986.

Gindin, Sam. "Free Trade and Competitiveness: Developing a Left Alternative." *Working Papers*, No. 4. Ottawa: Canadian Centre for Policy Alternatives, 1985.

Globerman, Steven, and Aidan Vining. "Canadian Culture under Free Trade." *Canadian Business Review, 13,* No. 2, Summer 1986.

Glyn, Andrew, "Capital Flight and Exchange Controls." *New Left Review*, No. 155, January-February 1986.

Gonick, Cy. *The Great Economic Debate.* Toronto: James Lorimer & Co., 1987.

Gonick, Cy. *Inflation or Depression: The Continuing Crisis of the Canadian*

Economy. Toronto: James Lorimer & Co., 1975.

Grayson, J. Paul. *Plant Closures and De-Skilling: Three Case Studies*. Ottawa: Social Science Council of Canada, 1986.

Green, Francis. "Some Macroeconomic Omens for Reagan and Thatcher." *Capital and Class*, No. 30, Winter 1986.

Gunderson, Morley, et al., eds. *Unemployment: International Perspectives*. Toronto: Centre for Industrial Relations by the University of Toronto Press, 1987.

Hager, Wolfgang. "Little Europe, Wider Europe and Western Economic Co-operation." *Journal of Common Market Studies, 21*, Nos. 1 & 2, September/December, 1982.

Heilbroner, Robert L. *The Worldly Philosophers*. New York: Simon and Schuster, 1961.

"The Hollow Corporation." Special Report. *Business Week*, No. 2935, March 3, 1986.

Holmes, John, and Colin Leys, eds. *Frontyard, Backyard: The Americas in Global Crisis*. Toronto: Between-the-Lines, 1987.

Howe, Carolyn, "The Politics of Class Compromise in an International Context: Considerations for a New Strategy for Labor." *Review of Radical Political Economics, 18*, No. 3, 1986.

Kahler, Miles. "European Protectionism in Theory and Practice." *World Politics, 36*, No. 4, July 1985.

Katzenstein, Peter J. *Small States in World Markets*. Ithaca: Cornell University Press, 1985.

Keohane, Robert. *After Hegemony: Co-operation and Discord in the World Political Economy*. Princeton: Princeton University Press, 1984.

Keynes, John Maynard. *The General Theory of Employment, Interest and Money*. New York: Harcourt, Brace & World, 1964.

Keynes, John Maynard. "National Self-Sufficiency." *Yale Review, 22*, June 1933.

Kirsh, Sharon L. *Unemployment: Its Impact on Body and Soul*. Toronto: Canadian Mental Health Association, 1984.

Krieger, Joel. *Reagan, Thatcher and the Politics of Decline*. New York: Oxford University Press, 1986.

Kuttner, Robert. *The Economic Illusion*. Boston: Houghton-Mifflin, 1984.

Laxer, James. *Leap of Faith: Free Trade and the Future of Canada*. Edmonton: Hurtig Publishers, 1986.

Labor Research Association. *Economic Notes*, various issues, 1986 and 1987.

Lanoie, Claude. "Comparisons of the Canadian and United States Food and Beverage Industries." *Food Market Commentary, 7*, No. 3, September 1985.

LaPierre, Laurier, ed. *If You Love This Country: Facts and Feelings on Free Trade*. Toronto: McClelland and Stewart, 1987.

Lazar, Fred. *The New Protectionism: Non-Tariff Barriers and Their Effects on Canada*. Toronto: James Lorimer & Co. for the Canadian Institute for

Economic Policy, 1981.

Leslie, Peter. *Federal State, National Economy*. Toronto: University of Toronto Press, 1987.

Lipsey, Richard G., and Murray G. Smith. *Canada's Trade Options*. Toronto: C.D. Howe Institute, 1985.

Litvak, Isaiah A. "Free Trade with the U.S.: The Conflicting Views of Canadian Business." *Business Quarterly*, Spring 1986.

Lumsden, Ian, ed. *Close the 49th Parallel*. Toronto: University of Toronto Press, 1970.

Lundberg, Erik. "The Rise and Fall of the Swedish Model." *Journal of Economic Literature, 23*, No. 1, March 1985.

MacDonald, Neil B. *Locational Advantages in the Farm Machinery Industry*. Ottawa: Royal Commission on Farm Machinery, 1968.

MacEwan, Arthur. "International Debt and Banking: Rising Instability within the General Crisis." *Science & Society, 50*, No. 2, Summer 1986.

Macmillan, Katie. *The Canadian Common Market*. Calgary: Canada West Foundation, October 1985.

McQuaig, Linda. *Behind Closed Doors*. Toronto: Penguin Books of Canada, 1987.

Magnusson, Warren, et al., eds. *After Bennett: A New Politics for British Columbia*. Vancouver: New Star Books, 1986.

Magnusson, Warren, et al., eds. *The New Reality: The Politics of Restraint in British Columbia*. Vancouver: New Star Books, 1984.

Marx, Karl. *The Poverty of Philosophy*. New York: International Publishers, 1963.

Matthews, Ralph. *The Creation of Regional Dependency*. Toronto: University of Toronto Press, 1983.

Miliband, Ralph, et al., eds. *Socialist Register 1985/86: Social Democracy and After*. London: The Merlin Presss, 1986.

Miliband, Ralph, et al., eds. *Socialist Register 1987: Conservatism in Britain and America: Rhetoric and Reality*. London: The Merlin Press, 1987.

Nayar, Deepak. "International Relocation of Production and Industrialization in LDCs." *Economic and Political Weekly, 18*, No. 31, July 30, 1983.

Nelson, Joyce. "Canada Dry: Pipedreams and Freshwater Politics." *This Magazine, 21*, No. 5, October 1987.

Nelson, Joyce. "Losing It in the Lobby." *This Magazine, 20*, October/November 1986.

New Democratic Party. "An Alternative Strategy: Fair Trade vs. Free Trade." Ottawa, March 1985.

Norrie, Kenneth, ed. *Disparities and Interregional Adjustment*. Toronto: University of Toronto Press for the Macdonald Royal Commission, 1985.

North-South Institute. *Women in Industry*. Ottawa: North-South Institute,

1985.

Ontario Public Service Employees Union. *Free Trade and the Public Sector*. Toronto: OPSEU, August 1986.

Palmer, Bryan D. *Solidarity: The Rise & Fall of an Opposition in British Columbia*. Vancouver: New Star Books, 1987.

Pammet, Jon. H., and Brian W. Tomlin, eds. *The Integration Question*. Toronto: Addison-Wesley, 1984.

Parboni, Ricardo. "The Dollar Weapon: From Nixon to Reagan." *New Left Review*, No. 158, July/August 1986.

Pateman, Carole. *Participation and Democratic Theory*. Cambridge: Cambridge University Press, 1970.

Phillips, Paul, and Stephen Watson. "From Mobilization to Continentalism: The Canadian Economy in the Post-Depression Period." In Michael S. Cross and Gregory S. Kealey, eds. *Modern Canada: 1930-1980s*. Toronto: McClelland & Stewart, 1984.

Pinder, John, ed. *National Industrial Strategies and the World Economy*. Towowa, N.J.: Allanheld, Osmun, 1982.

Radwanski, George. *Ontario Study of the Service Sector*. Toronto: Ministry of Treasury and Economics, December 1986.

Ray, D. Michael. "The Location of United States Manufacturing Subsidiaries in Canada." *Economic Geography, 17,* No. 3, July 1971.

"The Reindustrialization of America." Special Issue. *Business Week*, No. 2643, June 30, 1980.

Resnick, Philip. *Parliament vs. People*. Vancouver: New Star Books, 1984.

Riches, Graham, *Food Banks and the Welfare Crisis*. Ottawa: Canadian Council on Social Development, 1986.

Riddell, W. Craig, ed. *Adapting to Change: Labour Market Adjustment in Canada*. Toronto: University of Toronto Press for the Macdonald Royal Commission, 1985.

Ross, George, and Jane Jensen. "Crisis and France's 'Third Way.' " *Studies in Political Economy*, No. 11, Summer 1983.

Rotstein, Abraham. *Rebuilding from Within; Remedies for Canada's Ailing Economy*. Toronto: James Lorimer & Co. for the Canadian Institute for Economic Policy, 1984.

Rugman, Alan M., and Sheila Douglas. "The Strategic Management of Multinationals and World Product Mandating." *Canadian Public Policy, 12,* June 1986.

Saul, John Ralston. "The Secret Life of the Branch-Plant Executive." *Report on Business Magazine, 4,* No. 7, January 1988.

Saunders, Christopher, ed. *The Political Economy of New and Old Industrial Countries*. London: Butterworth, 1981.

Savoie, Donald J. *Regional Economic Development*. Toronto: University of Toronto Press, 1986.

Sharp, Mitchell. "More Free Trade." *Policy Options, 8,* No. 5, June 1987.

Sharpe, Andrew. "Can Canada Compete?" *Canadian Business Review, 12,* No. 4, 1985; *13,* No. 1, Spring 1986.

Shipman, William D. *Trade and Investment Across the Northeast Boundary*. Montreal: Institute for Research on Public Policy, 1986.

Sideri, S. *Trade and Power*. Rotterdam: Rotterdam University Press, 1970.

Sinclair, Scott. "Free Trade and Regional Development Policy." Toronto: Coalition Against Free Trade, September 10, 1987, unpublished paper.

Sklar, Holly, ed. *Trilateralism*. Montreal: Black Rose Books, 1980.

Stairs, Denis, and Gilbert R. Winham, eds. *The Politics of Canada's Economic Relationship with the United States*. Toronto: University of Toronto Press for the Macdonald Royal Commission, 1985.

Statistics Canada. *Arts and Culture: A Statistical Profile*. Catalogue No. 87-527.

Steger, Debra P. "Recent Developments in Canada-U.S. Trade Relations." *Review of International Business Law, 1*, No. 1, April 1987.

Stone, Frank. *Canada, the GATT and the International Trade System*. Montreal: The Institute for Research on Public Policy, 1984.

Swankey, Ben. *The Fraser Institute*. Vancouver: Centre for Socialist Education, 1984.

Therborn, Goran. *Why Some Peoples are More Unemployed than Others*. London: Verso, 1986.

Tichy, Gunther. "Strategy and Implementation of Employment Policy in Austria." *Kyklos, 37*, No. 3, 1984.

"31 Million Reasons to Fight Unemployment." *OECD Observer*, No. 144, January 1987.

Turk, Jim. *Free Trade with the United States: The Implications for Canada*. Publication No. 16. Ottawa: Canadian Centre for Policy Alternatives, 1986.

Turk, Jim. "GATT Will Get Us Too—The Implications of Multilateral Free Trade." *Free Trade or Self-Reliance*. Toronto: GATT-Fly, 1987.

Wachtel, Howard. *The Money Mandarins*. New York: Pantheon Books, 1986.

Walters, Peter. "Distributing Decline: Swedish Social Democrats and the Crisis of the Welfare State." *Government & Opposition, 20*, No. 3, Summer 1985.

Warnock, John W. "Free Trade Fantasies: The Case of the Farm Implements Industry." *This Magazine, 9*, Nos. 5 & 6, November-December 1975.

Warnock, John W. *Partner to Behemoth: The Military Policy of a Satellite Canada*. Toronto: New Press, 1970.

Warnock, John W. *The Politics of Hunger: The Global Food System*. Toronto: Methuen, 1987.

Warnock, John W. *Profit Hungry: The Food Industry in Canada*. Vancouver: New Star Books, 1978.

Warren, Jack W. "Auto Part Manufacturers Battle Imports." *Canadian Business Review, 12*, No. 4, Winter 1985.

Watkins, Mel. "The Staple Theory Revisited." *Journal of Canadian Studies, 12*, No. 5, Winter 1977.

Whalley, John, ed. *Canada-United States Free Trade*. Toronto: University of Toronto Press for the Macdonald Royal Commission, 1985.

Williams, Glen. *Not for Export: Toward a Political Economy of Canada's Arrested Industrialization*. Toronto: McClelland & Stewart, 1986.

Wilson, Elizabeth. "Thatcherism and Women: After Seven Years." In Ralph Miliband et al., eds. *The Socialist Register 1987: Conservatism in Britain and North America*. London: Merlin Press, 1987.

Wolfe, David A. *The Delicate Balance: The Changing Economic Role of the State in Canada*. Dissertation, University of Toronto, 1980.

Wolfe, David A. "Mercantilism, Liberalism and Keynesianism: Changing Forms of State Intervention in Capitalist Economies." *Canadian Journal of Political and Social Theory*, 5, Nos. 1 & 2, Winter/Spring 1981.

Working Committee on Social Solidarity. *A Time to Stand Together . . . A Time for Social Solidarity*. Ottawa: The Working Committee on Social Solidarity, November 1987.